W. R. Cornish was born in Adelaide, South Australia, in 1937. He was educated at Adelaide University, and Wadham College, Oxford. He has been Lecturer in Law at the London School of Economics since 1962. In January, 1969, he takes up an appointment as Reader in Laws, University of London, at Queen Mary College.

The Jury

by W. R. Cornish

Allen Lane The Penguin Press London 1968

Contents

Preface

Jury service is an experience which comes unexpectedly upon people once or twice in a life-time. Once they have overcome initial irritation at the disruption of their lives and puzzlement at the unfamiliar surroundings most jurors find the duty an absorbing one, involving important responsibilities. This book is intended in particular for those who have performed jury service or are liable to do so and who wish to find out what it involves, what is known about how juries function and what the merits and demerits of the system are. Without ever having served as a juror, I have tried to bear in mind how jury service appears to a juror, and in this I have been very much helped by the numerous jurors who have been prepared to spend time discussing their time at court with me. I have also had invaluable assistance from other quarters. Numerous legal practitioners, court officers and academic colleagues, both here and abroad, have been willing to provide information, argument and criticism. I am most grateful to them all.

W.R.C.

1 · Introduction

In England, the system of trial by jury is often regarded as the foundation of an impartial and acceptable system for administering justice. The members of a jury are a group of independent citizens. They have no interest in the case before them, nor is their judgment coloured by regular experience of the business of the courts. Nonetheless, the jury system is becoming increasingly controversial. Critics claim that in a number of different ways present-day juries do not always serve the true aims of justice. Juries are accused of acquitting too readily in criminal cases. The verdicts in some cases can be explained only on the basis that the jury did not understand the evidence or the judge's summing-up. The danger that jurors may be bribed or threatened is causing serious concern, and police protection for jurors has been needed on a number of recent occasions. In defamation cases, the high damages awarded by juries are said to impose unfair restrictions on the freedom of the press to comment on matters of public interest.

At the same time the powers and responsibilities of juries are being altered by judicial interpretation and new legislation. The Court of Appeal has rejected juries as the proper instrument for assessing damages in personal injury cases. In criminal cases, juries are now permitted to return verdicts by majorities of at least ten to two in certain circumstances. Other changes in the jury system are in the air. The Government intends to implement the report of a Home Office committee which has proposed many changes in the qualification and selection of jurors. The principal recommendation is that the present property qualification should be abandoned and that all adult citizens should be liable for jury service.

In one sense, trial by jury has for some time been in decline. The method is being used in a smaller and smaller proportion of all the cases tried in English courts. Many criminal cases are now dealt with in Magistrates' Courts, and most civil actions are dealt with by a judge sitting alone. Where new tribunals have been created outside the framework of the ordinary courts for the purpose of deciding particular kinds of disputes – for instance concerning national insurance, or the fixing of fair rents – the jury system has not been introduced. But it would be wrong to suppose from this that the jury is a dying institution. Each year some 175,000 people in England and Wales receive jury summonses, and 110,000 of them are empanelled for service. The truth is rather that their use is being increasingly channelled into one area of the law: the trial of major criminal offences. It is here that the need to provide a court that is impartial, representative and free of responsibility to the state is felt most strongly.

In the past the jury has been at the centre of the common-law trial system. Court procedure, the conduct of advocates, the rules of evidence, the substantive law itself have all been moulded so that cases can be presented in a fair and intelligible way to a tribunal of laymen. As the jury is altered, or replaced by different tribunals, there may need to be consequential adjustments in other aspects of the judicial process. The aim of this book is to describe the present functions of juries in the English courts and against this background to consider how far the system does achieve its objects.

FROM WITNESSES TO ADJUDICATORS

Change is by no means a novelty in the jury system. As an institution it has undergone a remarkable process of adaptation since its first introduction in the early Middle Ages. It is now axiomatic that the jury decides the facts of a case on the evidence presented to it in court, and not on personal knowledge which the jurors have gleaned for themselves. Yet the original trial juries acted in just the opposite way. Their function was to return a group verdict on the matter in dispute based on their knowledge of the affairs of their neighbourhood.

INTRODUCTION

The origins of the jury system are uncertain. A classic account by the historian Brunner speaks of it as an importation by the conquering Normans in 1066. He traced its roots back to the 'group inquests' of the Carolingian kings. But there is no evidence that the Normans did use the 'group inquest' before the conquest. On the other hand, the Danes accepted group accusation of crime at the end of the tenth century, and records from the same period tell of cases in which land disputes were settled by the sworn verdict of a group of neighbours. It seems rather more likely that the Normans inherited the jury concept as an existing English institution. Any conclusion on the issue must be speculative, and it may be that the jury system developed from a variety of sources.[1]

Certainly William the Conqueror used the inquests of a group of neighbours when, for administrative purposes, he needed information; most notably this was the means of compiling the Domesday Book. The whole force of this procedure came from the fact that the members of the jury group were required to swear an oath as to the truth of their findings; and false swearing was regarded as a terrible thing. A century later Henry II brought the 'group inquest' into regular use in the machinery of justice. He established the 'jury of presentment', or 'grand jury', with the duty of seeking out suspected wrongdoers in the neighbourhood and presenting them before the king's itinerant justices for trial. He also introduced 'petty' or trial juries in the royal courts; their function was to provide a workable alternative to older ritualistic methods of trial such as 'trial by ordeal', 'trial by battle' or 'trial by the swearing of oaths'. Petty juries were soon in regular use in the king's courts, especially when trial by battle and by ordeal had fallen under ecclesiastical disapproval. But only very gradually did the jurors begin to shed their character of informants returning their verdict on the basis of their own knowledge of the affairs of the neighbourhood. In the later Middle Ages, as society became more complex and jurors were less likely to have sufficient personal knowledge to decide a case for themselves, the judges began to admit witnesses who stood apart from the jurors and to permit them to give evidence to the court. This practice slowly became the established rule. It was not until the eighteenth century that the principle seems to have been finally established that a juror should not sit on a case of which he had previous knowledge. The jury has thus existed in its modern form for only some three or four centuries. It has always been bad history to trace the system back to Magna Carta, and even the juries which were being introduced in the thirteenth century were only an early species in the chain of evolution.[2]

LEGAL AND LAY JUDGES

The jury system is one means by which laymen, in the sense of non-professional lawyers, have been incorporated as judges in the administration of justice in England. It is not the only method. Justices of the peace have a history almost as ancient. The office was established in the fourteenth century. Justices were appointed by the Crown throughout the counties, and there has never been a requirement that they have a legal training or any other educational qualification.[3] The justices provided a voluntary corps which played a major role in administering such local services as existed before the establishment of modern local authorities in the nineteenth century. They also exercised judicial functions, and as their administrative tasks decreased in number so their judicial duties increased. Not only do they now have wide powers for the hearing of criminal charges, including almost all charges against juveniles, but they also deal with family cases such as separation and maintenance and a variety of other matters.

There are other lay judges. In ordinary civil courts non-legal assessors may be used to advise judges in a specialized field in which they are experts. For instance, Admiralty cases are sometimes tried by a judge sitting with two nautical assessors to give him expert advice. Moreover, the modern growth of special tribunals outside the framework of ordinary courts has involved the widespread use of non-legal adjudicators. They are often, but by no means invariably, selected for their knowledge or experience in the sphere in which the tribunal operates.

All these lay judges perform functions which differ from those of a jury. The members of a jury are selected without regard to any skill, and the brief duration of their service prevents them from acquiring the kind of experience which justices of the peace or the members of a tribunal will amass with time. A jury never sits alone as a judicial body, as does a bench of justices, but always with a judge. There is a division of functions between judge and jury which may be roughly summed up in the well-known adage: 'Law is for the judge to decide, and facts for the jury.' The verdict which the jury returns on the facts will be a simple announcement of a conclusion, not supported by reasons showing how it was reached. Most other tribunals deliver a reasoned judgment. Some justices of the peace and administrative tribunals reach decisions without giving their reasons, but it is true to say that verdicts of juries are particularly inscrutable. Finally, it has been a traditional rule, only recently breached, that the jury's verdict should be unanimous. In all other courts and tribunals composed of more than a single judge, it is customary to follow ordinary committee procedure: decisions are reached by bare majority vote. Where professional lawyers act as trial judges, they are appointed to serve either full-time or part-time.[4] The full-time trial judges are those of the High Court, the County Courts and the three permanent criminal courts (the Old Bailey in London, and the Crown Courts in Liverpool and Manchester). Stipendiary magistrates also serve in a full-time capacity. The appeal judges are the Lords Justices of Appeal, who sit in the Court of Appeal, and the Lords of Appeal in Ordinary, who sit in the House of Lords. In addition there are such special offices as those of the Lord Chief Justice and the Master of the Rolls. The most important judicial appointments are made by the Crown on the advice of the Prime Minister, and the Lord Chancellor is responsible for the rest. Save in the case of stipendiary magistrates, who are not necessarily barristers, the choice is made from among those barristers who are of sufficient seniority and ability to merit the office. As the total number of practising barristers is only about two thousand, the field of candidates at any one time is small.

This system of appointment by one member of the Government in power is in marked contrast with American practice. In the United States, many judges are elected by popular vote, and in some cases they have to stand for re-election from time to time. In England, once a judge is appointed to a full-time office, he holds it 'during good behaviour'. Recently, this independence has been qualified for some: compulsory retiring ages have been laid down for the newly-appointed. In such cases, any financial hardship resulting from retirement will be alleviated by substantial pensions. The English system also differs from that of most West European countries, in which there is a separate judicial profession. The trained lawyer is still a young man when he takes up his first appointment as a judge, and he expects to work his way gradually through a series of judicial positions of increasing importance. In England, once a man acquires judicial office his chances of promotion are small. Stipendiary magistrates cannot expect to move to any other court, and only recently has there come to be any real chance of a County Court or criminal court judge going on to the High Court bench. High Court judges can hope for appointment to Court of Appeal or the House of Lords; but even then it is only as a Lord of Appeal in the House of Lords or as holder of one of the special offices mentioned above that he will get a better salary.

The office of stipendiary magistrate is the one full-time judgeship for which solicitors are eligible as well as barristers. This office was established in London, and then in certain other cities, to provide a replacement for the bench of lay justices of the peace in a Magistrates' Court. Stipendiaries were first introduced in the eighteenth century, but the system has not gained wide popularity.[5]

Part-time judges function in both civil and criminal courts. Where for some reason the permanent judges are unable to cope with the volume of work, special commissioners, normally senior barristers, are appointed as auxiliaries. The criminal law also makes use of part-time judges on a much more general basis at Courts of Quarter Sessions, since these courts are rarely in permanent session. Borough Quarter Sessions are presided over by a Recorder, who is appointed on the nomination of the Lord Chancellor and must be a barrister of at least five years' standing. County Quarter Sessions consisted for many years of a representative bench of the justices of the peace of the county, electing their own chairman. Over the last thirty years it has become almost universal practice to appoint a legally qualified chairman. In some cases, the justices of the sessions themselves elect the holder of some other judicial office, such as a County Court judge; or they may apply to the Lord Chancellor, who will appoint a barrister or solicitor of at least ten years' standing. Recorderships and chairmanships of Quarter Sessions provide some opportunity for a man to show his abilities as a judge before being given a permanent position on the bench, and many full-time judges are appointed after experience of this kind.

JURIES IN OTHER COUNTRIES

This book is concerned mainly with the English judicial system and the jury in English courts. Even so, it is useful for purposes of comparison to glance for a moment at the introduction and development (and in many cases the supersession) of the jury system in other parts of the world. It spread from England to Scotland within a century of its establishment by Henry II. Scots juries differ from those in England in two important ways: they are larger bodies (of fifteen members), and their verdicts may be given by a bare majority.[6] Colonization by the British also led to the introduction of juries in many places. Where the British acquired a territory which lacked any established legal system, the common law was introduced; as soon as circumstances permitted, trial by jury was instituted as an essential part of common-law procedure. Thus in much of Canada and in Australia and New Zealand, courts were soon using some form of jury trial. In these places, with their high proportion of British settlers, the jury system has proved reasonably satisfactory. There have been some interesting experiments in some parts of these countries, for instance by the introduction of majority verdicts, and in the use of much smaller juries in civil cases: New South Wales has had a four-man civil jury since 1844. As in England, its use in civil and minor criminal cases has gradually declined, though not to the same extent in each country. In places such as the first West African colonies, the jury was introduced for the whole populace, but such foreseeable obstacles to success as anti-African prejudices, inter-tribal partisanship and extensive bribery of jurors led to its abandonment in the later nineteenth century for civil cases, and to severe curtailment or supersession by trial with assessors in criminal cases. This disillusioning experience made the British wary of introducing the system into a number of later-established African colonies, such as Northern Rhodesia, Nyasaland and Tanganyika.[7]

Perhaps the most significant exportation of the jury was to the American colonies, for they won their independence at a time when the jury system was being generally acclaimed as a fundamental guarantee of individual liberty. Trial by jury was therefore enshrined as a constitutional right. This has meant that litigants have never lost the right to demand that many civil and all serious criminal cases be tried with a jury. Juries are therefore used much more frequently in America than in England. Indeed, it has recently been estimated that some 80 per cent of all criminal jury trials in the world take place in the United States. Not only is trial by jury guaranteed in the Constitutions of the Federation and the States, but various important changes have been made in the system itself, most of which are designed to limit the powers of the judge. American juries differ substantially in their constitution and duties from their English counterparts.[8]

In some colonies the British acquired a territory with an established legal system. If this was the case, it was not at once replaced by the common law. If the existing system was European – as in South Africa and Ceylon, where the Dutch had already introduced Roman-Dutch law – there was a tendency to add English features gradually to the administration of justice. In both countries, one early change was the establishment of jury trial. On the other hand, if the native judicial system was non-European, as in India and Kenya, it was preserved only for the indigenous population, the colonists themselves being governed by the common law. In such places, the jury functioned only in the sphere of administration of the common law, and in India the common law was gradually extended to non-Europeans. So, consequently, was trial by jury, and by the time India had won her independence it was in use in a number of states, though not in every case throughout the whole state.[9]

In most of these countries, racial, political and other

factors have dictated the introduction of other methods of trial. In India, the Law Commission was forced in 1958 to recommend the total abandonment of juries because bribery of jurors was so widespread. In South Africa racial bias was not uncommon, and the Government has acquired power, in some criminal cases, to order trial by judge sitting with two legally experienced assessors, usually barristers. It is significant that the first instance of this arose in 1914 under the Riotous Assemblies Act. The range of such offences has been widened to include other political offences, and the same system of trial is prescribed for all cases in which accused and victim are of different races. Moreover, the jury system seems to be out of favour generally. Even a defendant not subject to the prescription just mentioned must elect expressly for trial by jury and today this right of election is seldom exercised.[10]

The belief that the jury system provided a unique guarantee of democratic justice led not only to its inclusion in the American Constitution, but also to its introduction into European systems of law which were quite unrelated to English common law. As the old autocratic monarchies of Europe were overthrown, or forced to accept some form of representative government, juries were introduced. First France, then Belgium, Norway, Denmark, Germany, Austria, Italy and Spain introduced juries into criminal procedure. Even Japan made provision for the system when adopting the German criminal code in this century, but the provision has been more or less ignored.[11] In fact, wherever jury trial has been grafted on to an existing workable system, the graft has refused to 'take', and initial enthusiasm has waned. In some places it has been totally or partially abandoned in favour of a system of trial with a bench of judges and lay assessors. This occurred for instance in Germany in 1924 and in Denmark in 1936. Elsewhere the jury concept has been so radically altered that it has come to resemble a system of trial with lay assessors, as has been the pattern in France since 1943. The motives for abandonment have varied. In some countries, the system has been unacceptable to totalitarian regimes such as that of Italy in 1931, and of Spain after the Civil War. But in others, the difficulty seems on the whole to have been one of temperament rather than one of political illiberality, resulting in failure to achieve a balance of power between judge and jury which will produce reasonably satisfactory results. As we shall see, the English judges were able to evolve, in the course of day-to-day experience of legal problems, their own rules defining the proper spheres of activity of the jury. It has proved extremely difficult to transplant into an already established and alien system of law those detailed rules of practice and procedure which make the English system of jury trial workable in its own native climate.

INFORMATION AND RESEARCH

Most people have only a sketchy idea of the courts which operate in this country, of the manner in which they are constituted, or of the kinds of case which they hear. For all that, there is a widespread belief that the courts provide an impartial forum for disputes. The presence of juries, especially in major criminal trials, has done much to build and maintain this optimism. It is not easy for any developed society to convince its members of the unbiased nature of its judicial institutions.

This, then, is the first ground on which the continued use of the jury system can be justified. Moreover the system has a built-in mechanism for sustaining the public trust which supports it. For it continually draws ordinary members of the community into the workings of the courts, instructs them briefly in the processes of the law, and then returns them to their ordinary lives generally well satisfied with the community duty which they have undertaken, and with the functioning of the administration of justice.

The second principal line of argument in favour of the jury stems from those special characteristics which allow the jury considerable freedom to reach whatever verdict seems just, taking the case as a whole. No check is made to ensure that the jurors have understood the directions given them; they deliberate in secret; they give no reasons for their verdict. They are therefore free to refrain from strict application of the law to the facts, either because they dislike the law or because by departing from it they can express some special sympathy or criticism.

Despite the support of the general public and of many

lawyers, critics of the jury system are becoming more vocal. In a recent broadcast, Lord Devlin observed that 'a jury has for so long been regarded as an essential part of our way of criminal justice that until recently any man who advocated dispensing with it would have been regarded as a crank. But all of a sudden it has become a debatable subject.'[12] In the first place, trial by jury is a cumbersome and expensive method of trying a case; at the very least, this places the onus of proving its value on those who wish to see it continue. But the most substantial arguments against the jury turn on just those aspects of the system – secrecy of deliberation and absence of declared reasons for the verdict – which secure many of the advantages claimed by supporters. The basic objection of the opponents is that the jury, as an entirely untrained body, lacks the ability to understand and judge a case adequately. The critics, with Judge Jerome Frank at their head in the United States and Professor Glanville Williams in this country,[13] have emphasized that the random process by which its members are selected must produce some juries with little or no experience of assessing witnesses or of following the development of a case as it is presented under the formal conditions of a court-room. The most trenchant opponents allege that the jury has survived only because the secrecy of the jury-room has been so carefully preserved that the worst has never been known outside it.

Arguments about the attributes and abilities of English juries are likely to reach stalemate for lack of accurate knowledge of how they function; hence the now frequent appeal for research into juries. It is clear that a wider variety of people than ever before consider that such investigation would be justified; indeed, that it would be not a symptom of social malaise but evidence of social maturity to put the institution under responsible scrutiny. It is one of the purposes of this book to consider which matters could most usefully be investigated and what possible consequences might follow the results of research.

The United States is now the established leader in objective studies of the jury system. For forty years lawyers and psychologists there have been conducting experiments designed to test aspects of the ability of non-specialist groups to assess evidence. All earlier investigations have now been dwarfed by the researches of the Chicago Jury Project. For fifteen years a team of lawyers, psychologists and sociologists at the University of Chicago has been working with judges and court officials throughout the United States on a number of different studies. Their series of projects will, when finally reported in full, provide a body of knowledge quite unparalleled in its scale and depth.[14] Already this work has sparked off new interest in English universities, and in both Oxford and London research projects are now under way.

The American studies suggest that there are four important avenues of research:

1. *Recording and analyzing discussion in the jury-room.* This has so far been impossible in England, since it is regarded as fundamental that the jury should be free to deliberate in secret and return a verdict without indicating how it was reached. The Chicago investigators began experiments in Kansas with the cooperation of a federal court, in which the deliberations of actual juries were tape-recorded. However, news of this activity quickly produced a national outcry and a Senate Committee investigation. Shortly afterwards, some thirty states enacted statutes forbidding jury-tapping. In England, deliberate and unsanctioned listening-in constituted the ancient crime of eavesdropping until its recent abolition;[15] even now it is probably contempt of court. But there is no constitutional bar preventing collaboration between the courts and the appropriate Government departments in an effort to institute jury-room investigations under properly controlled conditions.

2. *Interviewing jurors before or after service.* It is probably contempt of court in England to interview a juror in connexion with his service between the time of his being summoned and the completion of his duty. However innocent the intent, an approach to a juror in these circumstances could easily be misinterpreted as an attempt to influence the verdict and is therefore likely to be regarded by the judges as an improper interference with the due administration of justice. If a juror is interviewed after his service is over, the same objection cannot be maintained. Moreover, trial jurors take no oath of secrecy, in contrast with those who used to sit on grand juries, though they are customarily

warned by notices in jury rooms not to speak about their service to others, either during or after the trial.[16] In 1922 the foreman of the jury in the *Armstrong* poisoning case gave a newspaper interview directly revealing the course of the jury's deliberations in the case. The Lord Chief Justice, Lord Hewart, deprecated this conduct in the strongest terms, without saying whether it amounted to contempt of court.[17] Since then the editors of newspapers and journals have been chary of publishing jury-room memoirs, though they have never wholly disappeared from the press. In the past few years, public disquiet over a number of jury cases has produced quite a spate of personal recollections of jury service, some of them including references to the way in which decisions were reached in the jury-room. In 1966 the B.B.C. broadcast interviews with jurors which dealt with cases heard and how verdicts were reached. A distinction ought to be drawn between publishing a juror's experience of an actual, identifiable case, and serious research covering a number of cases, which are not afterwards identifiable, for the purpose of testing general hypotheses about the working of the jury. The post-trial interview has been used for much of the American work, and undoubtedly can produce interesting information. If its object is to discover how the jury reached its decision then the fallibility of memory and the effects of emotional involvement must be allowed for.

For the purposes of this book I have myself interviewed a considerable number of jurors, and discussed many aspects of their service with them. The interviews were given of their own free will, and the results are not sufficiently exhaustive to merit any form of detailed quantitative analysis. Even so, the interviews did provide a valuable insight into the attitudes, experiences and problems of jury service; therefore I have felt it useful to refer to them at various points throughout the book.

3. *Comparing the verdicts reached by juries with the views of lawyers about the same cases.* This method is employed in the most extensively reported portion of the Chicago work. Five hundred and fifty-five judges throughout the United States agreed to send in reports of jury trials which they had conducted, and in this way the results of 3,576 criminal cases have been exhaustively analysed in a book entitled *The*

American Jury.[18] Each judge's report enabled a comparison to be made between the verdict actually reached by the jury and the way in which the judge would have decided the case himself. The judges were asked to give any reasons they could adduce to account for differences where they occurred and to answer a number of other questions designed to indicate whether the jury had understood the evidence, and to isolate the recurrent factors which cause judges and juries to reach opposite results.

A substantial area of difference did emerge. In 19 per cent of the cases juries acquitted where the judge would have convicted; and in a further 5 per cent they convicted on a less serious charge than the judge thought appropriate. There was a much smaller variation in the opposite direction: the juries convicted when the judge would have acquitted in 3 per cent of the cases; and they convicted on a more serious charge than the judge thought proper in a further 1 per cent.[19]

This suggests that in America roughly one criminal case in every four might have produced a different result if it had been tried by a judge – a most striking variation. No attempt has ever been made in England to collect similar information in any systematic way, although the Lord Chief Justice did conduct a poll of the Queen's Bench judges in response to a visit from one of the Chicago investigators. The answers showed that cases in which judges would have acquitted, but in which the jury convicted, were 'very rare', but estimates of the number of cases in which the jury acquitted but the judge would have convicted varied from 3 to 10 per cent.[20] These figures give only general impressions, and they cover only the experiences of the High Court judges who sit in Assize Courts but not those of Recorders and Chairmen of Quarter Sessions. The measure of difference in all the superior criminal courts should now be investigated, and it may diverge considerably from the Chicago results. The point has already been made that jury trial in the United States is itself a markedly different institution; in particular the judge has less power to control and influence the jurors than in England.

4. *Performing or playing recordings of trials to experimental juries*. This technique has one special advantage over those

so far mentioned; it permits observation of a number of different juries hearing the same case. If the researcher is testing the importance of one particular factor – say the inclusion or exclusion of evidence of an accused person's past criminal record – then it is a simple matter to present the same case to a variety of 'juries', both with and without the evidence in question, and with no other variation in the trial except different 'jurors' as participants. The technique has been employed in the Chicago Project in experiments designed to test the effect of different kinds of legal direction on the defence of insanity.[21] Similar experiments now taking place at the London School of Economics are designed to test the effect on jurors of certain rules of evidence.

Of course, the experimental jury is subject to the limitation that the participants know that they are not trying a real case; the fact that they bear no responsibility for settling the rights and liabilities of actual citizens is bound to introduce an incalculable factor. One can at least say that those who have taken part in running such experiments, both in America and in this country, have been impressed by the serious and highly responsible way in which experimental jurors react to a carefully simulated recording of a trial. In any case, the results of experiments can be checked against results produced by other methods. The techniques of research which have been outlined are not mutually exclusive; each may be used to test hypotheses suggested by findings derived from other sources.

The primary purpose of the ensuing three chapters is to explain the law and practice relating to the jury system in England, after which merits, demerits, improvements and alternatives may be discussed. One chapter is devoted to the present system of selecting jurors, and to proposed changes; another deals with the jury's part in a trial, and the influence which it has had on court practice; this is followed by an investigation of the complex interplay of the respective roles of judge and jury. Chapter 5 moves from analysis to evaluation, and is concerned with the jury as a constitutional protection against governmental and other interference with the impartial administration of justice. Then follow two chapters devoted to the jury's role in the criminal courts; these explore the factors which may influence jurors' judgment in criminal cases generally and also their attitudes and abilities in particular kinds of prosecutions. Chapter 8 turns to civil cases, with particular reference to areas of the law, personal injury and defamation actions, in which juries have until recently been commonly used for particular reasons. Chapter 9 deals with special uses of the jury, in coroners' courts and on other tribunals. The final chapter draws together threads from the detailed discussion of the earlier chapters which are relevant in considering the role of juries and other tribunals in the future.

2 · Jurors

The jury system aims to provide the courts with a tribunal that is both impartial and representative of the ordinary citizen. These twin objects are worked out in detail through the rules for the qualification and selection of jurors. If jurors are to be impartial then no one – neither the state nor any individual or faction – should be able to affect the process of selection. We shall see that in England little has been done to provide formal methods of securing impartial selection; a good deal has been left to the discretion of the summoning officers as to how they actually carry out their task. There have been few complaints, so established practices have run on without alteration. Some changes, however, are now about to be made. They will help to ensure that in the choice of jurors justice is seen to be done as well as done.

The sectors of society that are actually represented on juries will be discovered only by looking at the rules for qualification and exclusion. Here again the existing rules, which since 1825 have included a specific property qualification, have been allowed to continue on into an age in which they seem hopelessly anomalous. But in this case changes have been slow because they raise a fundamental conflict between the desire to make juries truly representative and the fear that not all citizens are intellectually capable of the extended and onerous duties of jury service. Nevertheless a substantial revision of the qualification rules is imminent, and it is therefore to the property qualification that we first turn.

At the beginning of the nineteenth century juries were in no way representative of the populace as a whole. A man was tried by his peers only in the sense that the members of the jury were not government servants and did not hold any regular office. Just as the right to vote in parliamentary elections was confined to the owners of freehold land of a certain value, so jurors were chosen from roughly the same class. But the qualifications for jury service were less precise. Much was left to the discretion and customary practice of the petty constables (the parish officers who drew up the jury lists) and the under-sheriffs and others who summoned the jurors. The visit of the Assize judge to each county was an important social event, and in consequence it was common for the jurors at Assizes to be drawn from the aristocracy and the gentry. Quarter Sessions, being less of an occasion, were mainly served by juries of small farmers and tradesmen.[1]

Because the composition of juries was subject to so much discretion, allegations of handpicking were inevitable, especially in criminal cases where the Crown had some special interest.[2] Sir Robert Peel, as Home Secretary, achieved a number of much needed legal reforms, mostly of the criminal law and its administration. Among the earliest of them was the Juries Act 1825. This Act aimed to provide a standard qualification for jury service, and to consolidate generally some eighty-five different statutes relating to juries. Under the Act the principal qualification for jury service was the holding of certain interests in land. A man became liable to serve as a common juror if he occupied a dwelling of at least £20 annual value for rating (£30 in London and Middlesex). This still remains the principal qualification, though the Act also renders a person liable for jury service if he owns freehold land having an annual value of at least £10, or a tenancy for twenty-one years or more having an annual value of at least £20, or if he occupies a house having at least fifteen windows.[3] The property qualification for jury service was liberal by 1825 standards, for the requirements were less stringent than those for most Parliamentary electors, until the Reform Act of 1832. Peel sought to make the qualification of jurors both certain and uniform, but he was not able to interfere with the old, vague customs of the city and borough courts. They continued to follow their traditional practices until 1922. Nor did the Act affect coroners' juries; there are still no exact qualification rules governing them (see p. 245).

Although the qualification provisions of 1825 are still effective today, there has been a gradual increase in the number of people occupying separately rated dwellings, and as rateable values have increased, the occupants of many more houses have qualified as jurors. Nonetheless, jury service has remained the one public duty for which a property qualification is required, during a period in which other public rights and responsibilities have come to be shared by all adult citizens.

During this century, two Home Office committees have considered the qualification rules. In 1913, Lord Mersey's Committee recommended no more than a small reduction in the minimum rateable values of the property qualification.[4] But in 1965 Lord Morris's Committee concluded that it was 'inherent in the very idea of a jury that it should be as far as possible a genuine cross-section of the adult community', and therefore that the qualification for service should be 'citizenship as evidenced by inclusion in the electoral register as a Parliamentary elector'.[5] Shortly after it was published, the Government announced its intention of implementing the Morris Committee's report as a whole. But other legal reforms of administration of justice, particularly the Criminal Justice Act 1967, have so far taken up the available Parliamentary time. This Act did contain important provisions concerning juries: the disqualification from jury service of persons with previous criminal convictions (substantially as recommended by the Committee); and the acceptance of majority verdicts of at least ten to two (not within the Committee's terms of reference);[6] but the substantial part of the Committee's report has not been acted on. Nonetheless the Home Secretary has repeated that legislation dealing with jury qualifications and related matters may be expected within the reasonably near future.

Why has the change been so long in coming? There were two quarters from which pressure might have come: workers and women. The T.U.C. in its early years argued that juries should be made representative of the whole population. In 1913, the Mersey Committee was perturbed by evidence of working-class feeling against the middle-class bias of juries.[7] But agitation from trade unions was never more than sporadic, and an explanation was not difficult to discover: until 1949, there was no compensation for loss of wages while serving on a jury. For a working man a jury summons could mean an arduous financial burden.

Organizations for women's rights have been more persistent. The first battle was to have women admitted to juries at all. This demand was among the many different civic and professional rights for which women fought so strenuously in the period before the First World War. It was conceded in 1919 and was thus among the first batch of victories.[8] Thereafter the relatively small number of women householders ensured that it would be unusual to find a jury containing more than three or four women jurors, and all-male juries are still common. In the last decade the number of women marked for jury service on the electoral rolls has remained constant at 11 per cent.[9] Women's organizations have continued to keep this imbalance in the public eye and the appointment of the Morris Committee to review the whole question of qualification for jury service was largely the result of their efforts.

Another factor which militated against a change in the 1825 rules was that periodic increases in rateable values gradually extended the number of those qualified for service. Yet for a long time this extension was very slow. As recently as 1956 Lord Devlin was able to characterize the typical juror in a celebrated phrase, as 'male, middle-aged, middle-minded and middle-class'.[10] At the same period market-research organizations were using the density of 'J's on the electoral register to determine the social status of different areas throughout the country.[11] It was estimated that about one and a half million persons were qualified to serve. But since then there have been widespread rating revaluations. In 1963 eight million houses and flats had their rateable value increased from less than £30 to more than £30.[12] The middle-class colour is rapidly fading from Lord Devlin's picture. The property qualification now excludes the occupants of the poorest housing and those who are not separately rated. This still produces variations. In one West London borough, the proportion of persons marked 'J' to the total number on the 1967 electoral register was 9 per cent. But this proportion represented an average between different wards. In one ward the figure was as high as 17 per cent, in two others as low as 4 per cent.

There is no acceptable reason why mere house occupation should form the basis on which desirable jurors are selected. Not surprisingly, the Morris Committee received no convincing evidence that householders have any special abilities as jurymen. The real question was whether to turn the jury into a true cross-section of the adult community, or to restrict it to those who might be expected to show some special degree of experience, responsibility or ability. The Committee chose the former course, attracted by the notion of jury duty as a concomitant of the privilege of citizenship, and fortified by the view of most of those who gave evidence that juries as at present selected are able to understand the issues put to them and to reach properly considered verdicts. But that was by no means the universal view. Some witnesses, including the Metropolitan Commissioner of Police and the Association of Chief Police Officers, thought that the quality of jurors had deteriorated. This presumably reflects the increasing anxiety in police and other circles that juries are too ready to acquit persons accused of crime.[13] No doubt the police have been encountering particular cases in which the jury's acquittal has been hard to accept, and this could be because modern juries have a wider social representation than in the past. But we shall see that no figures have been kept which would show whether the acquittal rate has recently increased, so that there is no objective means of checking the police view. It represents no more than the impression of an interested party.

The Chicago Jury Project has provided some evidence of how the social status and sex of American jurors affects their contribution to the deliberation of a jury. One report shows that jurors have a marked tendency to choose as their foreman a man of one of the high social-status groups, a proprietor or white-collar worker; and that the foreman, not unexpectedly, plays a larger part in the deliberations than other members of the jury. The report shows that ordinary labourers and housewives make fewer contributions to the course of discussions than other jurors, but that the differences are more pronounced in civil cases than in criminal. But as far as actual verdicts were concerned, it was not found possible to predict the verdict that a juror would favour by basing one's guess on such general characteristics or criteria as occupation, education, sex or age. Too many factors of individual personality seemed to be operative. But it was shown in experimental cases concerning a person accused of crime who pleaded insanity, that persons belonging to a minority ethnic group – Negroes – more often favoured a verdict of not guilty by reason of insanity than the rest of the jurors, and that jurors of higher socio-economic status showed an above-average tendency to vote for a verdict of guilty. The report demonstrated that persons of higher status had no greater power than others to win over dissidents to their own way of thinking. As far as differentiation between the sexes is concerned, one experiment showed that men and women jurors tended to adopt the same positions as have been observed in other psychological studies of the interaction between men and women in groups. Men tended to initiate bursts of discussion which were directed to solving the problem in hand. Women tended rather to react to the contribution of others, and generally to assume a social-emotional role in the discussion.[14]

It may well be that, as with the American experiments, it would not be possible to show that changes in the age or sex ratio of jurors produced any predictable results overall. These are among the factors being studied in the present experiments at the London School of Economics. The 'jurors', who listen to a tape-recorded trial, are selected from the whole adult population without reference to a property qualification; they are of necessity drawn on a voluntary basis. The results from the first set of experiments show that women jurors as a group show no greater tendency to than men to acquit a defendant charged with a relatively minor theft. There is some tendency for persons under thirty to favour an acquittal, compared with those in higher age groups. This is also true of those with higher educational qualifications and with higher occupational status. These same groups also change their minds more frequently than others in the course of the discussion of the case. But it must be emphasized that these results are only of the first batch of experiments. They are now being investigated and checked in further similar experiments.

Even if the Morris Committee's recommendation would introduce on to juries many people who have greater sympathy with criminal defendants or require to be more thoroughly convinced of the case against them than the typical juror of the present day, it does not follow that the recommendation should not be implemented. It may well be that there are certain kinds of case that are too emotional or too difficult to be adequately tried before the new juries: this is a matter to be discussed in Chapter 8. But, in general, the jury system aims to have cases decided by a representative group of ordinary citizens, so that verdicts can reflect the judgment and moral sense of the community. The Committee must be right in principle to say that juries ought to represent the whole population to whom other rights of full citizenship are given: this is an essential part of the concept of a jury. If it does not work satisfactorily, the time has come to find other tribunals for the courts, not to tinker with the methods of constituting juries.

Special juries

The Morris Committee did not favour the selection of specially able or experienced juries either in general or for particular kinds of case. This confirms a trend in the law that was established only in 1949. Before that there were two classes of trial jury: common and special. In the past special juries have fulfilled two rather different functions: as informed judges of facts requiring knowledge of some special non-legal field, and as jurors of higher social status than normal. Special juries of the former kind seem to have been employed from the thirteenth century onwards. There are medieval cases recorded of London juries of cooks and fishmongers summoned to try persons accused of selling bad food, and many instances of mercantile disputes being settled by merchants who knew the trade in question. This was natural in a system under which jurors were expected to decide the case by applying their own knowledge. Until the latter part of the eighteenth century the general common law lacked a developed set of commercial principles. But under the Chief Justice of the King's Bench, Lord Mansfield, great strides were made in remedying this deficiency, and the technique which he adopted was to hear commercial cases with a special jury of City merchants. The Chief Justice's jury had a regular membership and on occasion the jurors were invited to dine with the judge. Mansfield used the verdicts that they returned to formulate general propositions of mercantile law. At a time when Parliament rarely used its legislative power to develop new law of this kind Mansfield's imaginative use of specially qualified jurors was a practical means of keeping the law in step with the needs of a rapidly expanding trading nation.[15]

Special juries also became popular in other cases where there was no need for technical or professional expertise. In the late seventeenth century it became customary for the Court of King's Bench to order the summoning of juries composed entirely of persons of higher social status than was required for common juries. It was settled by a statute of 1730 that in the Court of King's Bench such a special jury could be requested by any litigant, provided he was prepared to pay the requisite fee. These special juries were available not only in civil cases but also in criminal prosecutions, and, as we shall see (p. 131), their use in sedition trials at the time of the French revolution was virulently denounced. Part of the trouble was the absence of any established qualification for special jurors, and this allowed the Government to get its nominees on to the jury without much difficulty. The Juries Act 1825 at least prescribed that special juries should be of the rank of 'banker, merchant or esquire', and in 1870 property qualifications were added, which prescribed certain minimum rateable values above those for common jurors. There was a gradual widening of the class from which special jurors were drawn. The Mersey Committee, in 1913, heard complaints that the quality of special juries was being lowered by the inclusion of too many publicans. The Committee took the matter seriously enough to recommend that a special minimum rateable value should be prescribed for licensed premises, although this suggestion never became law.[16]

In the early years of this century, special juries still had some popularity: their use in criminal cases had practically died out, but they were sought in personal injury cases in the belief that people of higher status were likely to think in larger terms when it came to assessing damages. They were also popular in defamation actions, where an element of class or political prejudice was often useful to one side or the other. But it was difficult to justify a system by which one side could hope to influence the result of his case merely by paying for a different tribunal, and the special jury was eventually abolished in 1949. An exception was made to keep special juries from the City of London in the Commercial Court of the Queen's Bench Division. The spirit of Lord Mansfield was not altogether dead, but the use of juries in commercial matters was by that time rare, and no special jury has sat in the Commercial Court since 1950.[17] The Morris Committee has recommended its final abolition.

At a later stage we shall return to the question of how far the proper administration of justice is jeopardized by the lack of skill and knowledge of ordinary jurors. Obviously the danger is greatest in complex cases involving unusual or technical subject matter. One solution we shall have to consider is the revival of specially qualified juries, not in the spirit that was behind the provision of jurors of higher social status, but on the model of the commercial jury, which had sufficient special knowledge of the field in question to understand the issues and make an informed judgment upon them.

Selection by ability

In a number of other countries where the jury system has been introduced, a property qualification for jurors has not been thought suitable. The situation in the United States is particularly instructive. There the requirement of occupation of property has gone, but other steps are taken to select jurors who are thought to be suitable for the job. In many states, selection is made by jury commissioners who are appointed annually by the courts. In some places the commissioners do their job by asking prominent local citizens for names of suitable jurymen, in others they send out questionnaires to potential jurors inquiring about such matters as age, citizenship and schooling. Some even conduct personal interviews. In certain states, for instance in parts of California, investigation of prospective jurors is quite sophisticated. Persons under consideration have to answer multiple-choice question papers designed to test literacy, knowledge of basic legal terminology and procedure, and even intelligence, memory and perception.[18] The United States Supreme Court has held that it is not inconsistent with the concept of the jury as a 'cross-section of the community' to select jurors on the basis of intelligence and verbal comprehension, even though this has the effect of eliminating a disproportionate number of persons belonging to certain social or economic groups.[19]

There is a school of thought in America that believes that these methods should be carried still further. Psychological tests have been developed for the purpose of analysing such factors as emotional stability, ability to judge behaviour critically, and willingness to judge honestly and carefully on the evidence. Use of such tests would provide more objective criteria for selection than the personal estimates of jury commissioners who conduct interviews or act on the recommendations of others.[20]

These pioneer transatlantic ventures suggest that once we have experience of juries selected at random from the community, a reaction may set in; the desire to select jurors for their general ability to do the job may well gain strength. The Morris Committee was in fact set up partly in consequence of an incident in which an unintelligent juror had spoken privately to a witness without appreciating the significance of what he was doing.[21] The Committee must therefore have had the question of intellectual ability very much in mind. It examined the American approach carefully. But it was not prepared to go far along the road to careful pre-selection.

As we shall see, it recommended that certain basic requirements of mental and linguistic ability be laid down, but otherwise the Committee faced the prospect of a truly representative jury with steady optimism:

We think that in any healthy community there will be a high sense of duty, a fundamental respect for law and order, and a wish that principles of honesty and decency should prevail. A jury should represent a cross-section drawn at random from the community, and should be the means of bringing to bear on the issues that face them the corporate good sense of that community. This cannot be in the keeping of the few, but is something to which all men and women of good will must contribute.[22]

OTHER LIMITATIONS ON ELIGIBILITY
FOR JURY SERVICE

From the Juries Act 1825 onwards, a number of statutes have defined the various grounds of exemption or disqualification for jurors – largely matters of age, employment in certain occupations and past contacts with the law. These rules are now badly in need of rationalization and modernization, and the Morris Committee has put forward suggestions which would do much to improve the existing law. At present, there are certain grounds which disqualify a person from serving as a juror, and others which entitle him to claim exemption. In general, disqualification and exemption produce similar consequences. A person who falls into either category may object to having his name marked on the electoral roll as a juror, and a litigant may challenge him for cause (see p. 45) when he is about to be sworn in court. But such a person has no right to claim that he should not serve as a juror once he has been summoned.[23] Nor can a verdict be upset on appeal because a juror who should have been disqualified, or could have been excused, does serve.[24] The Morris Committee has proposed a system under which those to be eliminated on special grounds should be classified under three heads: those *disqualified* from service; those *ineligible*; and those *excusable*, who have a right to claim exemption from service. Because the removal of the property qualifications would take away the necessity of marking potential jurors on the electoral roll, these grounds would be investigated in a questionnaire which those about to be summoned for service would be required to answer. If a potential juror proved to be disqualified or ineligible he would be unable to serve; if excusable he could choose whether to do so or not.[25]

Age limit

The upper age limit for jurors was fixed at 60 in 1825. In 1913, the Mersey Committee recommended that it be raised to 65. This was done during both world wars but on each occasion there was a reversion to the lower limit after the war was over. Most witnesses before the Morris Committee thought that the limit should be 65, and the Committee agreed. There was however some debate as to whether it should be put even higher. The Committee thought that the normal retiring age from employment was a reasonable limit. Judges and magistrates retire at 75 and 72 respectively, but at least it can be said that they have plenty of experience of attending to court proceedings for hours at a stretch. In any case, it is now recognized that these limits may be too high, for the Lord Chancellor has announced his intention of lowering them.

At present a person qualifies for jury service at 21, but he has also to satisfy the property qualification and so the number of young people who actually serve on juries is small. If the property qualification were removed a quarter of an average jury would be under 30. The Morris Committee considered whether the lower age limit should be raised, but thought that there was not sufficient reason for doing so. They pointed out that nearly half of those tried in the higher courts in 1963 were under the age of 25 and nearly two-thirds under 30. Not surprisingly, they avoided any suggestion that the principle of like trying like should be pushed to logical extremes, but still they felt that it would be no bad thing if the views of young people were heard on juries.[26] The Latey Committee on the Age of Majority has subsequently recommended that persons should be treated as being of full age for various legal purposes when they become 18 rather than 21. And the Speaker's Conference has suggested that the voting age should be lowered to 20. There is much to be said for these proposals, but it is unlikely that there will be great enthusiasm for lowering the age for jury service below 21. Marriage without consent, full ability to make contracts and deal with property, and membership of the electorate are matters of personal right. Jury service is first and foremost a duty to judge others; it is often quite a complex task which calls for maturity and general experience.

Disabilities limiting the usefulness of jurors

The present law does not expressly exclude those suffering from physical or linguistic disabilities which would seriously interfere with their performance as jurors. The matter is left to the discretion of summoning and court officials who will see to it that a juror is excused if, for example, he is deaf or dumb, or unable to read English. Sometimes these disabilities are not discovered until it is too late to take appropriate steps. In one case it emerged that a man was convicted of sheep-stealing in Wales by a jury on which there were two jurors who could not speak English. The Court of Criminal Appeal followed its regular practice and refused to quash the conviction.[27] More should certainly be done to exclude persons who are subject to such unquestionable disadvantages, and to make it clear to those summoned that they must bring such disabilities to the attention of the court. The Morris Committee has recommended that various categories of people should be ineligible for service: the deaf, the blind and those suffering from any other physical handicaps which would make it difficult for them to carry out their duty satisfactorily, in-patients in mental hospitals and persons unable to speak, write or read English.[28]

Criminal convictions

A man with a criminal record may well have special reasons for failing to discharge his duty as a juror in an honest and disinterested way, and it is right that some convicted offenders should be excluded from service. Moreover, a criminal may be specially susceptible to threats or bribes. By a strange quirk in the process of legislative reform, a change in the jury laws made in 1870 had the effect of restricting the class of persons disqualified from jury service because of their previous criminal record to those guilty of 'infamous crimes', that is buggery and cognate offences. It is highly unlikely that Parliament intended only to keep out that very small group of offenders, but in 1950 the Court of Criminal Appeal examined the statute and held that this was how it should be interpreted.[29] The Morris Committee agreed that people with serious criminal records should be disqualified and proposed that a person who within the previous five years had been in prison or other detention with a sentence of three months or more (without the option of a fine) should be disqualified. In some places it was the practice to show the jury list to the police so that criminals known to them could be eliminated. The Committee disapproved of this practice; it could be interpreted as giving the police a hand in selecting the jury. So it was necessary to devise another method by which criminals could be discovered and disqualified. The Committee decided that it could be done only by asking potential jurors themselves to supply the information. If the Committee's report is implemented as a whole then the question will be one on the general question-naire sent out to each person who is about to be sum-moned. It would be an offence to give false replies and if sample checks were made against criminal records there would be some sanction to back the large measure of trust on which the system would operate.[30]

However, the recommendation that people with criminal records should not serve has become law in advance of the rest of the Morris Report, as part of the provisions in the Criminal Justice Act 1967 intended to strengthen the admini-stration of criminal justice against attack by bribers and intimidators.[31] The Act goes further than the Morris Committee: any person who has served part of a prison sentence of at least three months is disqualified for ten years; any person who has served part of a prison sentence of five years or more is disqualified for good. The disqualification will prevent a man from serving even though he has been marked ' J ' on the electoral roll. He will be liable to a fine of up to £250 if he serves, but the verdict returned by his jury would not be rendered void by his participation. The Act requires the summoning officer to send potential jurors a notice of the new provisions, but this detached notice is of course less satisfactory than the inclusion of the relevant question in the official questionnaire; this cannot come about until the Morris Committee's general recommendations have the force of law. Another reason for hoping for full imple-mentation of the Report is that as the law now stands there is an unnecessary distinction between civil and criminal cases: a potential juror with a criminal background disquali-fying him from serving in criminal courts is still permitted to serve on a civil jury.

Commonwealth and alien immigrants

Aliens are at present excluded from jury service and would remain so under the Morris Committee's system, since they are not entitled to vote. However, Commonwealth and Irish immigrants are at present qualified once they are on the electoral register and have satisfied the property qualification. The Committee recommended that a minimum of five years' residence in England should be introduced.[32] This precaution seems justifiable though the period may be rather long. The Committee considered that a newly arrived immigrant would probably lack the kind of knowledge and contact with life in this country necessary in assessing witnesses and in making value judgments on issues such as whether driving was dangerous. The new requirement of literacy will exclude immigrants who still have difficulty with the English language after the five-year period.

Professional and other positions

It is generally agreed to be a bad thing to allow more people than is absolutely necessary an exemption from jury service because of the services they render in their professional capacity or by fulfilling some public office. In England there is a long and somewhat agglomerate list of such grounds for exemption, though it is by no means as easy to claim exemption here as in some parts of the Commonwealth and the United States. Lawyers, policemen, members of Parliament, peers, county councillors, doctors, firemen, priests, nuns and many others, even members of the Mersey Docks and Harbours Board and Elder Brethren of Trinity House, are exempt. But such people as accountants, architects, businessmen and school teachers cannot claim exemption by reason of their profession; and so the law does not, as is sometimes claimed, remove all those best qualified by their jobs to weigh evidence and reach conclusions upon it. The Morris Committee took a firm line against unnecessary exclusions. They stressed that if all the adult population were to be made liable for service then few would be summoned more than once or twice in a life-time, and that therefore professional inconvenience should rarely be a ground of excuse. However, they felt that there were special reasons for excluding members of certain professions. Those who have some close connexion with the administration of justice may take advantage of their experience and knowledge to thrust their views upon the rest of the jury. Therefore they should be totally ineligible. This would apply to a wide range of persons from judges to prison visitors and traffic wardens. The Committee thought that exclusion should continue for ten years after a person had given up one of these occupations.[33] Ministers of religion and members of religious communities were considered to fall under the same head, though it is hard to see why it was necessary to exclude them totally rather than to give them the right to seek exemption. Others again should be entitled to be excused, either because they perform some special duty to the state (M.P.s and servicemen), or because they are concerned with the immediate relief of pain and suffering (doctors, nurses, dentists, veterinary surgeons).[34]

Other grounds of excusal

Summoning officers have been given statutory authority to excuse a person from jury service if he can show some good reason why he should not serve.[35] They deal with most cases which arise in response to a jury summons. But court officials and judges also exercise a similar power, though this is not expressly based on any statute. When a juror raises his objection only on reaching court it is desirable that the court should have power to excuse him. It is specifically laid down that a person has a right to be excused from attendance on the grounds of illness, or, if a woman, 'for medical reasons'.[36] Other grounds which commonly lead either to complete exemption or at least to deferment to a more convenient time are: having to look after children or invalid relatives; running a one-man business which would have to be closed down; having holidays already arranged; losing the seasonal bonuses of certain kinds of employment. Ordinary business inconvenience is often put forward as a reason for excusal, but is not normally regarded as sufficient. The system appears to operate satisfactorily, and the Morris Committee has recommended its continuance and expressed the hope that summoning officers will be generous in the exercise of their power.[37]

Under the present law, jurors who have completed a period of service have some right to be excused from serving again within certain periods. These vary for different courts and different counties.[38] In addition, judges sometimes excuse jurors for life or for a long period of years when they have finished serving on a particularly long case. Their power to do this has been called in question. The Morris Committee considered that under its proposed system the very large number of potential jurors would make it possible for all who have served to be entitled to claim exemption for the next five years; it suggested that records should be kept by summoning officers for that period in order to check such claims. The Committee also thought that the judges' power to excuse for longer periods should be expressly conferred by statute.[39]

SUMMONING

The property qualification has made it necessary to select jurors in two stages: first, by drawing up a list of those eligible, and secondly, by summoning a number from that list from time to time as a court requires them. For a long time the jury list had to be separately drawn up by a parish or borough officer, but now that the electoral roll is a register of all the adult residents in a district, it has come to be used instead. Those who satisfy the property and other qualifications are sought out in drawing up the electoral roll each year, and separately marked with a 'J'. A person is normally sent a letter of warning before his name is marked for the first time. He is informed that if he has a ground upon which he can object, he must do so within a given time, and if necessary go before the justices to sustain his objection. The system is liable to a certain degree of inaccuracy, for instance where the wife owns the house but the husband is assumed to be the occupier and so is marked for jury service.

The process of selecting jurors for service from the general list is performed by the summoning officers for each court. The sheriff of the county has traditionally summoned jurors for Assizes and County Quarter Sessions. In practice his duties are delegated to under-sheriffs, who are usually local solicitors in private practice. Those towns which have their own Borough Quarter Sessions have an official known as the clerk of the peace to perform the duty.[40] Clerks of the peace are commonly town clerks or other local government officers, though some are solicitors. When a court requires jurors it issues a precept to the summoning officer, which is a demand that he summon an appropriate number of jurors. Sometimes this number is stated, and sometimes it is left to his discretion. More than the precise number needed have to be summoned to allow for excusals, challenges and other uncertainties.

It is a rare occurrence for a court to find itself without enough jurymen. If it does happen, there is an ancient procedure known as 'praying a *tales*', by which the judge may command the summoning officer to select 'so many (in Latin, *tales*) of such other able men of the county then present' in the precincts of the court as are needed to make up the full number of jurors. It was recently held that a complete jury cannot be collected in this way; there must be some properly summoned jurors (*quales*) to whom the talesmen can be added.[41] The Morris Committee has recommended that this surprising procedure, by which a man can find himself spirited out of the street and sworn on to a jury without warning, should be restricted: it should only be possible to make up a quarter of the jury in this way.[42] This seems a fair balance of convenience. There must be some protection against the court having to close for lack of jurors, otherwise summoning officers will feel obliged to have ready a large number of reserve jurors who will have to waste a lot of time because of an unlikely chance.

The jurors who are summoned are known as the panel. The summoning officer has a legal obligation to see that the proportion of women on the panel is the same as that in the list of jurors from which they are drawn, subject to the proviso that where possible their number should be at least fourteen. In fact this rule has been widely neglected in recent years.

The summoning officer is expected to make a disinterested selection of persons to be summoned. Despite recommendations by the Mersey Committee in 1913 that a proper system of uniform and mechanical selection of names be established, the matter has been left to the discretion of individual officers. The Morris Committee discovered that their methods varied considerably from place to place; some worked completely at random, some took a few names from each street or page of the electoral list, some worked alphabetically through it. Some deliberately summoned from one area at a time, to make it easier to serve summonses and arrange travel. One whimsical solicitor revealed how, as an articled clerk left to do the summoning work for his principal, he used his power to remove the mother of a young lady whom he was courting from her watch-dog position at home.[43]

Any method of selection which is restricted to areas much more limited than those allotted to the court may produce a social or occupational bias in juries, and this is quite contrary to the concept of the jury as a random cross-section of citizens. There could be other dangers. For instance, those intent on bribery or intimidation might find the task of tracing jurors easier.

It is right that jurors should be selected on a truly random basis throughout the area allotted to the court. The Morris Committee received evidence that one clerk of the peace used a computer to obtain a selection that was scientifically random, and found the process simple, efficient and economical. In the United States, mechanical selection is combined with mechanical methods of preparing and addressing summonses to the jurors selected. The Morris Committee urged the Home Office to do what it could to have such a system introduced throughout this country.[44]

SERVICE AT COURT

The panel and the ballot

The summoning officer completes his duty by returning to the court a list, known as the panel, which sets out the names, addresses and occupations of the jurors who have been summoned and not excused. At present a litigant can obtain a copy of the panel, for the price of a shilling, from the summoning officer and so find out the group from whom his jurors will be selected.[45] This gives a little information upon which he can decide how to exercise his rights of challenge. By providing addresses, it also assists a person who wishes to make an improper approach to a juror. It is desirable in future that only the general area from which a juror comes be indicated, and that litigants see the panel only on the day of the trial.

Juries are made up from those on the panel by a ballot. The law prescribes that a ballot shall take place by drawing cards containing each juror's name from a box. However, the Morris Committee's inquiries revealed that the random choice implicit in this procedure is not always followed:

Some clerks prefer not to place the cards in a box, but to shuffle them like a pack of cards and then to draw off the top twelve. In some courts the ballot is not a genuine one at all, and clerks arrange for the limited number of women on the panel to be evenly divided between juries. Others deliberately arrange the ballot in such a way as to exclude women from certain types of case, and even to place on juries dealing with difficult cases jurors who seem from their occupation to be qualified to understand the issue.[46]

It is thus the case that not only summoning officers but also clerks of court have the opportunity to influence the final composition of juries, and that some do so, though no doubt with the most honourable motives. It cannot be right to leave such discretion to officials of the state, particularly in criminal cases. The Morris Committee were firmly of the opinion that all such practices should cease and that court officials should be obliged to conduct a proper secret ballot. Indeed all suspicion of manoeuvring should be avoided by some means, such as having one of the summoned jurors mix the cards in the box, and another draw them out.

Challenging

It is unlikely today that a litigant will wish to question the whole panel on the basis that the summoning officer has not made a disinterested selection, but if he does have such an objection then he may 'challenge the array'. The right is of great antiquity and was still being taken advantage of in the early nineteenth century. In one case in which a publisher was being charged with sedition, he was able to prove that the sheriff who summoned the jurors was a member of the association which had instituted the prosecution.[47] The old procedure on a challenge to the array was for two jurors to be selected as 'triers'; they would hear the allegations and decide whether the challenger had 'shown cause'. But in 1948 it was laid down that the judge would hear and decide the issue.[48]

Where challenges occur today they normally take the form of an objection to an individual juror. This is called 'challenge to the polls'. The juror may be challenged in either of two ways. In criminal cases, the accused has a right to challenge up to seven jurors peremptorily, that is without giving any reason. This number was settled in 1948.[49] Previously in crimes such as treason and murder the number had been much larger. The Crown does not have this right. Instead it may ask a juror to 'stand by' until all the others in court have been called. This is just as good as a right to challenge peremptorily except where there are not enough other jurors available. After an accused has challenged seven jurors he may not ask other jurors to stand by.[50] His rights may therefore be more limited than those of the prosecution.

The right to challenge peremptorily does give the accused some influence over the question of who should try him. In recent times the practice has not been greatly used. A sample of Old Bailey cases heard in 1964 showed that in 110 cases juries were challenged in only 14; objection was taken to 26 jurors, 11 men and 15 women.[51] To some extent this has been because the clerks of some courts have been prepared to see that a juror is not called to the jury-box if counsel for one side, with the consent of the other, has requested that he be omitted.[52] However, there is now evidence that the practice of peremptory challenging is becoming more popular.

If a survey were made of defendants and counsel who had challenged peremptorily, a wide variety of reasons for their challenges would emerge. Sometimes women jurors are challenged to get an all-male jury. This has for long been common in sex cases, and the practice is growing in drunken-driving cases.[53] Sometimes jurors following a certain occupation are removed for fear that they will see the thinness of the defence too clearly, for example, accountants in fraud cases.[54] It is not often that an accused will have any special knowledge about a particular juror, so that challenging has to be done on general hunches.

There are no peremptory rights of challenge in civil cases, but in both civil and criminal cases each side has a right to challenge any juror 'for cause', that is by showing sufficient reason. Jurors who are shown to have an interest in the case, or to be so biased as to be unable to give a fair hearing, or are disqualified or exempt under the qualification rules, are among those who may be challenged for cause.[55] In practice, the right is even less effective than that of peremptory challenge. Again, a litigant is unlikely to know more about most jurors than the sparse information given on the jury panel: name, sex, address and occupation. He has no right to question the juror in court until he has established some basis for his objection by other evidence. It is not entirely unknown for litigants to interview the jurors on the panel in advance to discover their attitudes to particular matters, but it is not settled whether such conduct amounts to a contempt of court; in Canada it has been held wrongful for a defendant to communicate with a juror before or during his trial.[56]

One of the best-known points of difference between the conduct of jury trials in the United States and in England is the marked contrast in the method of exercising the right of challenge. In the United States it is common practice for each juror to be examined – either by the judge or by the litigants – on his or her personal history, opinion and beliefs, in order to decide whether a challenge should be made either peremptorily or for cause. In this way American lawyers learn a great deal more about the membership of their juries, and it is reckoned an important part of an advocate's technique to know how to question jurors and which to challenge. Even then, it appears from recent research that crucial questions are sometimes not put and jurors who are somewhat prejudiced get on to the jury. The process can be cumbersome and time-consuming. At the trial of Jack Ruby in Dallas for the murder of Lee Harvey Oswald, 162 prospective jurors were examined over fifteen days before a complete jury was sworn.

In making comparisons, it must be remembered that in the United States juries have been given greater powers, so that their membership is of correspondingly greater significance to litigants. The judge's sphere of influence is limited by restrictions on his power to review and comment on the evidence in summing up. And in some states the jury in a criminal case may decide the law and the punishment as well as the facts relating to guilt. There is a significant tendency for the examination of jurors to be formal and conducted by the judge, not the attorneys, in those states where the judge is also accorded the widest powers.[57]

The system in the United States accepts that if a right of challenge is to be a real one under modern conditions, then the litigants must be furnished with an opportunity to find out the antecedents and attitudes of the potential jurors. In contrast, the English system is a survival from earlier conditions in which a litigant could be expected to have general knowledge of most jurors' reputations. The English system does little more than avert the situation in which a litigant feels aggrieved because his case was tried by jurors whom he 'did not like the look off'. It certainly speeds up court procedure and avoids the difficulty of deciding which challenges for cause are sufficient.

The English approach is unlikely to be much modified, unless some specific abuse forces a change. Two possibilities must be borne in mind. One is the suggestion made on a number of recent occasions that unscrupulous defendants are using their peremptory challenges in criminal cases to remove jurors who look intelligent and who would therefore be less susceptible to bribes or intimidation. Certainly there have been recent cases in which challenges have been made to this kind of juror, and because several defendants have been in the dock together the number of challenges has been considerable. In one case where a number of approaches were afterwards made to jurors the seven defendants made thirty-five peremptory challenges. If the practice continues to develop, then serious consideration ought to be given to limiting the right to challenge peremptorily. If such a change were made, it might also be necessary to go into the pros and cons of permitting examination of the jurors with a view of establishing grounds of challenge 'for cause'.

The other possibility has to do with the manner in which the Crown exercises its right to stand by. Lord Dilhorne recently stated that when he was Attorney-General he had the jury panel checked for known Communists, so that they should not serve in a spy case.[58] The search produced one active member of the Communist Party, who was accordingly asked by the Crown to stand down from the jury. The implications of this are somewhat sinister. It is only a century and a half since the Crown was regularly accused of packing juries with sympathizers in political prosecutions. Moreover, it is obviously unfair that the Crown should be able to call on its vast resources of police and other knowledge in deciding whom it should challenge. For the moment, the disparity could best be reduced by removing or severely limiting the Crown's right to stand a juror by. If the Crown is to make use of its sources of information (and it is hard to see how it could be stopped), then it ought to do so only by a challenge for cause, establishing reasons in open court which must satisfy the judge trying the case.

Selection of the foreman

Just as the judge can exert great influence on a jury's verdict in his summing-up, so can the foreman once the jury-room is reached. Most of the jurors whom I interviewed had strong views about how their foreman had discharged his duty, and this indicates that for many of them the course of their deliberation was much affected by his handling of the discussion. In view of this, the lack of any established procedure for his selection seems odd. The Morris Committee found that the practice from one court to another varies widely: sometimes the judge or the court usher suggests to the jurors that they choose their foreman, sometimes the occupant of a particular seat is told to do the job, sometimes nothing is said at all.[59] I was told of juries which never chose a foreman, and others which nominated one only on returning to court with the verdict. The Morris Committee recommended that the task of selection be left in all cases to the jury themselves, and that, as they should be allowed as much time as possible to become acquainted with one another before making the choice, it was better to lay down no definite point in the proceedings when the foreman must be selected. In New Zealand, however, the judge is bound to direct the jury to retire and select its foreman once it has been empanelled.[60] The practice is generally thought to be satisfactory and could well be introduced here for those cases in which a jury starts hearing a case as soon as it is made up. Many juries, however, have to wait around for some time before starting a case; if they were instructed to get acquainted during that period, with a view to selecting a foreman, not only might they succeed in discovering the best man for the job, but their discussion could well assist in forming them into a cohesive group.

Treatment at court

Almost everyone summoned for jury service suffers some interference with the ordinary routine of his daily life, but people are inconvenienced in very different degrees. Summoning officers have a discretion to excuse people for whom jury service would be specially difficult, such as mothers of young children, owners of one-man businesses, and holiday-makers. This discretion cannot be exercised too liberally, or jury service would be reduced to a duty undertaken only by volunteers. So there are many who simply have to put up with the inconvenience. There is a danger that those who are irritated or worried by it will not give proper attention to the proceedings in court. The jurors whom I interviewed, however, consistently gave the impression that any annoyance they felt when first summoned for service was counteracted by the intrinsic interest of the proceedings and their feeling that they must do their best to discharge their serious responsibility.

There are some jurors, however, who are left with a residual feeling of resentment which may well flare up if proceedings are run inefficiently or inconsiderately. Businessmen in particular are readily put out by unnecessary attendances or unexplained waits in jury-rooms, the sort of inefficiency that they would not tolerate in running their own affairs. There can be no doubt that there are many jurors who are left feeling that they have not been treated as considerately as they might have been. There has been a steady trickle of letters in the press over the years complaining about inadequate information concerning the length of service and such important incidentals as facilities for parking and meals, cavalier treatment by some court officials, physical discomforts in jury-boxes and jury-rooms, where it is sometimes difficult even to see or hear properly.

Many courts have allowed established procedures to run on without apparently doing much to reduce the small discomforts and irritations of jurors. One instance is the common practice of summoning all the jurors to court on the first day of the session, merely for the purpose of dividing them into juries and telling all except those needed on that day to return at a later date. When this practice was eventually abandoned at the Old Bailey in 1965, it was estimated that between £15,000 and £20,000 would be saved each year.[61] This perhaps indicates the extent to which jurors' time was consumed to little purpose. The Morris Committee were outspoken about the need to improve the personnel management aspects of administering the jury system. In particular they commented on the juror's first attendance at court:

When he first reports for duty, he encounters an atmosphere somewhat reminiscent of the army's reception of raw rookies. Numbered off into squads of twelve, told enough to ensure that he will be on parade at the right place at the right time, but told very little more, he settles down to await events and, like any new conscript, eagerly accepts whatever rumours are circulating about the likely duration of his service or other matters of direct interest to him.[62]

A number of jurors whom I interviewed contrasted this sort of attitude with the measured courtesy and deference that they received from counsel once they were in the jury-box trying a case.

The Morris Committee recommended as a first remedy, the obvious expedient, common in the United States, of sending each juror an explanatory handbook with his summons.[63] This would set out details about the times at which the court sits, where to report, the facilities that are available, the provisions for payment and similar matters of administration. It ought also to include some general points about service in court, such as the respective duties of judge and jury, whether or not verdicts have to be unanimous and guidance on the selection of a foreman. Assistance should also be given on whether to take notes, and how to ask questions during the hearing. The Morris Committee did not favour the last two suggestions, because they felt that both matters should be left to the individual judge, who would make recommendations to the jury if he felt so inclined. This approach stems from a common belief among lawyers that jurors are likely to waste time and be distracted both by note-taking and by asking questions. But lawyers do not, perhaps, appreciate how often jurors are disturbed by lack of guidance on both matters.

It would also be desirable that the handbook should give some explanation of why delays at court are sometimes necessary, and it should promise that unnecessary time wastage will be avoided wherever possible – a promise that should be fulfilled by administrative improvements. The time has come when methods of avoiding delays at many courts should be fully investigated by management consultants who are professionally equipped for the job. The organization of court business now is based on the assumption that the judge's time is the most valuable quantity. In consequence all those concerned in a case – parties, counsel, witnesses and jurors – may have to wait around so that the trial may start immediately the preceding case has finished. It should not be assumed without careful exploration that valuable resources are best conserved by never leaving a judge with time on his hands.

The Morris Committee was quick to point out that a handbook could be used to help prevent errors occurring in the procedure at the trial from the jurors' lack of knowledge of what they ought and ought not to do. Three kinds of serious problem can arise very largely because of jurors' inexperience: a juror may serve when he ought to have asked to be excused, for instance because he knows a party or a witness, or cannot easily understand English; a juror may come in contact with some person involved with one side or the other in the trial; or the jury may take into account facts that ought to be disregarded, or may reach its verdict by some unjust or unacceptable process. If one of these occurrences comes to light during the trial the judge may deal with it by investigating what has happened and abandoning the trial, or by dismissing the juror concerned and proceeding with the remaining members, or by ignoring the occurrence. Until 1963, it was not possible to proceed with less than a full complement of jurors if each side did not consent (a rule which put the continued good health of each juror at a premium). But in that year, the judge was given power, irrespective of the parties' wishes, to continue a criminal trial provided that nine jurors remain.[64]

If the improper occurrence comes to light after the verdict

has been returned, then it may be necessary to upset the verdict. But the appeal courts are reluctant to do this. They will investigate allegations that there has been some communication, for instance, between a juror and a prosecution or defence witness. They will also upset a verdict if there was some significant formal defect in the procedure, perhaps because the jury bailiff retired with the jury, because a document which contained the accused's record was mistakenly given to the jury, or because all the jurors were not in court when the foreman announced the verdict.[65] They are, however, extremely reluctant to allow an appeal because of some defect in the composition of the jury, or in the way in which the verdict was reached. The case in which the Court of Criminal Appeal refused to upset the verdict of a jury which had on it a Welshman who did not speak English has already been mentioned. Similarly the Court has not acted where it has been shown that a juror knew of the accused's dubious antecedents, or produced a list of his previous convictions in the jury-room, or that the jury drew lots for its verdict[66]. Only very rarely has this sort of allegation produced the desired result of upsetting the verdict. It is not that the Court of Appeal will never investigate allegations of this kind. But there is a well-established, and at first sight artificial, rule which severely limits its ability to do so: the court cannot receive evidence from a juror about any aspect of the manner in which the verdict was reached.[67] If some outsider can give evidence about a juror's prejudiced state of mind, or of some event in the jury-room, then the court will hear him, and will consider whether the allegation is sufficiently serious to justify allowing the appeal. But it is rare for there to be such evidence.[68]

One concern of the Court has been to maintain verdicts against means of subsequently jeopardizing their finality and certainty. But it is important to remember Lord Atkin's remark in this context: 'Finality is a good thing, but justice is a better.'[69] However, finality is not the only consideration: it is necessary to ensure that it is not worth anyone's while to approach jurors in an attempt to find out if a verdict was improperly reached, or to induce them to say so with the aid of threats or bribes. No one can tell how far this fear is a real one. But the increase in attempts to interfere with jurors during the trial of serious criminal cases in the past few years suggests that attempts might be made to interfere with jurors after their service if there were advantages in doing so. If the court did investigate what a juror alleged to have happened in the jury-room, it would be able to check the accuracy of the allegation against the recollection of the other jurors, so that the chance of upsetting a verdict by a fraudulent statement would be slight. It is obviously unsatisfactory that a man should remain convicted where the jury pursued some undesirable or outrageous course in reaching agreement. The Court of Appeal has clearly felt this, for, while saying nothing to encourage an appellant to produce a juror who can give evidence of improprieties in the jury-room, it has taken care to find out the nature of the alleged defect in any case that has come before it. The fact of the matter is that so long as the jury system is maintained there remains an inherent danger that some error of this kind will occur. Careful instruction may help to keep down the number of cases in which something goes wrong, but it can never be as effective as wide experience of proper court procedure. And this can only be gained by regular service in court.

Payment

The most serious grievance which used to arise from service on a common jury was that there was no payment for service at all. On the other hand, special jurors, who as a class could much better afford to bear the expense, were paid because the litigants were obliged to pay a fee for the special jury. In 1949, a long overdue reform was introduced whereby jurors became entitled to claim expenses and losses of earnings up to certain prescribed amounts. At present a juror may draw a travel allowance, a daily subsistence allowance of 12s. 6d. (increased where he is away for more than eight hours) and compensation for loss of earnings and other expenses up to £3 5s. od. a day.[70] This maximum figure means that persons who normally earn more will, if their pay stops, suffer financial loss from jury service. This is particularly hard in cases which last for several weeks. The point was made strongly in the Great Train Robbery case, when some jurors complained to the court about the considerable financial hardship that they were suffering. At that time nothing could be done. Now the maximum has been raised to £6 10s. 0d. a day after the tenth day of service, if the court directs that the increase be paid. But is this enough? It is hard to see why any person called for service should have to suffer financial loss because of it. There should be no limit. A juror who wishes to make a claim above a certain amount ought simply to be obliged to prove his loss more carefully than would otherwise be required.

It is sometimes suggested that instead of a system of reimbursement for loss, we should change to a system of remuneration, under which each juror would earn a fixed sum each day. There seems no reason why in principle a person should not receive a fee for performing a public service of this nature. But it would not be a method of providing a uniform advantage to all who serve. Some jurors suffer no loss of earnings while they are away at court. White-collar employees, in particular, often continue to draw their pay. Manual workers are more likely either to lose their pay entirely or else have the difference between the reimbursement they receive from the court and their normal rate of earnings made up by their employer. Even then there may be losses of overtime and other special rights. Again, the self-employed may simply lose the value of the work they could otherwise have done, and may have to hire a substitute. A uniform payment would be an unexpected bonus for some and compensation for others. It is more desirable that the funds available be devoted to ensuring that no one suffers any actual loss from jury service. Only when that position is attained should the question of payment for services rendered be considered.

The cost of the jury

The introduction of the system of reimbursing jurors for lost pay has added considerably to the cost of running the jury system. No figures are available of the amounts devoted to this end for the country as a whole, but the High Court's accounts for 1965–6 show that £3,000 was spent on jurors, and that Court held only forty-two jury trials in the year. The total number of jury trials in 1965 was approximately 7,000. It must be stressed that reimbursement for loss of earnings has only increased the cost of the jury system. Expenditure was substantial even before 1949. The system requires a considerable administration to make it function. Electors having the property qualification have to be marked on the electoral list. Jurors have to be summoned. Jury bailiffs are specially employed to watch, guide and assist jurors at court. Jury rooms have to be provided for their deliberations. Sometimes the police are required to keep an eye on them out of court hours for fear of intimidation or bribery. In the recent 'Torture' case at the Old Bailey seventy-two officers were doing full-time duty on this work. The presence of a jury is generally reckoned to slow down the course of proceedings – in civil cases where there is a choice of trial with a jury or by judge alone, the courts will set aside eight days for a jury trial when a case is estimated to take five days with a judge alone. As far as criminal cases are concerned, the Law Society has recently stated that 'the average cost of a trial at Quarter Sessions or Assizes must be at least five times as great as it is in Magistrates' Courts and often considerably more, and it occupies a far greater measure of public and private time.'[71] Trial by jury is not cheap and it is not quick. These are not factors which will weigh heavily if the jury is shown to be a superior tribunal to the alternatives, but they do suggest that the case for retention of the jury system needs to be made out positively.

3 · Trial method and practice

Trial by jury was for so long an integral part of the courts of common law that it has deeply affected many aspects of court practice. This chapter describes the extent to which the jury has now been superseded by other types of court, and at the same time examines the degree to which procedural rules are the product of jury trial, and require to be maintained only in so far as that system remains the method of constituting the court. This requires some exploration not only of the procedure at the trial itself but also of the pre-trial steps that lead up to the hearing. One aspect of trial practice – the law of evidence – is so intimately connected with the presence of juries that it will be separately discussed at the end of the chapter.

CRIMINAL CASES

The courts

There are two ranks of criminal courts. The superior courts – Assizes, Quarter Sessions, the Central Criminal Court in London and the Crown Courts in Liverpool and Manchester – are always composed of judge and jury. The inferior courts are the Magistrates' Courts, consisting either of a stipendiary magistrate, or a bench of lay justices, advised by their legally qualified clerk. The present principle is that a defendant is in general entitled to demand trial by jury before a superior court on any offence for which the maximum penalty is more than three months' imprisonment. Traditionally the more serious, or 'indictable', offences were tried in the higher courts, and the lesser, 'summary', offences before the magistrates.

It is still true that the most heinous types of indictable offence have to be sent for trial at a superior court, but the middle range of offences – for example, property offences which do not involve violence or breaking into a dwelling – are now frequently dealt with summarily, if the accused consents. This development has been proceeding steadily for over a century. During this time, both kinds of criminal court have been almost constantly under the pressure of increasing work. Not only has the number of legal provisions establishing criminal offences grown steadily, but increased police efficiency in detecting criminals and expansion of the crime rate itself have made the extension of the criminal courts essential. The number of superior courts in session at any one time has grown considerably, but the increase would have had to be many times greater were it not for the transfer of cases involving the less serious indictable offences to the magistrates.

Summary trial of indictable offences was first established for adults in 1855 for the offence of stealing objects worth less than five shillings.[1] The experiment proved successful and the maximum amount was increased in 1879 to £2 and in 1915 to £20. In 1925 the monetary limit was entirely removed. During the same period other crimes were added until a substantial list evolved. In the 1950s the higher courts were under acute pressure of work, and in 1959 a Home Office Committee under the chairmanship of Mr Justice Streatfeild recommended that property offences involving breaking and entering premises other than dwelling houses should be added to the list of indictable offences triable summarily. This suggestion became law in 1962 and immediately the magistrates had to deal with more than 16,000 such cases each year.[2]

If an offence is indictable, but may be tried summarily, the magistrates before whom the case first comes may decide that the allegations made are sufficiently serious to exclude summary trial, in which event the case will be sent for full trial on indictment before a jury. Otherwise, if the accused consents, the case will be tried by the magistrates. There are also some offences which are classified as summary, but which carry more than three months' imprisonment as a maximum penalty. In these cases also, the accused must be offered the right to elect for full trial before a jury. In addition, there are also certain offences where the legislature has expressly laid it down that the offence may be tried on indictment or summarily; different maximum penalties are laid down for each.[3] In these cases the police or other prosecutor makes the decision about the form of trial when laying the charge, but it is subject to the approval of the magistrates. As before, should the maximum penalty for the summary offence be more than three months' imprisonment the accused still has his right to elect for trial by jury.

Summary trial is generally preferred by the prosecution unless there is a special factor such as the seriousness of the crime or the accused's long record of previous offences. When the system was introduced for stealing offences in the nineteenth century it produced an immediate increase in the number of persons charged with the offences. Similarly, the Streatfeild Committee were told that the police commonly charged persons against whom there was evidence of a breaking offence with only a lesser offence, such as larceny or attempted larceny, so that, if the accused consented, the whole case could be disposed of in a Magistrates' Court. This led to the Committee's recommendation that the breaking offences should be triable summarily as well as on indictment.[4] At the time of writing, an even more substantial review of the working of Assizes and Quarter Sessions is being undertaken by a Royal Commission chaired by Lord Beeching. It may well recommend a widespread relocation and reorganization of these courts. Again an adjustment of the proportion of cases tried summarily and on indictment may be one consequence of the investigation.

For an accused, the choice between magistrates and a jury is sometimes a difficult one. An important advantage of summary trial is that the sentencing powers of magistrates are limited. In general, they may not sentence to any form of imprisonment or detention for a period of more than six months, and their power to impose a fine is restricted to a maximum of £400. However, it has to be remembered that these limits are not final: if an indictable offence is tried summarily and it then appears that the accused's previous record warrants a greater penalty than the magistrates have power to impose, they may send the case to Quarter Sessions for sentencing. The speed of summary proceedings will appeal to the man detained in custody. Their relative cheapness will appeal to the accused who is paying in full or in part for his defence; and the chance of less publicity will appeal to many defendants. But against these attractions must be set the principal advantage of jury trial – the greater likelihood of getting off completely.

Special features of the case may sway the choice one way or the other: it may belong to a class of case where juries are thought to be specially ready to acquit, for example certain motoring and sexual cases. There may be some factor which can be used to elicit special sympathy from a jury, such as a pregnant wife who will appear as a witness, or something which will arouse prejudice against the prosecution, such as an allegation that the police dealt brutally with the accused. It may be that the local bench of magistrates is taking a particularly tough line with certain kinds of offence. On the other hand the line of defence may seem too subtle to be easily presented to a jury, or there may be some feature of the case which is likely to arouse a jury's feelings against the accused. A London stipendiary magistrate recently stated that some defendants were being advised by solicitors to elect for full trial because legal aid had been granted and the advice had therefore been given with the higher fees in mind. The magistrate, being unable or unwilling to cite specific instances, had to face the full indignation of the Law Society.[5] But such a temptation is an inevitable consequence of a system under which the state gives aid to litigants and at the same time leaves the choice of court to their legal advisers.

There is little accurate information available about the kind of defendant who opts for trial by jury. In his study of serious motoring offenders, Willett found that only 8 per cent of his sample elected for trial, but among those the proportion of manual workers was low. A number of reasons are likely: absence of legal advice, ignorance that motoring organizations provide legal aid, a desire to avoid long-drawn-out proceedings. What did appear to Willett was that the cases which went for full trial were not distinguished by special features indicating the defendant's innocence.

Closer study is certainly needed of the defendants who opt for trial by jury, and their reasons for doing so. Professional lawyers do see definite advantages in one court or another for certain kinds of case, but the choice of a jury is only properly open to those who can afford the expenses attendant on jury trial and to those who have legal aid. The recent changes in the legal aid system for criminal cases,[6] by which some defendants to whom aid is granted will have to pay a contribution towards the cost of their defence, may discourage applications for a jury still further.

A picture of the criminal work undertaken in Magistrates' Courts would be incomplete without mention of the fact that persons under seventeen are almost invariably tried in a Juvenile Court, whether the offence is indictable or summary. A Juvenile Court is a Magistrates' Court specially constituted and subject to special procedures. Only in three cases will a juvenile stand trial in a superior court before a jury: where he is charged with homicide, where he is indicted jointly with an adult, or where, if he is over thirteen, he chooses full trial. At present this occurs in less than 2 per cent of the cases in which juveniles are charged with indictable offences. Yet in 1965 no less than 29 per cent of all defendants charged with indictable crimes were under seventeen. The growth of Juvenile Courts is therefore of great importance in the general shift of work from the superior courts into the summary jurisdiction of the magistrates.

To sum up, trial by jury is now reserved for that small proportion of all criminal prosecutions in which adult offenders plead not guilty to charges of serious crime, and there is either no option to be tried by the magistrates, or else this opportunity is not taken. For every charge on an indictable offence there are five on summary offences. A large proportion of indictable offences are disposed of in Magistrates' Courts. In 1960, this proportion was 82 per cent of all offenders and 74 per cent of adult offenders. In 1965, after the extension of the list of indictable offences triable summarily, it had risen to 88 per cent of all offenders and 80 per cent of adult offenders. Of the cases which reach the higher courts a large number do not require any trial of the facts because the accused pleads guilty. A survey conducted by the Association of Chief Police Officers shows that this occurred in 64 per cent of the cases sent for trial to the superior criminal courts in 1965.[7]

Juries are therefore required to try a mere 4 per cent of all the indictable offences charged. The rest are removed from their province by pleas of guilty or summary trial. This process leaves a reservoir of cases including those in which the question of guilt is most hotly contested and delicately balanced on the evidence. And these are the cases which need the most careful trial.

Committal proceedings

Where a criminal case is to be tried on indictment before judge and jury, there is a formal preliminary step, known as committal proceedings, which takes place before examining magistrates. The purpose of committal proceedings is to require the prosecution to satisfy the magistrates that there is at least enough evidence against the accused to establish a *prima facie* case against him. There is no equivalent step where a charge is tried summarily before magistrates. It is thought that the defendant needs special protection before he undergoes full trial before a jury, because there is often a delay of weeks before his trial, during which he may remain in custody; and because full trial is a serious affair in which the defendant may run the risk of far greater penalties than a Magistrates' Court may impose.

Some important changes in the system of committal proceedings have recently been made. The Criminal Justice Act 1967 has made provision for variations in the procedure, which before the Act always followed a standard pattern. This pattern and the problems it created must be described before the purpose of the changes can be appreciated. Until the 1967 Act, the procedure at committal proceedings was as follows: the prosecution, which had already taken statements from potential witnesses, called those who could give relevant evidence to give oral testimony before the magistrates. This was taken down by a court official, read over to the witnesses and signed by them: in this form the evidence was known as a deposition. The defendant had the right to cross-examine the prosecution witnesses, and he might also give evidence himself or call his own witnesses. In practice he usually reserved his defence until the trial. The magistrates would then decide whether the prosecution had made out a *prima facie* case.

Even this modern form of committal proceedings had been in use for little more than a century. In order to understand its emergence, it is worth briefly tracing the development of machinery for the institution of criminal proceedings from the early Middle Ages. The original prosecuting authority was the jury of presentment, or grand jury, created by Henry II in the Assize of Clarendon, 1166. Its duty was to 'present' those of the neighbourhood suspected of crime to the king's itinerant justices for trial. It was a large body of local landowners and soon proved to be too cumbersome an instrument to carry on the task of criminal investigation effectively. In the fourteenth century, this duty passed very largely to the justices of the peace, though the right of any private individual to institute a prosecution has always been recognized in England. The grand jury was retained but its function became supervisory: it sat at the beginning of each Assizes and Quarter Sessions to decide whether the bills of indictment against accused persons were 'true bills', that is whether the prosecutor had made out a *prima facie* case. But in the sixteenth century it was laid down that the justices must take down statements in the form of depositions from those whom they interviewed in the course of their investigations. These early depositions, recorded in private, came to provide the material on which the grand jury often relied in deciding whether there was a *prima facie* case. The grand jury deliberated in secret, so that there was no public pre-trial hearing at all. It could call in a witness and examine him in private without the prosecution being present to cross-examine. This led to a good deal of corruption of witnesses.[8]

In the nineteenth century, the growth of police forces in turn rendered the justices superfluous as prosecutors, and their private proceedings were turned into the modern form of committal proceedings in 1848. The grand jury then became entirely redundant, but it continued to incommode the procedure of the higher criminal courts until 1933.[9] Then the need for economy forced its abolition, though its passing was the subject of much doleful regret from the bench and elsewhere.

The functions of the grand jury were not, however, completely obliterated. Instead they were transferred to the judges of the High Court. It is possible today to prefer a voluntary bill of indictment before a judge without the need for committal proceedings. The judge decides whether a *prima facie* case has been made out at a private hearing upon the written statements of witnesses whom the prosecution has interviewed. Depositions do not have to be taken. In practice the procedure is rarely followed. Were it otherwise, it would be plain that here lies a method of circumventing the protection provided by committal proceedings. It is used sometimes where there have been committal proceedings, but they are in some way incomplete – because for instance, of the death of a magistrate. In this way, the need to start again from the beginning can be avoided. So, too, it provides a useful way of adding a new accused to a number already committed for trial, in circumstances where it is desirable that all should be tried together. One of the men concerned in the murder of the three London policemen in 1966, Harry Roberts, was indicted by the voluntary bill procedure. He was arrested only after the other two accused had already been through committal proceedings.

Before the 1967 Act there was much discussion of two problematic aspects of committal proceedings: the amount of time that they absorbed, and the prejudice which might have been caused in the minds of the jurors who afterwards heard the case by reports of what took place before the magistrates. In order to allow the accused to know the case against him, and to protect him from having to stand an unmerited trial, many hours of laborious work went into cases at the committal stage. Often the proceedings achieved no more than a formal record of evidence which the prosecution witnesses had already given to the police and which they would have to give again at the trial if the accused did not plead guilty.

The fear that reports of committal proceedings by the press and in radio and television broadcasts might prejudice the jurors who tried the case caused comment each time that there was a widely publicized trial. The danger was twofold: that jurors would arrive at court having read or heard reports of committal proceedings which contained the

prosecution's opening statement of the facts – not necessarily confirmed by the evidence, or the testimony of the
prosecution, but not the defence, witnesses; and that a
particular piece of evidence might have been given at the
preliminary hearing which was not admissible at the trial,
for example the accused's previous convictions. The issue
was given much publicity by the view expressed by Mr
Justice Devlin, in summing up to the jury at the trial of Dr
Bodkin Adams, that it would have been wiser to have held
the committal proceedings in private. It was widely known
that evidence had been given before the examining magistrate which was intended to support a second charge against
Dr Adams. However, this charge was dropped at the trial.

The judge's remarks did for a time lead to more committal proceedings being held *in camera*. In addition, the
Tucker Committee was set up to inquire into the question of
the publicity given to committal proceedings. The Committee declined to recommend that the hearing should be
held regularly behind closed doors.[10] Instead they favoured
keeping the proceedings open to the public but severely
restricting press and radio reports. The basic issue before
the Committee – how far juries are in fact influenced by
reports of committal proceedings – was a matter which
could not be resolved by direct evidence. The Committee
stated baldly: 'the question is one incapable of proof either
way' and acted on the speculations of their witnesses. The
matter could, however, have been investigated if a breach of
the secrecy of the jury-room had been permitted for research
purposes.

It is worth reporting that, of the jurors whom I
interviewed, only a few recalled having read reports of committal proceedings of the case which they tried. Those
who had were involved in cases which aroused considerable
public interest. None of them felt that they had been much
influenced during the trial by the reports which they had
already read. Most jurors seemed very strongly impressed
by the events of the trial itself: the witnesses, the accused,
counsel, the judge. It is likely that the immediacy of the trial
would in most cases reduce the prejudicial effect of any
information gleaned from a newspaper report read casually
in the ordinary course of life before the juror knew that he

would be concerned in the case. But that is not to say that prejudice will be entirely eliminated, and knowledge of particular facts such as the accused's past record are unlikely to be forgotten. Most jurors interviewed said that the knowledge of the accused's previous convictions had or would have influenced them towards a conviction. The Tucker Committee's recommendation was thus a precautionary measure which it was sensible to take until such time as there is firm evidence showing that the likelihood of prejudice to jurors is fanciful.

The Committee's report was heavily criticized for imposing a limitation on the freedom of the press to report all matters heard in open court, and thereby to act as guardian against abuses and improper practices. The press itself led the campaign. A number of supplementary arguments were advanced in support. It was said that well-publicized committal proceedings were useful in quelling wild rumours about a case. It was also said that publicity may bring forward some new witness, in particular one who will help the defence. This is obviously important if it does in fact occur. The Tucker Committee asked to be informed of instances, and were referred to twenty-one cases. They made efforts to investigate them all, but were unable to find a single case in which the new witnesses had made a vital difference.[11]

The measures in the Criminal Justice Act 1967[12] are designed both to reduce the time and effort spent in committal proceedings, and to limit the scope of newspaper and broadcast publicity. The basic pattern of the proceedings has been retained, but either side is given the power to introduce evidence in the form of a written statement from a witness rather than by calling the witness to give oral testimony. This is permissible only if the other side does not object. The intention is to prevent the necessity for a prosecution witness attending the preliminary hearing where the defence does not wish to see and hear him in the witness-box. Moreover, where the defence raises no objection to the entire evidence being in documentary form, the case will be sent for trial without the examining magistrates considering the statements at all, except where the defendant is not legally represented, or his representative submits that the statements do not show a *prima facie* case against him.[13] This allows a legally represented defendant the further choice of waiving committal proceedings altogether once he has seen the written statements of prosecution witnesses.

It remains to be seen how great a saving of time will result from these new provisions. The various pressures on legal practitioners to do as complete a job as possible may mean that the regular practice will still be to require the prosecution witnesses to give their evidence orally. Certainly some solicitors regard the chance to observe the prosecution witnesses as a great advantage in weighing up the strength of the case against their clients, and they have been quick to counter proposals that committal proceedings should be wholly abolished. Some years must elapse before we can see whether the attachment to this tactical advantage is a deep one.

The Criminal Justice Act also implements the Tucker Committee's recommendations that press and broadcasting coverage of committal proceedings be severely restricted. In one respect, however, the Act is less rigorous. It recognizes that the one justification for so considerable a limitation of press freedom is that possible prejudice to defendants in the minds of jurors should be avoided. If, therefore, a defendant should for any reason desire publicity for the committal proceedings he is entitled to a court order lifting the restriction. What is more, he is entitled to the order even if he is being dealt with together with another defendant who does not want publicity.[14] If no special order for publicity is made, press and broadcast reports of committal proceedings are now restricted to the barest outline: the charges, the names, addresses and occupations of the defendant and witnesses, and certain details of the outcome of the proceedings. If the defendant is not sent for trial on any charge, then the ban is at an end, as it is also when the trial itself finishes.

It may be that the time has now come to consider more drastic reform of the whole pre-trial procedure. The central problem is to provide a means of checking that the police do not exercise their wide powers to investigate and prosecute in objectionable ways. In many countries the problem is tackled through the establishment of a separate government office which bears the duty of considering whether the police dossier on a case warrants the institution of a prosecution, and may also be concerned in the collection of evidence – particularly in the difficult matter of the interrogation of suspects. One system exists in Scotland, where the Crown Office, acting in each sheriffdom through the Procurator-Fiscal, sifts the evidence collected by the police and takes statements (precognitions) from their witnesses before deciding whether a prosecution should be instituted. In England the Director of Public Prosecutions occupies a somewhat similar position but the scope of his duties is much more limited. His office deals with certain classes of difficult and controversial crimes, and with cases referred to it by government departments, the police and others. Once the effects of the most recent changes in committal proceedings can be measured, serious consideration should be given to extending the powers of the Director to control the process of instituting prosecutions in all cases. It may be that this would provide a more effective check on the abuse of police power than the duty of the examining magistrates to find that there is a *prima facie* case.

It would of course be necessary to ensure that the defendant did not lose his right to know the case against him which he must answer. No doubt he would lose the right to see and cross-examine prosecution witnesses in advance. But how far does a dress-rehearsal of this kind serve the real interests of justice in a trial system where so much depends on the impression given by oral witnesses? What might be of greater real value would be to require the statements taken by the police from all those whom they interview before the trial to be handed to the defence. Indeed this is a change which ought to be introduced whatever other changes are made in the system.

The trial

Once the trial of an indictable offence before a jury has begun, it proceeds without interruption. Only exceptionally will the court adjourn one case before it is finished and start another. A court working with jurors must organize itself in this way, for it would be highly inconvenient for the jurors to be called away from their ordinary jobs intermittently, and the strain on memory would be impossible. In Magistrates'

Courts, adjournments occur more often, particularly when a court is under considerable pressure of work. The result may be that a case drags on for an undesirably long period; the interruptions may result in aspects of the case being forgotten or neglected.

When trial by jury was first introduced into criminal proceedings, it was a basic principle that the defendant could be tried in this way only if he 'put himself on his country' by pleading not guilty to the indictment. If he refused to plead, the practice evolved on subjecting him to a torture known as *peine forte et dure*. He would have weights of increasing heaviness placed upon his body until he either gave in or expired. Tortures of various kinds were still being used to extract a plea in the eighteenth century, and *peine forte et dure* was finally abolished in 1772.[15] Nowadays if a defendant refuses to plead, a jury will be empanelled to try the question whether he is fit to do so (see p. 244). If he is found fit to plead, he will be treated as having pleaded not guilty and the trial will proceed.

The substantive part of the trial begins with an opening speech by counsel for the prosecution in which he outlines his case. The prosecution evidence is then given. Most evidence comes from oral witnesses. Once a witness has completed his evidence-in-chief, the accused or his counsel may attack it by cross-examination, and then the witness may be re-examined by his own side to clear up points arising out of cross-examination. Only when the Crown's case is closed does the accused or his counsel begin to outline the defence and to produce evidence to support it. It is a traditional part of the game-like nature of the English criminal trial that it is open to an accused to keep his line of defence secret until this moment. But a recent breach in this principle has been made so as to require a defendant to give the prosecution advance notice if he intends to raise an alibi in defence.[16] The defendant is free to give evidence or not as he chooses. If he fails, the prosecution may only point out to the jury that he might have done so; but the judge may usually go further and comment unfavourably on the fact that the defendant refused to go into the witness-box. When the defence evidence is complete each side addresses the jury on the strength of its own case and the weakness of the opposition. Since 1964, it has been the invariable rule that the prosecution must address the jury before the defence does so.[17] The judge then sums up to the jury, directing them as to the law, referring them to the portions of the evidence which are relevant in deciding the facts, and summarizing the issue for their decision.

The jurors must then consider their verdict, and usually retire to do so. It is improper for their foreman to announce a verdict of guilty which the jury had agreed upon before the summing-up.[18] The jurors may not separate once they have begun their deliberations. If they want to ask the judge questions at any stage of their discussion they are free to do so, and their communication to him will be heard in court and defence counsel will be permitted to comment upon it.[19] In the first instance the jury must attempt to reach a unanimous verdict. But since the recent change, if after two hours, or a longer time if the judge thinks it appropriate, they cannot agree, they will be instructed that they may return a verdict by a majority of at least ten to two. If at any stage during the trial one of the jurors has to be discharged, the permissible majorities are nine to two on an eleven-man jury, or nine to one on a ten-man jury. The trial judge is not obliged to send back a jury that cannot reach a unanimous verdict to see if it can return a majority verdict; he can at once accept that there has been a disagreement and discharge the jury.[20] Before the introduction of majority verdicts, it was a misdirection if the judge suggested to the jury that they might compromise and return what was actually a majority verdict.[21] Now the judge must take care not to suggest that jury may be more divided than the prescribed limits. If the verdict is guilty, then the jury is required to tell the court whether it is by majority and what the majority was. This is important, for the Criminal Division of the Court of Appeal may take into account the fact that the verdict is only by a majority when considering whether it is a safe and satisfactory finding.[22] If the verdict is one of not guilty, the jury will not be asked whether all the jurors concurred in it. This rule is an attempt to limit any prejudice to the accused which might arise if it were known that he was only acquitted by a majority. One judge has stressed that just because a jury has been directed (after the requisite period of deliberation) that it need not be unanimous, it does not follow that any subsequent verdict is by a majority. This at least prevents damaging headlines, such as 'Man acquitted by a majority'.

Juries quite frequently take several hours to consider their verdict. The longest time taken in recent years was sixty-seven hours in the Great Train Robbery case. Until 1870, juries were put under pressure to reach a verdict by leaving them without food, drink or heat. In a case in 1858, a new trial was ordered, because the jury had had food and drink passed up on a string.[23] Jurors today are given an allowance for subsistence, and the judge will normally permit them to have food and drink brought to them at their expense, while they are deliberating. Another ancient practice, now defunct, was that if any jury was still deliberating at the end of an assize, the assize judge would have the jurors placed in a cart and carried to the next assize town so that they could return their verdict to him there. Today it is improper for the judge to put the jury under any sort of coercion to arrive at a verdict. On one occasion a judge told the jurors that if they did not do so in ten minutes he would have to leave town and they would have to be locked up until he returned next morning. They convicted in six minutes, and the convictions were quashed on appeal.[24]

Once the jury has returned its verdict, if the accused is found guilty on any charge, his previous record, if any, will be read out and he may make a plea in mitigation. The judge may ask for a report as to his medical condition or social circumstances. Finally he will be sentenced by the judge; the jury plays no direct part in determining the punishment.

It will be seen from this brief description that the judge has little to do with the collection and presentation of the evidence. This is the responsibility of the prosecution and the defence. The court will compel the attendance of witnesses and the production of documents, but this is normally upon the application of one side or the other. A trial judge does have power to call a witness at any time before he begins summing-up but it is not frequently exercised. The judge also plays little part in the examination of witnesses. He is free to do so if he thinks it advisable, but the Court of Appeal has from time to time criticized trial judges who have assumed the role of prosecutor or asked questions indicating that they thought that the accused was guilty.[25] This is in pointed contrast to a country such as France, where the primary responsibility for examining witnesses lies upon the presiding judge.

The English approach has roots which stretch back to the thirteenth century, when the royal judges were striving to mould trial by jury into an effective substitute for older modes of proof, such as trial by battle and by ordeal. As we have seen, the first jurors were neighbours who decided disputes on their own local knowledge. Inevitably cases began to arise in which not all the jurors were equally well acquainted with the subject matter of the case. At this stage, the judges were faced with a choice: they could either take a verdict from the group as a whole, or they could examine the jurors individually to find out which had the most knowledge of the case, before coming to a decision themselves on the information given by the knowledgeable jurors. There are reports of thirteenth-century cases in which judges can be seen following the latter course rather than the former. But the practice did not become regular, and soon it was established that the jury's sole function was to return a group verdict. A case in 1367 made it clear that the verdict had to be the unanimous view of all the jurors. This set the stage for the gradual introduction of separate witnesses and the transformation of the jury into a body which adjudicated on evidence produced in court.

In France, a similar issue faced the courts in the thirteenth century, and it was resolved in the opposite direction. An inquisitorial system developed by which royal judges examined individual witnesses and then reached their own conclusions. In time this led to the establishment of a vast judicial bureaucracy. Even at a time when it was a novel idea to inquire into the facts rather than to appeal to divine revelation of the truth by a battle or an ordeal, the superiority of the French method of eliciting the facts must have been apparent. Professor Dawson has suggested that the reason why it was not adopted by the English kings and their judges lay in the fact that in the thirteenth century the power of the royal administration had become unusually strong, and the problem was to devote the available trained manpower to maintaining the system. The king's justices were few, and they did not have the time to conduct lengthy investigations into particular cases. At a later stage, when a larger supply of men with legal training became available,

the need for specialists was restricted because means had been found by the Angevin kings to distribute widely throughout the population the burdens and responsibilities of government. Methods of delegation established so early were followed and extended as the work-load continued to mount. This was true even of the central courts of common law, which were soon taken over by some extremely able specialists.[26]

The decision to rely on group verdicts of juries eventually led to the accusatorial character of the English criminal process, and this has conferred on us today the advantage that cases are tried by judges and juries who have not become concerned in the extraction of evidence and ought therefore to be able to bring a valuable element of objectivity to the trial. Failure to adopt an inquisitorial system has also meant that the defendant has never been under an obligation to answer questions in court if he chooses not to do so, nor (subject to the new exception in respect of an alibi) to reveal any defence in advance of the trial itself.

However, the full significance of these principles can only be appreciated if considered in conjunction with the many obstacles which were placed in the way of a defendant presenting his own case to the court. Individual witnesses were gradually permitted to give evidence in court, but litigants and their spouses were not allowed to do so, because of their interest in the outcome of the proceedings. Only in the seventeenth century did an accused person gain the right to call his own witnesses, and he himself was not permitted to give evidence until as late as 1898, save for some minor exceptions.[27]

Another serious hindrance was that an accused originally had no right to counsel. Gradually this was conceded, first to argue points of law, then in the latter eighteenth century to cross-examine prosecution witnesses. But it was not until 1836 that a person accused of felony was entitled to have counsel address the jury on his behalf. Only during the present century has this right to counsel become an economic possibility for many defendants, with the establishment and gradual expansion of the legal aid scheme. For the last seventy years the defendant has been substantially free of the legal restraints which prevented him from presenting his case as he thought best. The time is now ripe for considering what modifications should be made to the system which has developed. Numerous suggestions have been made. The requirement that a defendant give the prosecution notice in advance of an alibi is the first to be given the force of law. It is a sensible change since it prevents the accused springing a surprise explanation of his whereabouts at the time of crime, which the police cannot check because the trial is already well advanced. Other suggestions have been made which would help the prosecution to establish the real facts, for instance, that special defences such as insanity ought to be notified in advance, so as to remove the element of surprise.

More controversial is the argument that an accused ought to lose his right not to give evidence. Some would require him to answer questions put to him by the prosecution or the judge; others would merely say that he should listen to such questions, and be at liberty to answer them or not at his own risk.[28] There are changes which could be of great assistance to an accused who is seeking to establish a genuine defence, and certainly no additional advantages should be given to the prosecution without seriously considering these as well. The police should be obliged to hand over to the defence all statements taken from persons who are interviewed in connexion with the crime. This should include statements which the accused himself has made. Provision should also be made for the assistance of forensic experts to be made available to an accused so that he can carry out an investigation which is necessary to his defence. Everything possible should also be done to ensure that an accused has proper opportunity to receive legal advice at the early stages of a police investigation when he is still a suspect, or has just been charged.

The case has been prominently made from police and other circles that the present attributes of the accusatorial criminal trial, in which the defendant can to some extent shelter behind surprise defences and can refuse to give evidence, are allowing criminals who ought to be convicted to be acquitted by the jury. While this is no doubt true, the force of it should not be allowed to obscure the fact that more could be done to assist defendants to know their legal rights, and to provide them with true help to establish a genuine defence.

One other aspect of the criminal trial that deserves comment is the preponderance of the spoken word over the written. Evidence, argument and summing-up are largely oral. Historically, this was dictated by the presence of a jury, for literacy has never been a qualification for service, and illiterate jurors, once common, do sometimes reveal themselves even today by their inability to read the card on which the oath is printed. Literacy is essential in some cases – in complex fraud cases, for instance, jurors are given many documents to consider. The Morris Committee has recommended that there be a literacy qualification for all jurors. It will no doubt be a long time before oral evidence and speeches lose their importance in favour of documents in criminal trials; but it is a method which places great strain on the juror's memory. Moreover, the evidence is not put in an order in which all the witnesses who can report on one event give their evidence on that event consecutively. Instead each event will be dealt with at different stages of the trial, and it may be difficult for a juror to remember back and carry forward. He gets no help in recalling earlier evidence on a particular point when a witness is dealing with it; only at the end of the case will counsel in their speeches and the judge in his summing-up draw together the web of evidence for the jury's benefit.

CIVIL CASES

Use of the jury

There has never been a time when all English courts have used trial by jury as the sole method for disposing of civil actions. In particular, the Court of Chancery did not use juries, though it did at one stage employ specially commissioned examiners, who were laymen, to investigate disputed facts and report to the Court.[29] Neither did the Ecclesiastical Courts, in spite of the important jurisdiction which they had over matrimonial matters and wills. In the nineteenth century, when the civil courts were substantially reconstituted, the jury was given new fields of operation. In 1858, the powers of the Court of Chancery were brought more closely in line with those of the common-law courts. One change was to confer on the Court a discretion to order jury trial if a litigant requested it. The Divorce and Probate Courts set up in 1857 were both given jurisdiction to sit with a jury – indeed a party might demand one. The modern County Courts were created in 1846 to furnish a more expeditious way of dealing with minor civil cases. Originally there were no juries, but in 1888 it became possible for a party in a common-law action to demand one. At first these juries were composed of only five members, but in 1903 the number was raised to eight.

These extensions of the use of juries were one of the last practical expressions of faith in the jury as an instrument for settling disputed facts in civil cases. But the response of litigants and the practitioners who advise them has not in the long run been very enthusiastic. In Chancery cases, the jury never gained much of a foothold, and while theoretically it has remained possible for trial with a jury to be held in a modern Chancery action, Chancery practitioners never ask for one. If one were sought, the case would be transferred to the Queen's Bench Division of the Court. In contested divorce and probate actions, juries did for a time gain some popularity. In divorce cases they were used where there was an irreconcilable conflict of evidence, or where damages were sought against a co-respondent. But today neither divorce nor probate cases are tried by jury in practice.[30] No divorce jury has sat in the High Court since 1956.

An even more striking decline in the use of civil juries relates to common-law actions. Until 1854 all actions in the common-law courts were tried by a jury. Then, the alternative of trial by a single judge became possible: but both parties and the court had to give their consent. At the same time the court acquired the right to direct another mode of trial in one kind of case where juries were particularly unsatisfactory – where the action involved taking accounts, the court could order it to be sent to an arbitrator. This latter exception was subsequently expanded so that the court could require a case to be heard by a single judge if it involved the prolonged examination of documents or accounts, or any specific or local investigation rendering trial by jury inconvenient. This provision has remained part of the law. Gradually further exceptions were made. In 1883 it was prescribed that before there could be a jury one or other side must ask for it. This change was merely one of emphasis – either litigant could still have a jury if he wanted it. But the new rule produced its effect. The proportion of Queen's Bench actions tried by jury fell from 80 per cent to around 50 per cent. While this became the general rule, certain kinds of action were specially treated: a jury remained the automatic mode of trial, unless both parties requested otherwise, in cases of libel, slander, false imprisonment, malicious prosecution, seduction and breach of promise of marriage – all cases that might involve the personal reputation of one of the parties.

In 1918, war-time conditions forced a further change. Except for the six types of action involving reputation, to which was added any case in which there was charge of fraud, a case could be tried by jury only if a party requested one and the court in its discretion assented to the request. There was a reaction against this limitation which led to a return in 1925 to the former rule that the request of one party was enough to secure a jury. But this too remained controversial, and the need to conserve court time and expenditure during the depression years caused a return to the 1918 provision in 1933. Since the Second World War the courts have been increasingly unready to exercise their discretion in favour of a jury, and practitioners have on the whole accepted trial by judge alone and have ceased to ask for a jury (see p. 227). For several years the number of Queen's Bench and Assize actions tried by jury rather than by judge alone has been under 4 per cent. The figure in 1965 was 1·7 per cent and in 1966 1·5 per cent.

Civil procedure before and at the trial

As with criminal procedure, trial by jury has done much to shape the present form of civil actions. The trial of a civil case bears many similarities to that of a criminal prosecution: in a typical contract or tort action, counsel for the plaintiff opens his case, and then calls witnesses and produces other evidence. The defendant then follows a similar course. Both sides address the court, and, if there is a jury, the judge delivers a summing-up. The jury retires to consider its verdict. In contrast with criminal cases, the jury decides both 'halves' of the action: not only the question of liability, but also that of damages. In a civil case a majority verdict can be returned only with the consent of the parties. This rarely occurs, for no arrangement is made before it is discovered that the jury cannot agree, and by then at least one party is unlikely to want a majority verdict. If the judge is sitting alone, he delivers judgement on the whole case, normally giving reasons for his decision.

There are other similar characteristics: the judge is not directly involved in the presentation of evidence, proceedings once begun are not unnecessarily adjourned, and oral testimony is of primary importance. The role of the judge is in marked contrast to the role of the judge in civil procedure in France. There the judge in charge of the case will be involved from the outset in directing the whole course of the proceedings, including the collection of evidence. He will gradually build up a dossier on it as his investigations pass from stage to stage. If relevant, reports of investigators appointed by the court will be included in it. The process is much more evolutionary and there is no stage equivalent to the 'trial', save the final submission of the whole record, supported by oral argument, to the full court for determination.

While the English system places much emphasis on the trial of the action, there is also a complex pre-trial procedure. In this the court plays a part, but the initiative remains very much with the litigants. The claim and the defence to it are in the first place developed by the exchange of written pleadings between the parties. The plaintiff delivers a statement of claim setting out the facts on which he bases his case. The defendant in return delivers a defence, stating which facts he admits and which he contests. A reply from the plaintiff may follow, and so on until all the allegations of fact between the two sides are shown to be agreed or disputed. In this way the issues of fact are as far as possible narrowed before a trial takes place.

Written pleadings developed in the Middle Ages when

juries were still summoned to decide the facts from their own general knowledge. Pleadings were, at one and the same time, a method of narrowing the question which the jury were called upon to decide, and, until independent witnesses became usual, a useful way of stating each litigant's version of the facts to the jury. This was because the pleadings became part of the record of the case and counsel could read from them to the jurors. As well as this, the pleadings assisted in distinguishing the questions of fact and law, and in settling the venue (neighbourhood) from which the jury must be drawn.[31] The system was permitted to degenerate into a maze of technicalities and intricate refinements. In the nineteenth century a set of drastic reforms swept away the cobwebs. Indeed in 1897 it became possible to proceed to trial without pleadings unless one side obtained a direction from the court that they should be delivered. In practice, however, an application for pleadings was customarily made and acceded to, and so the old procedures survived. What remains today is a system which, if it is used flexibly, provides a convenient method of fixing the real issues between the disputants. It is one which puts the onus of proceeding on them and not on the court, though the court exercises powers of supervision and provides sanctions to compel a dilatory party to act or risk losing the case.

The court also takes some part in the provision of evidence; it will summon witnesses, order the discovery and production of documents, and compel a party to answer written questions which are known as interrogatories – but always because it is requested to do so by one side or the other. At the trial the judge has no power to call a witness if either party objects.[32] This attitude of detachment from the presentation of the case shows itself particularly in the infrequency in which the courts depart from the established method of getting expert opinion before them. It is for each side to consult its own experts and if an agreed report is not forthcoming then each will be called to give evidence, and the court, although it will probably have no special knowledge of the matter in issue, will have to choose which testimony it prefers. The civil courts have power to appoint a court expert to investigate the problem and report to the court, where he may be cross-examined by any party, but this is a power which is very rarely used. It is significant that this power does not exist where the trial is with a jury.

The purpose of this short description of the procedure in civil actions has been to emphasize the extent to which present forms owe their basic shape to the fact that in the common-law courts the climax of the proceedings was traditionally a jury trial. Where a type of action was not one that used to be brought before a common-law court, it may even today have procedural characteristics which mark the difference. For example probate actions to determine the validity of a will were a matter for the Ecclesiastical Courts until 1857. A much stronger continental influence prevailed in those courts, and the judge occupied an investigatory position. In modern probate actions it is recognized that the procedure is still inquisitorial, so that, for instance, the judge has a power to insist that documents be produced for which a litigant could normally claim special privilege from disclosure.[33]

There is at present considerable criticism of the expense and delays involved in civil litigation in this country and the Law Commission may soon put this matter on their programme of subjects to be investigated. A book on trial by jury is not the place for a detailed discussion of possible reforms to procedure in general, but it is right to emphasize that at a time when almost all civil cases are conducted before a single judge, it is necessary to examine with care all the characteristics of procedure which were formerly dictated by the final trial before a jury. Some, such as the system of pleadings, have an independent value, but others may be ripe for modification. We shall return to some of them in Chapter 8, in the course of discussing in detail the role of the jury in particular areas of the civil law. The two most controversial aspects are the fact that the whole case must be prepared and costs run up in the collection of evidence before the court considers any part of the dispute between the parties, and the strictly accusatorial practice of requiring the parties to produce as witnesses any experts needed to give information or opinions to the court.

THE RULES OF EVIDENCE

The rules of evidence regulate the way in which facts can be proved in court. They are extensive, strict and in some cases highly technical. They began to emerge in the same period in which it was being finally settled that jurors no longer acted both as witnesses and as judges of the facts. The judges developed many parts of the law of evidence as a means of controlling the information which could be given to the court through separate witnesses produced by the litigants. One view is that the whole motive force behind the rules was the desire of the judges to prevent juries from misconstruing the available evidence. Professor Thayer, the leading exponent of this view, considered that 'the law of evidence was the child of the jury'. Other scholars have shown that some rules were originally introduced for other reasons, and it is true that some have been maintained for reasons which have nothing to do with the abilities of juries. But there can be little doubt that the need to exclude evidence which juries might misjudge, and the desire to instruct them on how to treat evidence which is admitted, have together been the principal reasons why English law has developed its present elaborate and formal rules of evidence.[34]

In contrast, foreign systems of law that have not been influenced by the common law, adopt generally a much looser attitude to the introduction and treatment of evidence. This has been the case even where the jury system has to some extent been introduced. In France, for instance, the whole law of evidence is comprised in a small number of procedural rules, which can be exhaustively stated in a short space.[35]

A general feeling that the underlying assumptions of the English law of evidence require re-examination has recently led to the whole matter being referred to two government committees: the Law Reform Committee is examining evidence in civil cases, and the Criminal Law Revision Committee, evidence in criminal cases. The results of this important review of the whole law are beginning to appear and the Government is wasting little time in promoting legislation to implement the recommendations. One fundamental problem of reform is how far rules which were developed in the common-law courts at a time when most cases, civil and criminal, were tried by jury are appropriate in courts where judges sit alone, or in Magistrates' Courts where the bench is composed of justices of the peace. There is a tendency to assume that professional judges have enough experience to be able to attach proper value to suspect or prejudicial evidence. There has been little consideration so far of the position of justices and the extent to which they should be treated like judges or like jurors. However, one significant development here is the refusal of the judges to require administrative tribunals to adhere strictly to the rules that apply in the ordinary courts.[36]

The present formal rules add complexity to trial procedure: time may be consumed in arguing about how a rule should apply; if the judge makes a mistake it may lead to a successful appeal. Many of the rules concentrate on the preliminary issue of whether evidence should be given at all, rather than on the weight that should be given to it in relation to the particular case. For these reasons reforms which would remove the present elaborate and strict rules and leave the court free to attach what weight it will to all the evidence are undeniably attractive. But it is not a policy which should be adopted without carefully considering how far professional judges are truly equipped to discount the prejudicial content of some kinds of evidence presently excluded from court altogether. Moreover, any movement towards the introduction of a more flexible approach will be hampered for the present by the wish not to create a wide gap between the rules of evidence which apply to trial by jury and trial by judge alone. It is obviously undesirable to allow the constitution of the court to affect the case that a person may put before it. And it is unlikely that there will be any very considerable revision of the rules of evidence applicable to jury trials. These rules, built up over a long period of experience, are one of the most revealing expressions of the limited trust which lawyers are prepared to place in juries. However, there is at least room for investigation into the manner in which juries would react if the rules were substantially changed, and this sort of study needs to be undertaken before the present enthusiasm for reform in the law of evidence is extinguished.

This chapter now explores in more detail some of the most important rules of evidence which have been developed in order to exclude evidence which juries ought not to hear ('exclusion' rules) and rules which direct juries how to assess the evidence which they do hear ('instruction' rules). The purpose of this brief outline is to demonstrate the complexity of the present law produced by rules designed for trial by jury, and to indicate the problems which the constitution of the courts present to those concerned with reforming the rules of evidence.[37]

'Exclusion' rules

English law regulates the ambit of evidence which can be given at a trial by the general principle that if evidence is to be admitted it must have some substantial relevance to the facts in issue in the case. Any legal system must grant the courts some power to exclude irrelevant material if they are to maintain efficiency and keep down costs. The difficulty is to strike a balance between giving the court sufficient background information to put the case in perspective and preventing essential facts from being obscured by side-issues. In common-law countries, the desire of judges that juries should not be distracted from the central issues has led them to police the rule requiring substantial relevance with greater vigour than occurs in other legal systems. The relatively brief and concentrated trial which is characteristic of common-law countries is greatly helped by the reluctance of judges to allow the exploration of evidential by-ways.

Evidence which passes this first test of relevance may nevertheless be inadmissible for some other reason. Some of these 'exclusion' rules have a purpose unconnected with juries. For instance, the rule that a confession of crime cannot be given in evidence unless it is shown to have been made voluntarily exists to prevent improper methods of interrogation by the police. It is part of the English solution of the problem of devising a fair method of questioning suspects. But most of the 'exclusion' rules exist to keep out evidence which though relevant might be given undue weight by jurors and other judges of questions of fact.

(i) *Competence of witnesses.* We have already noted the former drastic rule that a litigant, including even the defendant in a criminal trial, could not himself give evidence (p. 72). It was thought that his interest in the proceedings made him too untrustworthy for it to be safe to allow the jury to hear his evidence. Other justifications were also offered for this rule, for instance the temptation to perjury and oath-breaking which giving evidence would offer to a party. Not until the nineteenth century was it generally recognized that this blanket prohibition often kept a great deal of relevant information from the court, and that on balance it was better to hear a litigant's evidence and trust the jury to make an allowance for his interest in the outcome of the case.

There are now few rules which totally exclude a person from being a witness. One limitation concerns the evidence of young children. In civil cases children must give sworn testimony, and to do this the judge must be satisfied that they understand what is implied by the oath or affirmation which they make. In criminal cases, a child may be permitted to give unsworn testimony if the judge finds that the child, while not understanding the significance of an oath, nevertheless knows what is meant by telling the truth.

It is always difficult to assess a child's evidence because so little is known about the ability of children in general to perceive events and remember accurately what they have seen. There is certainly a widespread fear that children may lie or indulge in fantasies even in court, without appreciating the significance of what they are doing. It has been demonstrated that the accuracy of a child's perception and memory improves noticeably between the ages of eight and fourteen,[38] but further research could assist revision of the present law: is there any one age at which most children become sufficiently perceptive for them to be trusted as witnesses, or should we continue with our system by which the judge makes a quick, rough assessment of the particular child? Are there certain kinds of evidence which a child is particularly able to comprehend and recall? Are there methods of eliciting evidence from a child which are specially likely to lead to accurate recollection?

As well as providing a basis on which the formal rules might be revised judges and magistrates would be provided with useful information from which to supplement their intuitions about the behaviour of children. It might even prove possible to pass the information on to juries in some circumstances. It is also desirable that some investigation be made of the attitude which juries adopt to children's evidence. We shall see (p. 96) that the law requires that the jury be instructed to find that a child's evidence is corroborated if the evidence is unsworn, or if the child is concerned in a sexual offence. If it appears that juries regularly exhibit special sympathy for a child witness, just because of the child's age, then it might be wise to provide that a corroboration warning should always be given.

(ii) *Hearsay*. Evidence is hearsay when a witness reports a fact to be true not because he himself perceived it but because he learned it from some other indirect source; for instance, witness X says that Y told him that he saw Z climbing through a certain shop-window. The principle is capable of many refinements. There is a general rule that hearsay is not admissible in evidence. The rule is justified on various grounds, the most substantial of them being that hearsay is not the statement of a witness before the court who can be subjected to the usual tests of reliability: cross-examination by the opposing side, observation by the court of the witness's general manner, the emphasis that he gives his words, his tone of voice and so on. Behind this is the belief that a jury cannot be trusted to take into account the defects of such evidence. As early as 1811, Sir James Mansfield, Chief Justice of Common Pleas, put it:

In Scotland, and in most of the Continental States, the Judges determine upon the facts in dispute as well as the law; and they think there is no danger in their listening to evidence of hearsay, because when they come to consider of their judgment on the merits of the case they can trust themselves entirely to disregard the hearsay evidence, or to give it any little weight which it may seem to deserve. But in England, where the jury are the sole judges of the facts hearsay evidence is properly excluded, because no man can tell what effect it may have on their minds.[39]

The hearsay rule may prevent a witness from giving a lucid account of his story, and cause the feeling that he has been prevented from putting it completely or coherently. It may also have the effect of excluding evidence of great relevance. As a result the judges, moved by the desire not to lose an important piece of evidence in a particular case, have created numerous exceptions to the rule. More recently, a number of statutes have added further important exceptions, and in the civil law the rule itself is now more honoured in the breach.

The exceptions created by the judges are renowned for their over-fine distinctions. For instance, if a person is not available as a witness because he has died, other people may be called to give evidence of certain kinds of statements that he made while alive, even though they are hearsay. If the statement was 'against interest', that is, prejudicial to the maker of the statement in some way, it will be admitted, but the statement must be an admission of pecuniary or proprietary liability. It is not enough that the statement will damage the man's reputation; and it may even be the law that an admission by the maker of the statement that he has committed a criminal offence would not be enough.

Another kind of statement which is admissible as hearsay is the dying declaration of a man as to the cause of his death. If another person is charged with his murder or manslaughter then the declaration may be given in evidence by someone to whom it was made. The justification for the exception is said to be that a man is more likely to speak the truth when faced with the immediate prospect of death – a view which is certainly more pious hope than proven fact. Because of this, the exception will only apply if the dead man is shown to have had 'a settled, hopeless expectation of death' at the time of making the declaration, and some cases show curiously different attitudes among judges as to just when this is so. In one case, the dead man's head was almost severed, but there was no proof that he believed himself to be dying. The evidence could accordingly not be given. In other cases death did not follow for some days after the statement, but nevertheless the statement was allowed to be given in evidence.[40]

There are many other exceptions to the hearsay rule. When the American Commissioners came to devise Uniform Rules of Evidence it was found necessary to define thirty-one exceptions. In England, the House of Lords recently refused to create a new exception. Records kept by a motor manufacturer of the cylinder numbers of cars had been tendered in evidence. The records were hearsay because the information had been supplied by workmen employed at the time when they were made and these workmen were not giving evidence. The House did not regard it as proper for the judges to create further exceptions to a rule already overloaded with them. Lord Reid said: 'The only satisfactory solution is by legislation following a wide survey of the whole field, and I think that such a survey is overdue. A policy of make do and mend is no longer adequate.' However, in the first instance it was a reform of just this kind which was enacted, for Parliament created a new exception to the hearsay rule to admit trade and business records.[41]

The first reform of the hearsay rule by statute occurred in 1938, when the Evidence Act 1938 created a general range of exceptions to the rule for civil cases. Where statements were put into documentary form, the documents could be produced in evidence in certain circumstances, if the person who wrote the document was no longer available to go into the witness-box. But it is significant that the Act gave the judge a special discretion to exclude this kind of hearsay where the case was tried by a jury. In 1967, the Law Reform Committee recommended that in civil cases the rule should be still more widely relaxed. The most important of the Committee's suggestions was that 'first-hand' hearsay should be admitted: a witness should always be able to give hearsay evidence of information given him by someone else, if that person had direct personal knowledge of the facts concerned. This is about to become law. The passing of the civil jury since the 1938 Act is perhaps marked by the fact that the judge is given no power to exclude 'first-hand' hearsay in a jury trial.[42]

In criminal cases, where juries are so much more frequent, it is likely that reform of the hearsay rule will proceed much more cautiously. The fear remains that juries are ill-equipped to take account of the many ways in which hearsay evidence can be defective or misleading. The reforms in connexion with civil cases show that it is often assumed that judges have enough practical experience to take account of the dangers. It would have been useful to preface reform with some attempt to discover how juries, judges and justices would treat hearsay if it were admitted, in order to see whether the rule is justifiable at all, and, if so, whether there are factors which make it possible for the different kinds of court to deal fairly with certain kinds of hearsay.

(iii) *Opinion*. Allied to the notion implicit in the hearsay rule that a witness should be confined to stating facts which he has perceived, is the rule that a witness is not normally permitted to express an opinion. He cannot, for instance, state that a person accused of being unfit to drive through drink was drunk, though he may state all the facts which led to his belief – raucous singing, unsteady gait and so on. The rule does not apply to expert witnesses. A medical expert, for instance, could give his opinion about how far the defendant's capabilities were affected by alcohol, because he is called to give the court assistance on such technical matters. Moreover, it is sometimes very difficult to try to differentiate between fact and opinion, and English practice has not been ready to attempt their separation in many cases where in American law elaborate tests have emerged for doing so. Nevertheless, the rule exists very largely because 'the jury would be tempted blindly to accept a witness's opinion', and could probably be ignored when the courts are constituted by experienced judges who are aware of the possible pitfalls.

(iv) *Findings of other courts*. Another related rule, which has recently been largely reversed, prevented evidence being given at the trial of an action to show that a party has already been found to have performed a particular act by another court, in the course of hearing a separate case concerning the same event. For instance, in a civil action for damages following a car accident, the plaintiff could not prove that a criminal court had already found the defendant guilty of dangerous or careless driving on the occasion in question. He had to set about proving the defendant's negligence by producing his own witnesses and other evidence. This general practice was settled to be the law by the Court of Appeal in *Hollington* v. *Hewthorn*.[43] It was justified on a number of grounds: the verdict or judge's finding in the earlier proceedings was only an opinion as to the effect of the evidence given in court; it could also be regarded as hearsay. The rule had developed in a period when juries were still common in civil cases. The difficulty in presenting a jury with evidence of a previous relevant conviction was that the jurors would not know what weight to give to it; there was a danger that they would treat it as absolute proof and disregard any contrary evidence which suggested that it was mistaken. Now that juries have largely disappeared from civil cases, the question is whether professional judges are able to attach the correct significance to evidence of the earlier conviction. A judge is certainly more likely to be aware that he has only been presented with the opinion of another court and of the various possible reasons why that opinion may not be correct. He will also appreciate that if the courts are to provide certain and final answers to questions raised before them, they ought, in the absence of strong reason, to avoid reaching inconsistent results.

The Law Reform Committee concluded that the law ought to be changed and a conviction ought to be admissible evidence in a subsequent civil case that the accused committed the act of which he was found guilty. This will become law when the Civil Evidence Bill is passed.[44] Its effect is to put the burden of proving that the conviction was wrong on the defendant: he has to produce some evidence which will in effect show why he ought not to have been convicted. In some cases, the plaintiff will gain a useful advantage in negotiating an earlier and more favourable settlement, and this may prove to be the most substantial effect of the change in the law. For if the defendant actually challenges the conviction at the trial, the cautious plaintiff will not rely on the conviction by itself but will, if possible, produce witnesses to support it. Where trial judges are faced with cases in which they have to weigh a conviction against contrary evidence provided by the defence it remains to be seen how strong they require the defence evidence to be. The balancing task is a difficult one, but it does not only depend on the ability of the judge to perform it. It must also be governed by the extent to which he thinks that it is desirable to achieve consistent results on the same questions of fact between one court and another. This is a general question of policy on which it will probably prove necessary to obtain guidance by direction from the appeal courts; the answer is not to be found in the new legislation.

One reason why the Law Reform Committee took the rule in *Hollington* v. *Hewthorn* as one of their first subjects for consideration was that there had been certain cases which were clearly designed to stage a retrial of a previous criminal case. The first concerned Mr Alfred Hinds, who in 1953 had been convicted of taking part in a robbery of Maples' furniture store. A police inspector involved in the prosecution afterwards published a newspaper article in which he said that Mr Hinds was guilty; Mr Hinds thereupon sued him for libel. The inspector was unable to rely on the previous conviction for robbery and had to set about re-proving the truth of his statement. The jury in the libel case were not satisfied that he had done so, and found for Mr Hinds. Thereafter, two of the men convicted of taking part in the Great Train Robbery brought similar actions, and in one case the newspaper which had published the assertion of guilt decided against the difficult and expensive task of re-proving complicity in the robbery. Instead it admitted that the statement was defamatory but asserted that the plaintiff's reputation was so unsavoury that he deserved no substantial damages. The jury accepted this contention by awarding only nominal damages. In these cases one cannot know how the juries would have been affected by proof of the earlier convictions if it had been possible to admit them as evidence. It can scarcely have escaped the knowledge of the jury in the *Hinds* case that the plaintiff had been convicted for the robbery, although strictly they had no evidence of it. But there can be little doubt that the plaintiffs would all have been advised that their chances of success would have been reduced considerably if the previous verdicts could have been admitted, because they would no longer have been able to put the defendants at such a tactical disadvantage.

The Law Reform Committee took the view that this kind of action must be stopped in future, and the law is to be changed so that if a defamation action raises the question of whether a person did or did not commit a criminal offence, and it is proved that he has been convicted or acquitted of the offence, this will be taken as *conclusive* proof on the issue. It will no longer be possible to bring about a retrial of the earlier case by this means.[45]

(v) *Character and misconduct.* In criminal cases, the prosecution is not usually permitted to impugn the defendant by producing evidence of his bad character, previous criminal record or other misconduct. This principle has for long been looked on as fundamental to the protection of the accused against conviction by mere prejudice. Its basis is the obvious fear that juries and other judges of fact will be unable to attach due weight but no more to the information. It is very much a rule for juries because it can only be applied consistently before a tribunal such as a jury, which is constantly changing its members. In Magistrates' Courts, where criminal proceedings are governed by the same rule, the magistrates will nevertheless come to know the faces and records of those who appear before them at all regularly. The rule excluding evidence of character and convictions necessarily operates unevenly at the summary level.

The rule is not absolute. If the accused chooses to give evidence about his good character he puts his character in issue, and the prosecution is then usually entitled in retaliation to call and to cross-examine witnesses with the object of establishing that his reputation is not all that he would have the court believe. Another exception concerns so-called 'similar fact' evidence: where there is evidence that the accused has committed other crimes or wrongful conduct of a strikingly similar nature to that with which he is charged, the evidence of the other acts may be given in order to show that the accused was following some regular course or system of conduct, or to attack a defence, such as that he made a mistake, or that there had been an accident, or that he had been wrongly identified. These are occasions where the similar facts do not simply show that the accused had criminal tendencies; rather they show that the crime with which he was charged fitted into a particular plan, or that it would be a remarkable coincidence if the defence that he is setting up applied equally to the other misconduct. For instance, when the 'Brides-in-the-bath' murderer, Smith, was charged with causing the death of his first 'wife', the prosecution was permitted to prove that his two subsequent 'wives' had died in the same peculiar circumstances in order to demonstrate that it was highly unlikely that the first 'wife' had died by accident rather than by Smith's systematic design. The precise circumstances in which the judges will permit similar fact evidence to be given have proved difficult to define, and this is another area of the law which has given rise to a procession of cases, all of which are not easily reconciled.[46]

Another set of exceptions concerns the situation where the accused goes into the witness-box to give evidence on his own behalf. When in 1898 it became for the first time permissible for him to do so, it had to be decided how far he should be subject to the general rule that any witness can be cross-examined about his character so that the court may judge how far he deserves to be believed. It was settled that the accused should be free from cross-examination about his past character and conduct, but certain exceptions were made. They include the situation where the accused has chosen to attack the credibility of prosecution witnesses, and where he has given evidence against any other person charged with the same offence. The latter of these has a special justification – one of two persons charged together should not be free to give evidence that all the blame lay with the other and leave the box with his apparent credibility unstained. The former gives rise to great difficulty, for the judges have thought it only fair in certain cases to allow the accused with impunity to give evidence of a defence which necessarily involves attacking the reputation of a prosecution witness. For example, the defence may be that the woman in a rape case in fact consented to intercourse. Such an allegation is permitted without allowing in the accused's past record. In other circumstances, the judges have fluctuated in their views as to what attacks on the prosecution give a right to retaliate against the accused's reputation. But where such retaliation is allowed the accused will be obliged to choose between refraining from saying that a Crown witness has manufactured evidence and having the whole of his past record put to him in the witness-box. Given that the general policy of the law is one of exclusion, with only very limited exceptions, there is a strong case for allowing the accused to attack the character of prosecution witnesses without jeopardizing his chance to keep his own record out of the case.[47]

But at present the whole policy behind this part of the law is under review by the Criminal Law Revision Committee. A number of those who consider that juries are regularly acquitting defendants who ought to be convicted, including some of the new wave of highly professional criminals, take the view that juries ought to be given the accused's record, at least if it is for the same class of crime as that with which he is charged and is reasonably recent. Often this is coupled with the view that the accused ought not to be able to preserve silence by not giving evidence, and that counsel, as well as the judge, ought to be free to comment to the jury on any reluctance to answer questions in court.

Professor Cross has wisely pointed out that our present ignorance of the way in which juries do deal with evidence of previous record when they receive it makes it very difficult to know how far it would be safe to trust them more generally with the information.[48] The jurors whom I interviewed were almost unanimous in thinking that knowledge of previous convictions would have been an important factor in increasing their certainty of the accused's guilt. Several recalled the relief they felt when, having convicted without knowing that the accused had a record, they then heard it read out before sentence. It appeared that juries do sometimes speculate about whether an accused had previous convictions. Some jurors informed their fellows that an accused had not given evidence because he had attacked the evidence of the police and was therefore afraid that his record would be put to him in cross-examination. They might thus have managed to sway doubters into convicting. One told of a jury which came to recognize the appearance of the police form stating previous convictions and took account of its very existence if they saw it in the hands of the prosecution. This supports the usual assumption that evidence of previous convictions is prejudicial, and that the wiser course is to exclude it. Many jurors found that they had to decide whether there was just enough in a weak defence for them to be unable to say that they were convinced of the accused's guilt beyond reasonable doubt. In such circumstances, consideration of previous convictions could well tip the scales.

It is one aim of the present experiments being conducted at the London School of Economics to provide more accurate information about the effect of letting in previous convictions. Using the technique of playing a recorded trial to a series of 'juries', variations are introduced with respect to the defendant's record. The process needs to be repeated many times in order to get reasonably certain results and as

yet the experiments are some way from completion. However, the first indications seem to be that in a trial for theft,
in which the evidence puts it on the borderline between
conviction and acquittal, the juries that are told that the
accused has convictions already for the same sort of offence
are noticeably more ready to convict the accused than those
that do not know of the record. But the juries that are told
that the accused has convictions for dissimilar offences (a
sexual crime and malicious damage to property) are a little
less willing to convict than the control group. There seems
to be a slight 'boomerang' effect, a feeling that it is unfair to
stack up irrelevant convictions against an accused. Certainly
this is an attitude taken by some of the 'jurors' in the course
of their deliberations. Currently the research is being extended to see how far these findings are confirmed in experiments using different kinds of trial. It is hoped that the final
results will provide at least some empirical information from
which to try to judge the desirability of allowing juries to
know the past criminal history of all defendants.

(vi) *Previous consistent statements.* A further ground of in-
admissibility is the rule excluding a statement made by a
witness on some occasion before the trial which is the same
as the story that he gives in evidence. There is a limited
number of exceptions – cases where proof of the previous
statement seems particularly telling – but beyond that the
rule is strict. Thus if a person who witnessed a road accident
makes an immediate statement of what he saw, and is afterwards called by either side at the prosecution of a motorist
involved in the accident, the terms of his earlier statement
cannot be put to him to establish that he has not changed his
recollection of the events. It is feared that the jury will
attach too much importance to the mere fact that a witness
has accurately repeated himself, in other words that the
very repetition will give added weight to the statement. This
approach, however justified it may be, prevents the court
from taking account of the fact that earlier statements are
more likely to be accurate. There have been many demonstrations by psychologists of the marked degree to which
memory fades and becomes distorted with time. Evidence
given at a trial which takes place some months, or in some

civil cases years, after the events with which it is concerned is always open to criticism on this score, whereas statements made soon afterwards do not suffer from the same defect. This is certainly an area in which it would be useful to know how modern juries would react if the rule were abandoned.

(vii) *Additional discretionary powers.* In addition to these strict rules, there are further situations in criminal cases when the trial judge may rule evidence to be inadmissible if he concludes that its worth as proof is outweighed by the likelihood that it will create an unfair prejudice in the minds of the jurors. For this reason evidence of how the accused reacted on being confronted and accused of the crime may be excluded; so too may cross-examination of him concerning his own past conduct, after he has attacked prosecution witnesses. Even 'similar fact' evidence, which falls technically within the exception allowing it to be given, may be excluded if it is too prejudicial. Although these powers are given by way of discretion to the trial judge, the Court of Appeal sometimes finds that he ought to have exercised one or other of them in the accused's favour.

(viii) *Admission for one purpose alone.* All the situations so far discussed show the care taken by judges to ensure that juries do not hear evidence which they may not be able to treat with proper circumspection. It is therefore surprising to find that there are other rules, which assume that if a jury hears a certain kind of evidence and receives a direction from the judge either to disregard it or to use it only as proof of one thing and not another, the jury will be able to do so. For instance, if an accused person attacks the character of a prosecution witness and then goes into the witness-box, he may have his own previous record put to him. The law requires the judge to instruct the jury that the accused's record must be taken only as evidence that the attack on the prosecution was unjustified, not as evidence that the accused is guilty of the crime charged.

Then there is an exception to the rule that a witness's previous consistent statement cannot be put in evidence. It can when the witness is the victim of a sexual assault, and the earlier statement takes the form of a complaint made shortly after the alleged attack by the defendant. However, the jury will be instructed to take the earlier statement into account when assessing the reliability of the witness, but not when considering whether the offence was committed. Yet again, where two defendants are being tried together for participating in a crime, it may be that evidence is given which is admissible against one but not against the other. Even though it may implicate the other in the crime, it is normally permitted to be given, the judge warning the jury not to have regard to it in assessing the guilt of the other accused.

It would hardly be surprising if many juries were found simply not to appreciate these subtleties and disregarded the limit placed on them. Of one case, where a jury was instructed to treat a piece of evidence as incriminating A, but not B who was jointly indicted with him (although it was damaging to B as well as A), the Court of Criminal Appeal remarked: 'the jury system could not work if it were not assumed that juries always do what they are told'.[49] In fact, the 'exclusion' rules exist very largely because it is assumed that if the excluded evidence were to be admitted the jury would not be able to follow instructions to attach only limited weight to it. In the situations where the jury is instructed to disregard a piece of evidence, either in part or completely, it is suddenly assumed that the jurors have highly developed abilities to put evidence neatly into some mental pigeon-holes but not others. It is most unlikely that they can properly carry out the instruction, if they understand it at all. How jurors react in such situations is one of the matters being tested in the London School of Economics experiments.

'Instruction' rules

The other main branch of the law of evidence consists of a series of rules concerned with the weight to be attached to evidence. Rules of this kind are either necessary or desirable in all courts however constituted; but they take a special form where trial is by jury, by becoming instructions which the judge is required to include in his summing-up.

(i) *Burden and degree of proof.* The judge must direct the jury which party bears the burden of proving the allegations of fact on each issue in the trial, and what amount of evidence will discharge this responsibility. In a criminal trial it is the prosecution which bears the ultimate legal duty of proving each element necessary to constitute the criminal act, and proof must be 'beyond reasonable doubt'. There are few exceptions. One is that the accused must prove the defence of insanity or diminished responsibility, if he raises it, but he has to do so only on the 'balance of probabilities'. In a civil trial, the burden of proof may well rest on different sides for different issues. The burden is usually discharged by making out the case on the 'balance of probabilities'.

If the judge expresses these rules to the jury by using some different phrase which he regards as an equivalent expression, his direction may be challenged on appeal. A line of cases testing the propriety of different formulations may develop. For instance, the direction that in a criminal trial the prosecution must prove its case 'beyond reasonable doubt' is an accepted formula approved by the House of Lords. But in the last twenty years judges have experimented with other phrases, such as the jury must be 'satisfied so as to feel sure', 'completely satisfied', or 'feel sure' of the prisoner's guilt. This led to a number of appeals in which different formulations were challenged. Some convictions have been quashed because the judge's direction has put the degree of proof to be shown by the prosecution too low, for instance, directions that the jury had to be 'pretty certain' or 'reasonably sure'.[50] This too is a matter under investigation in the London School of Economics experiments. So far, the indications are that the 'jurors' take little notice of the precise terms in which they are instructed. Even if they are told that they must find an accused person guilty on balance of probabilities they show a marked tendency to start discussing whether their doubts are reasonable.

(ii) *Corroboration*. English law has no universal rule that a fact cannot be proved by the unsubstantiated testimony of one witness, but it does recognize that there are certain situations in which it is dangerous to accept such evidence as proof. In some cases, the judge is required to instruct the jury not to convict unless it can find corroboration: this applies to unsworn evidence given by a child in a criminal trial, and evidence given in relation to specific offences such as perjury, exceeding a speed limit in a motor vehicle, and

TRIAL METHOD AND PRACTICE

procuring women as prostitutes. In other situations, the law simply requires the judge to warn the jury of the danger of convicting without corroborative evidence. Into this category comes the criminal accomplice who turns Queen's Evidence, because he may have special reasons for removing blame from himself; so too does the evidence against a person accused of a sexual offence, because it is known that sometimes false accusations are made in this class of case as the result of imagination, misconstruction or malice.

The requirement concerning the evidence of an accomplice is a good illustration of how these rules gradually acquire greater rigidity. Originally the rule was no more than a practical instruction which judges gave if they saw fit. Gradually its use became more and more regular, and eventually the House of Lords decided the 'corroboration warning' must be given, or else a conviction would be upset on appeal. But to decide who is an accomplice for this purpose can be complex, for it is not simply left to the judge. If there is some evidence that the witness was a participant in the crime, the judge must direct the jury to consider whether he did in fact take part. An intention to participate in some lesser offence is not enough. The jury is told that if it finds that the witness is an accomplice in this sense, then it would be dangerous to convict on his evidence without corroboration. In addition, the jury has also to be instructed as to the sort of independent evidence which the law regards as corroboration.[51]

Where a case is being tried not with a jury but by a judge alone, or by magistrates, the requirements of corroboration do not lead to such elaborate precautions, for there is no need to put the provisions of the law into the form required for a summing-up. In assessing whether adultery is proved in a divorce case, for instance, the judge will be reluctant to act on the uncorroborated evidence of one of the participants, but no rule of law prevents him accepting the evidence if he thinks that it is strong enough.[52] Nor is there any procedure which requires him to enunciate a corroboration warning to himself. There is therefore no room for an appeal from a misdirection through having failed to administer the approved verbal formula. This necessarily different approach is equally true of the other 'instruction' rules. When trial is by judge or magistrates, the 'instruction' rules serve as general guides to the assessment of the weight of evidence. They do not have to be reiterated in terms of an approved verbal formula which, if not adhered to, may found a successful appeal.

(iii) *Presumptions*. These are rules that specify the circumstances in which, if it is proved that certain facts existed, a further inference should be drawn from them. They protect against too little significance being attached to some kinds of evidence, just as the corroboration rules protect against the opposite tendency. Thus when juries regularly tried civil negligence actions, a presumption arose that where the damage was proved to have been caused by an object under the defendant's control, this was sufficient evidence to show that the accident arose from the defendant's lack of care if he gave no reasonable explanation of the accident: *res ipsa loquitur* – the thing speaks for itself. An example of a presumption from the criminal law was the rule that in a murder case if the accused was shown to have inflicted the injury, then as far as his intention was concerned he must be presumed to have intended the natural consequences of his acts. The judges in dealing with both these rules showed a tendency to apply them more strictly with time. The presumption *res ipsa loquitur* at first meant no more than that the jury *might* draw an inference of negligence from proof of the unexplained accident, but the Court of Appeal has since held that the jury *must* draw the inference if sufficient evidence 'rebutting the presumption' is not called.[53] The rule presuming that the natural consequences of an act follow from it was, in murder cases, hardened into the absolute role of law that if the accused was shown to have done a certain kind of act causing death, and a reasonable man would have expected its natural consequence to be at least grievous bodily harm to the deceased, the accused must be presumed to have malice aforethought, and to have committed the crime of murder. This new rule, established in *D.P.P.* v. *Smith*, was a departure from the basic principle that a person's guilt must be judged by reference to his own subjective state of mind, and it was heavily criticized for this reason. The judges seem to have been led to make the change by a desire that juries

should not think that they must acquit if there was no positive evidence of the accused's own state of mind. But the
rule in *D.P.P.* v. *Smith* went unacceptably far in trying to
provide a remedy. The Law Commission recommended its
abandonment and legislation has been passed which aims
to do so.[54]

Enough has been said to show how formal and strict rules
of evidence have developed in order to limit the kinds of
information that can be put before a jury, and to give directions on the weight that ought to be attached to evidence
once admitted. The present extensive review of the rules is
the result of widespread feeling that the law has grown up
erratically as a by-product of the evolution of the modern
trial system. The disadvantages are obvious. 'Exclusion'
rules lead to concentration on the question of what evidence
it is safe to put to the court at all, rather than on the value
to be attached to the relevant evidence as a whole. Since
general rules of exclusion will not work equally well in all
cases, exceptions are created. This tends to produce technical
and casuistic law, which readily provides grounds for successful appeals. Moreover, once relevant evidence is treated
as inadmissible, the situation may arise where a piece of
evidence is admissible for one purpose but not for another.
The judges have dealt with this dilemma by abandoning
their caution towards juries and expecting them to perform
sophisticated feats of mental agility in treating information
as relevant only to one particular issue.

'Instruction' rules, when used in a trial by jury, have
tended not only to become stricter and more elaborate, but
they have been applied in a formalistic way, with much attention being given to use of the approved verbal formula. If the
judge does not instruct the jury correctly, again the chances
of a successful appeal will be good.

Before a regular Court of Criminal Appeal was established
in 1907, there was generally no way in which a convicted
defendant could object to his trial on the grounds of a mis-
application of the law of evidence. Since that date, developments in the law of evidence applicable to criminal cases,
always the more elaborate branch of the law, have been
rapid. Appeals for technical faults in applying the rules have

been popular, because the Court of Appeal has no power to order a new trial if it finds in the appellant's favour. It must normally quash the conviction, unless it is satisfied that despite the error the jury could only have convicted him. A certain amount of the attraction of these appeals would have been dissipated if the prospective appellant could only expect another trial, conducted without the same mistake. Many Commonwealth jurisdictions have introduced provisions for ordering new trials which cover mistakes in applying the rules of evidence, and the results are not generally considered oppressive. But in England, resistance on the ground that no man should have to stand trial twice for the same offence has so far been successful.[55]

It is not surprising that, in the present review, reforms for civil cases have been quicker than for criminal cases. There is now no jury in most civil actions, and major changes such as the substantial relaxation of the hearsay rule have been quickly made. The question which remains to be asked is whether judges and magistrates trying civil cases are acting consistently and fairly in assessing new and difficult forms of evidence. This will only become apparent after some experience with the working of the new rules. In the criminal courts, reformers are still faced with enigmas about the ability of juries to deal with elaborate instructions and to cope with prejudicial evidence at present excluded. It is a great pity that the results of research were not available before the Criminal Law Revision Committee set out on its present task. Ignorance will probably make for cautious reforms, and caution may well mean the perpetration of further technicalities. Caution in the case of many of the rules is justified. The present rules after all express the day-to-day experience of judges working with juries over long periods of time. The limits of judicial trust which they embody are no doubt often warranted. It is probably inevitable that there will continue to be an elaborate code of evidence for criminal trials if the jury system is to remain workable. In the end this can only be an important argument against continuance of trial by jury.

4 · Judge and jury

At first glance it may appear that judge and jury have a simple, separate-but-equal relationship with one another: questions of fact are for the jury, questions of law for the judge. This proposition, so often the basis on which a judge builds his summing-up, disguises a much more complex state of affairs by failing to reveal any of the extensive powers of supervision which English judges have always been careful to exert over juries. One demonstration of this control has already been discussed: the rules of evidence are a means whereby the judges have limited the information which may be put before juries, and have directed juries how to attach due weight to the evidence that they do hear. There are other important aspects of the relationship. This chapter explores two of them: the extent to which judges have taken issues from the jury which would normally be regarded as 'questions of fact', and the degree to which judges are enabled by their position to persuade juries to their own point of view. Complete analysis of these matters will raise a number of complex issues, but it is only when they are explored that the true division of power between judge and jury becomes apparent. It is the considerable difficulty of transplanting this division of power abroad that has made the jury an unsuccessful export to foreign legal systems which have not adopted the common law. There can be little doubt that the jury system has been made to work as well as it does in England because the judges have had so free a hand to develop the rules under which it operates and to guide and influence juries from day to day.

The true meaning of the terms 'questions of fact' and 'questions of law' can best be approached through an example. Suppose that X is charged with living on the earnings of a prostitute. The prosecution alleges that X committed the offence by publishing a book of names, addresses and photographs of prostitutes, intended as an advertisement of what they had to offer, and received payment from the ladies concerned for doing so. If the occurrence of these events is in dispute, the jury will have the duty of deciding whether or not they did occur. Suppose that X denies that he is the man who ordered the printer to print the directory: the evidence on this may be direct – the printer may be called to say that X was the man who ordered the work to be done; and X may deny it. The jury's one function will then be to decide which witness to believe. But suppose that the origins of the directory are less clear – for instance, that the only evidence inculpating X is that of a newsvendor to whom X delivered a number of copies, but X says that although he delivered them he was not the person who had them printed. Here the jury will have to decide an inference of fact: does it follow from proof of the one fact (delivery to the vendor) that the other (ordering the printing) is likely to be correct? In this, the kind of judgement which is expected of the jury is rather different: it is not merely a matter of being able to tell whether a person is lying or mistaken, but rather of deciding from general experience how likely it is that one event took place because the other is acknowledged to have occurred. This too is treated as a question of fact.

Even if it is fully established that X had the directories printed and received payments from the advertisers, it is still not clear whether X is liable under the terms of the offence with which he is charged. Is producing such a directory to be regarded as 'living wholly or in part on the earnings of prostitution'? A judge might choose to deal with this intermediate question of definition in two ways. He might decide that it is a 'question of law', and determine the matter himself. This is what actually happened in the *Ladies' Directory* case,[1] the facts of which have provided the basis for the example just given. The judge there held that, as a matter of law, 'living on the earnings' included supplying services or goods for reward, if they were intended to further prostitution. In effect, additional words were imported into the legal definition of the offence. The judge's decision would have a general effect as a precedent, and could be stated as the law in a similar case in the future. But the judge might have chosen an alternative course, which would be to tell the jury to decide on the facts before them whether the accused had been living on the earnings of prostitutes. The question of further defining the words of the statute would then be left to the jury to be settled as a 'question of fact' for that case alone. The verdict would not have the effect of adding to the general law, for jury verdicts are not treated as establishing legal precedents.

One can never be quite sure which course a court will adopt. The matter is one of lawyers' custom and the court's decision as a matter of policy whether it is desirable or not to have a settled rule for future similar cases. But generally, where the words of a rule of law describe a class of actions, and the question is whether some particular act comes within their scope, the court will settle the question as a matter of law by way of further definition. In this way it was decided that producing a prostitutes' guide was 'living on the earnings' in the *Ladies' Directory* case. On the other hand, if the words of the rule of law call directly for a value judgment to be set upon an action, then it is likely that the question will be left to the jury to decide. We shall meet examples of this kind of rule at later stages of this book. Was driving dangerous? Did a publication tend to deprave and corrupt? Did a statement tend to lower a person's reputation in the eyes of right-thinking members of the public? The distinction between words describing a class of actions and words requiring a value judgment is one rather of degree than of kind. For the decision whether publishing a prostitutes' directory is or is not 'living on the earnings' involves two judgments: that there is a factual resemblance between this act and other acts more obviously described as 'living on the earnings'; and that publishing the directory deserves to be treated as a crime in the same way as the other acts.

That there is no magical difference between reserving such questions for the judge and handing them over to the jury is well illustrated by the following instance. An employer is in law under a duty to provide a safe system of work for his employees, and if an accident results because a particular employer has not taken reasonable care in discharging his duty, he will be liable in damages to an employee who is injured in consequence. When juries regularly tried such cases, the reasonableness of the employer's conduct was left to them without much further legal definition of what the law said was reasonable in a given situation. With the decline of juries, the trial judge has had to decide all questions before the court, and a tendency set in of laying down more precise rules as to what conduct was reasonable. Where the issue was whether the employer had provided sufficient safety equipment for an employee doing a dangerous job, the judges began to say that it was established in law by earlier cases that the employer's conduct was reasonable only if the equipment was on hand at the job and the employee had been instructed to use it. The House of Lords checked this tendency by advising judges to remember that they were fulfilling a jury function, and that 'reasonableness' should be decided in each case on its own facts.[2]

An example from the criminal law shows an equally interesting fluctuation in policy. The crime of murder will be reduced to that of manslaughter if the killing is shown to have been committed under provocation from the dead man. In law there is provocation only if the dead man's acts were so gross that they actually caused the accused to lose his self-control, and would also have caused a *reasonable man* to use violence with fatal results. The judges became dissatisfied that juries were being left to decide such a broad issue and in consequence began to define provocation more specifically. In particular it was established as a strict rule that mere words could never constitute provocation, so that a wife's confession of adultery to her husband could not convert his killing of her from murder into manslaughter.[3] The Royal Commission on Capital Punishment, which in a number of ways favoured the principle of leaving questions of evaluation to the jury with only a broad direction in law, recommended that this limitation should be removed: the jury 'can be trusted to arrive at a just and reasonable decision and will not hesitate to convict the accused of murder where he has acted only on slight provocation whether by words or otherwise.'[4] In 1957, this became law: '... the question whether the provocation was enough to make a reasonable man to do as he did shall be left to be determined by the jury. ...'[5]

In discussing the issue of applying the law to the facts and in showing how it may be settled by the judge or by the jury, depending on the particular circumstances, we have not wholly unravelled the intricacies of their relationship. Two glosses have to be taken into account. The first is that judges have sometimes laid down the rule that a question of the application of law to fact shall be settled by the judge and not by the jury, even though it is not intended that the judge's conclusion should be generalized into a principle of law, but should remain a conclusion on the facts of the case alone. The judge is deemed to be settling a 'question of law', but the phase means no more than 'question for the judge'. As we shall see (p. 225), this is the way in which the judge decides whether a person sued for malicious prosecution had reasonable and probable cause for bringing the prosecution in the first place. In the same way the judge decides questions of construction of a document – what meaning is to be given to specific words or phrases used in it – unless the words have some technical but non-legal use, in which case the question was one for the jury. Judges took for themselves most questions concerning the meaning of documents for the simple reason that in the past jurors were often illiterate. In addition, documents were often drawn up by lawyers, and so judges were in a better position than jurors to know the intended meaning of the words used.

The same sort of policy can be seen at work in another example: in a prosecution for perjury, it is necessary to show that the evidence given at an earlier trial and said to be perjured concerned an issue that was material to the earlier trial. A judge is more likely than a jury to be able to see whether the evidence was material to the subject of another proceeding, and so the question of materiality has become a question for him.

There are also certain issues which are quite nakedly treated as 'questions of fact', but which the judge deals with by himself. One is the proof of foreign law. If it becomes necessary to prove a rule of foreign law in English proceedings, this is done by calling a witness who is versed in the law of the country concerned to give evidence of the foreign law. It may be that each side will call a foreign legal expert, and that conflicting evidence will result. In such a case, the judge will have to choose between their opinions. The particular reason why this has been called a 'question of fact' is to prevent English lawyers treating a finding of foreign law made by a judge in one case from becoming a precedent binding another judge to the same conclusion in another case, even though he may take a different view of the evidence of the experts in foreign law.

Again, if it is necessary to decide whether certain evidence is admissible, and that in turn depends on disputed facts, the judge will have to decide. A common case concerns the rule that a defendant's confession of his crime is admissible in evidence against him only if it is proved that it was made voluntarily. The judge will settle whether this was so in the absence of the jury.

It must not be imagined from the complexities of this analysis that the jurors dealing with a particular case will be confused about the duties they have to perform. It is for the judge to instruct them about what they have to decide on the case before them. If confusions arise it is because his sum-ming-up lacks clarity or force. But it is worthwhile under-standing the division of function between the two; for it illustrates how English judges have been free, in the inter-mediate area of applying the law to the facts, to decide whether to allow the jury full sail or to keep it close hauled. In each case they have made a choice depending on the requirements of the particular issue: the desirability of making general rules more specific, distrust of a jury's judgment over a particular matter, its lack of a particular skill or experience, are all factors which have, on occasion, played their part in dividing up the duties of judges and juries.

THE JUDGE'S POWER TO REFUSE A VERDICT

The controls which the judge may exercise over the jury are, however, by no means limited to deciding, in accordance with precedent, what questions he shall settle himself. He has certain powers to supervise the jury's verdict and to refuse, if necessary, to accept it. These powers are wider in civil cases, for in criminal cases they are limited by the fundamental principle that a verdict of not guilty is final and cannot be questioned.

In civil proceedings, one side will bear the burden of making out his case on a particular issue; unless he does so, the other side will win. When he has put forward his evidence, his opponent may submit to the judge that no case has been made out for the opponent to answer. If the judge agrees that that is so, then his decision ends the action. The judge is normally reluctant to do this, and will require the defendant, in making the submission, to undertake not to call evidence in defence if the judge should decide against him.[6] The defendant is deliberately put at risk in order to discourage submissions of no case to answer. In summing-up, the judge also has an opportunity to direct the jury not to consider an issue because the side which has made an allegation has produced no evidence to support it. At the end of the whole trial, after the verdict, the judge has yet another opportunity to consider the question. At this stage he may consider not only whether there was some vital gap in the evidence of the side which is bound to make out its case, but also whether, on the evidence given by both sides, the case for one side is overwhelmingly strong. If a verdict is returned for the other, the judge may refuse to accept it because it is 'contrary to the weight of the evidence', 'weight' being used in the sense of the whole tenor or drift of the evidence, not in the sense of the balance of probabilities. He may then either direct a new trial, or enter judgment against the jury's verdict.[7]

The judge may exercise these powers in respect of 'questions of fact' in the narrow sense: whether events did or did not occur. But equally, if a judge is really dissatisfied with a jury's verdict on matters of inference, or of evaluation in applying the law to the facts, he is entitled to hold that the verdict was not supported by the evidence, or was contrary to the weight of the evidence. In some cases where the judges have thought that the jury is likely to be unreasonable, they have asserted the right to give their own preliminary ruling on the question. We shall see that in defamation actions the judge has power to decide whether the statement in issue is 'capable in law' of being defamatory. If it is not, then it will not be left to the jury to decide whether it was 'in fact' defamatory (see p. 213). Another example concerns the rule that an infant is only liable to pay on contracts for the sale of goods if they were 'necessaries'. What is a 'necessary' is in law only laid down in general terms: was it reasonably necessary for the infant to buy the article, having regard to his station in life, and his existing supply? In the mid nineteenth century, when juries were likely to contain a fair sprinkling of shopkeepers, the most unlikely articles were being found to be necessaries. In a case where the jury had decided that an antique goblet and jewelled cuff-links bought by a young man-about-town to give to a patron were necessaries, the Court of Exchequer Chamber ruled that the judge had power to decide first whether the articles were 'capable in law' of being necessaries.[8] The Court also held that the articles in question were not capable of being necessaries and so upset the verdict. Such actions rarely arise now, and are even less likely to be tried by jury, but the example is interresting because it shows clearly the way in which the judge might step in to limit a jury's power where he thought that the jurors might exhibit an unjustified prejudice.

In criminal proceedings, the situation is rather different. The prosecution is bound to prove all issues, with a few exceptions such as insanity. At the end of the prosecution case the defendant may submit that there is no case to answer. He is entitled to have that submission settled there and then, and he does not jeopardize his right to call evidence should he be unsuccessful. If the judge finds that there is no case for the defendant to answer he will direct the jury to return a verdict of not guilty. Sometimes he will merely indicate that the jury may like to stop the case against the accused, and it is not unknown for the jury to take an insufficiently clear hint the wrong way and return a verdict of guilty. Indeed, there have been occasions on which the jury has refused to budge from such a verdict.[9] The judge is then compelled to discharge the jury from giving a verdict at all. Another jury will be sworn, and customarily the Crown offers no evidence to it, so that the new jury must find the defendant not guilty. These manoeuvres are necessary because of the basic principle that once a man has been indicted before a jury and has pleaded not guilty, the charge against him cannot be determined except on a jury's verdict. This strict rule has meant that even where the prosecution is going to abandon its case by not offering any evidence against the accused, a jury must be empanelled to acquit him formally. A recent change in the law allows the judge to dispose of the case without having to swear in a jury in these circumstances.[10]

If the case proceeds to the end of evidence for both sides, and a verdict of guilty is returned, which the judge decides is against the weight of the evidence, he is bound in a criminal case to accept the jury's verdict. He may, however, facilitate an appeal by immediately granting leave to do so, and he may even refuse to enter judgment until the appeal has been heard.[11] Since it was set up in 1907, the Court of Criminal Appeal – now the Court of Appeal, Criminal Division – has always had power to upset a verdict of guilty that it considers unreasonable, or that cannot be supported on the evidence. Recently this power has been somewhat broadened. The Court may now quash a conviction if it finds that to let the conviction stand would be 'unsafe or unsatisfactory'.[12] The Lord Chief Justice has said that the change does no more than bring the statutory powers of the court into line with its established practice.[13]

If the case proceeds to the end and there is a verdict of not guilty, then no matter what the judge thinks of it, it is final, and no appeal lies against it even on a disputed point of law. The jury's power to acquit is sovereign.

An essential corollary of this rule is the principle that the judge may not direct the jury to return a verdict of guilty, provided that the accused has produced any kind of defence to the charge against him.[14] But to this aspect of the principle there is an important exception. Where the defendant has to prove a defence – as in the case of insanity or diminished responsibility – he must produce evidence to support it. If he fails to do so, the trial judge will not leave it open to the jury to return a verdict for the defendant on the basis of the defence. Moreover, even in the case of other defences, such as provocation or self-defence, where the ultimate onus is on the prosecution to disprove the defence raised, there is nevertheless a preliminary rule that the defendant must introduce some evidence to support his plea. If he fails the issue will not be left to the jury. In other words, the judge will direct the jury not to consider the defence if there is no evidence on which it could be based, even though, if some evidence were produced, it would be for the prosecution to prove the case as a whole and this would involve establishing beyond reasonable doubt that the defence was not substantiated.

Suppose that a defendant is accused of murder and admits the killing, but says that he acted in self-defence. If by the end of his cross-examination he is reduced to agreeing that he was really not defending himself at all, the judge will withdraw the issue of self-defence from the jury. The same would be true if he only gave evidence of acting in a way that could not amount to self-defence as a matter of law. When the trial reaches such a stage, the judge may, while leaving it to the jury to convict or acquit, indicate that in his view the evidence leads inevitably to a guilty verdict.

But, as Lord Devlin has recently pointed out,[15] some modern judges have taken the further step of actually directing the jurors to convict in such cases. This means denying them their constitutional right to acquit for any reason that they choose. It is true that if the jury defies the judge and acquits, he would be obliged to accept the verdict; but most jurors would be unaware, or at least unsure, of their ultimate power to do this if the judge told them that they must convict. Lord Devlin rightly points out the special danger that a judge may only decide that there is no defence because in his view the evidence is too clear for argument. This qualifies the basic rule that it is for the jury in a criminal case to decide whether the facts do establish the defendant's guilt. The qualification, once admitted, could gradually lead to a considerable usurpation of the jury's province by the judges. Certainly the old principle should only be abandoned by deliberate policy, not by creeping compromise.

SPECIAL VERDICTS

The judge may exercise a certain degree of control over the jury by asking it to return a special verdict, that is to give brief answers to a number of specific questions put by him.

This is common practice in civil actions such as libel, where there are usually a number of different issues to be made out, some by the plaintiff and some by the defendant. The special verdict is a method of ensuring that the jury does not ignore any issue which it has not fully understood and might otherwise disregard. On occasion, it may also be used as a way of establishing the facts, so that a point of law can be raised on appeal. Very occasionally it is also used in criminal cases for this latter purpose,[16] but the Court of Appeal has frowned on any unnecessary extension of the practice, because it is a means of preventing the jury from exercising its right to return a final general verdict of not guilty.[17] If there were a clash on the right to return a general and not a special verdict, the judge would be wrong to insist upon the latter, in either a civil or a criminal case.[18]

It has, however, been suggested that greater use should be made of special verdicts to ensure that juries are not ignoring issues in the course of their deliberations. For instance, it is thought that some juries have difficulty in grasping that a man is not guilty of theft until it is shown that he took the article with the intention of depriving the owner of it permanently, and may assume that a temporary borrowing is enough. This is certainly a danger, though avoiding it by means of a special verdict would have the effect of curtailing the jury's power to ignore the strict law and do what they think is right in the circumstances. A less drastic solution might be for the judge to give the jurors a written definition of the law that he has outlined to them so that they may refer to it in the jury-room.

THE JUDGE'S GENERAL INFLUENCE

So far we have discussed the judge's formal powers to control the verdict of the jury, and to exclude matters from its consideration. But most cases do not present serious problems about the application of the law to fact, nor does the possibility of a totally unacceptable verdict often arise. In day-to-day terms, it is the informal indications which judges give of their views, and the extent to which they are followed by the jury, that are of greater significance.

Some counsel attach great importance to the right of reply, that is, the right to deliver the final closing speech to the jury. But it is the judge in his summing-up who has the real last word, and it is likely that his view of the case will be influential. As well as directing the jury on the relevant law, the judge is free to comment as he likes on the strength of the case made out by either side. Since the early nineteenth century, it has also been judicial practice to review the evidence for the jury's benefit. The judge's discretion in dealing with the evidence and commenting upon it is limited only in a minor degree: he must direct as to which side bears the onus of proof, and give such other instructions, for instance on corroboration or a presumption, as the rules of evidence require. In a criminal case, out of fairness to the accused, there are certain comments that he ought not to make, for example, on the fact that the accused refused to say anything to the police when they questioned him.[19] He is also expected to refer to the case for the defence and the evidence which supports it. If he breaks one of these rules then it is likely that an appeal will be successful, but otherwise he is free to choose his own terms for summing-up.

In the nineteenth century methods of judicial influence were often somewhat crude. The annals of the Central Criminal Court are full of tales of the cursory Mr Commissioner Kerr, who was once reported to have disposed of a case with the words: 'Gentlemen of the jury, the man stole the ducks. Consider your verdict.'[20] Higher standards prevail today, for since 1907 the Court of Criminal Appeal has supervised the conduct of criminal trials. Some judges cultivate an ability to take a dispassionate and neutral position, leaving the whole question to the jury whenever there is any doubt in his own mind. Others have indirect ways of indicating their own views while paying due respect to the principle that the verdict is ultimately in the jury's hands. In this way the judge may in the end exert more influence than the man who pushes his opinion so strongly that he produces a reaction against him. The simple ordering of events in reviewing the evidence affords ample opportunity for the judge to show how strong or weak he considers the case presented by each side to be. Moreover, since the summing-up is entirely an oral procedure, a great deal turns on the judge's tone of voice, emphasis and inflexion.

The trial of Dr Stephen Ward on charges of living on

immoral earnings and procuring the services of prostitutes affords a recent example. It was commonly asserted that Mr Justice Marshall summed up against the accused on three of the counts. Ludovic Kennedy, who was present, wrote of it: 'It was not that the judge had omitted what was favourable to Ward – the record belied that. It was simply a question of emphasis. When the judge was pointing out to the jury those things in Ward's favour, he often did so in a flat, matter-of-fact voice. He appeared so uninterested in what he was saying that one could not be interested oneself: the mind automatically shut off from him. Yet when it came to matters which told against Ward, his tone changed: his voice and bearing became brighter, livelier, he held the attention where elsewhere he had lost it.'[21]

Many jurors *feel* that the summing-up has influenced them considerably. Of those I interviewed a considerable number specially commented on the wisdom and impartiality of the judge with whom they sat. They often contrasted him in glowing terms with counsel who had appeared before them. It is scarcely surprising that to people who were trying to act responsibly in performing a complex task without much experience he should appear to occupy an authoritative position. A number of jurors expressed added confidence in their verdict because it accorded with what they thought was the judge's view; and others (a more frequent comment) regretted that the judge had vouchsafed no view of his own which they could have followed. Frequently the issue as they saw it was whether there was just enough in the defence case to say that the prosecution had not shown proof beyond reasonable doubt; this was just the situation in which a judicial comment could sway the verdict one way or the other.

Judges realize their power to influence a verdict. Lord Birkett, in contrasting his work on the bench with that at the bar, confided in his diary: 'I still have the power of dominating juries; they do whatever I wish.'[22] Glanville Williams reports: 'I was told by a recorder, who was a strong supporter of the jury system, that when first appointed he used to sum up to the jury with absolute impartiality, and the result was that the jury, being left to do its own thinking, acquitted most of the defendants. To avoid these failures of justice the recorder changed his method and summed up in the direction he thought proper. The result was the expected number of convictions.'[23] It is scarcely surprising in a system under which judges are selected exclusively from practising advocates that some judges will continue to practise the art of persuasion from the bench.

But it must not be imagined that the summing-up always produces the result favoured by the judge. Graham Greene wrote of his experience on a jury which sat at Sessions for a week solemnly acquitting all who came before it, whatever the trend of the judge's summing-up.[24] Two matters in particular may reduce the effectiveness of the judge's remarks. First, the summing-up is given orally and has to be understood and remembered at one hearing.[25] There are no written directives which the jury can take away and mull over as their discussion in the jury-room develops. Secondly there is a natural tendency to disregard what is said about things which the jury cannot understand: nice distinctions over the precise meaning of a rule of law, and the judge's assessment of expert evidence may thus pass into oblivion.

The degree to which the judge is left free in England to direct the jury as he likes and to influence it as he wants is best appreciated by comparison with the fetters which encumber an American judge. In many states, the judge may not comment on the evidence; if requested by counsel, he must instruct the jury to give equal account to evidence given in written depositions as to the oral testimony of witnesses in courts; similarly, if asked he must direct that social or other prejudices should be excluded; if he refers to the jury's right to consider circumstantial evidence he must not exaggerate or minimize its effect.[26]

The American system has its own critics: a federal judge once described the trial judge as 'gagged, handcuffed, blindfolded, and paralysed from the waist up'.[27] The American Bar Association and the American Law Institute have called for the full restoration of the English system, which has survived in a few states. But this has met with no success. The question there, as here, is intimately connected with the system of selecting judges. We are content to rely on their aloofness, their small numbers and the fact that they are appointed to office for life. In the United States many judges are elected democratically: the problem of the biased or prejudiced judge looms much larger. The English system has evolved without the constitutional crisis which alone would have achieved any change in the kind of powers which the judges have given themselves to influence juries.

Two other aspects of American practice which differ from the English are worth attention. In some twenty states the judge's instructions to the jury are given before counsel address them – a further attempt to minimize the influence of the bench by taking the last word from the judge. It also has a certain logic. Under the English system the jury are not told by the judge what the rules of law are before they have heard counsel's arguments about how they should decide the case on the evidence.[28] In practice this dilemma is scarcely a real one. Indeed in America there is strong feeling that those states which still follow the English order have a more desirable procedure. The American Bar Association has recommended that it once more become the uniform method throughout the country.

Secondly, in many states the judge's instructions to the jury are written down – their wording is settled after submissions by counsel for each side. In view of what has already been suggested about the jury's failure to appreciate the force of some points in a summing-up, this practice should be given consideration in England.

THE JURY'S POWER TO IGNORE THE JUDGE

The formal powers to control verdicts which the judges have acquired, and their general freedom to assert persuasive influence over juries, is one side of the balance of power between the two. The other is the considerable freedom which is left to the jury to ignore the judge's instructions either deliberately or through a failure to understand them. The secrecy of jury deliberations, the lack of any requirement that reasons be given for a verdict once it has been returned, in particular, the fact that an acquittal of a criminal charge is completely unassailable, all combine to strengthen this freedom. As we noted at the outset, it constitutes the jury's most outstanding characteristic and will play a central part in much of the discussion throughout the rest of the book.

The fact that a jury is responsible ultimately to its collective conscience alone has been acclaimed as conferring a wide variety of advantages on the judicial system. Such advantages as have constitutional significance will be discussed in the next chapter, and special consequences in criminal cases in Chapter 6. But having just discussed the extent to which judges decide 'fact', we turn first to the question of how far juries determine 'law'. In this country, unlike some American States, juries are never directed that they are to decide what the rule of law is in its general terms. As we have already seen, they are, however, frequently left to make a vital value judgment in deciding how a rule should be applied to particular facts. And that is not the full extent of their influence. For if juries consistently refuse to enforce a rule of law it may fall into disuse. Moreover, it is possible to leave the terms of a general rule so vague that its true meaning can only be discovered by putting an actual case to a jury for its decision. Both these aspects of the matter deserve discussion.

THE JURY AS AN UNMAKER OF LAW

Although the verdict of a particular jury does not create a legal precedent, it may nevertheless not be entirely uninfluential as an expression of how ordinary citizens think that a provision of the law should be applied. If unexpected verdicts begin to occur regularly in the same sort of case, then it will become apparent that it is not that juries are taking some idiosyncratic view of the facts, but rather they are expressing disapproval of the rule of law which they are directed to apply. In theory, at least, this constitutes a valuable mechanism for ensuring that the law remains acceptable to the moral sense of the man in the street. Its particular importance relates to the criminal law, since it is a means of bringing law into disfavour, and eventually of achieving a change in the existing law. It should indeed follow that Parliament, in creating new penal legislation, must have regard to the likely reaction of juries. It ought to be borne in mind that a provision of which juries will not approve is unlikely to be regularly enforced.

This aspect of the jury system was of great importance when the criminal law was harsh and crude. In the eighteenth century there began the immense social change from an agricultural to an industrial community which brought with it a vast increase in urban population and much economic instability and poverty. An alarming growth of crime set in, especially in the cities, and on the roads and canals and at the ports where the new manufacturers were sent. The phlegmatic eighteenth-century Parliaments could see no other solution to the crime problem than increasing the severity of sentences.[29] By the turn of the nineteenth century over two hundred offences bore the death penalty, and convicts who were not hanged were liable to undergo the extreme hazard of transportation to Australia and elsewhere. If these Draconian laws had been enforced at all efficiently the country would have been grossly oppressed, but they were not. The administration of the criminal law was chaotic, with a wholly outdated police system of parish constables and watchmen, and prisons that were run by corrupt gaolers as offices of profit. In these circumstances those concerned with the actual process of trial were often disposed to prevent the conviction of an offender who had had the misfortune to have been caught and prosecuted. Many accounts of the criminal courts of the period show that grand jurors were often ready to throw out bills of indictment, prosecution witnesses would sometimes go back on their depositions rather than send a defendant to the gallows, judges would try to persuade defendants not to plead guilty and would look after their interests during the trial, petty jurors frequently refused to convict on the clearest evidence of guilt. Moreover, they would often find an accused person guilty of a crime which did not carry the death penalty, even where there was evidence supporting a charge on a capital offence. Forgers were found guilty only of possessing the forged notes. Thieves were found to have stolen goods of less value than the minimum for capital punishment. Sometimes the jury would so grossly undervalue the goods that their verdicts were commonly called 'pious perjury'. Even when an accused was convicted and sentenced to death, the judges had power to recommend a transportation or imprisonment or even a pardon, in place of execution, and this they frequently used. Grand and petty juries therefore played an important but by no means single-handed part in mitigating the most intolerable aspects of the criminal law during this period.

Of course, as a means of attaining justice the system was capricious. The criminal law did not apparently deter criminals, but at the same time like cases could be treated very differently. The readiness of the prosecutor to go through with the case, the prevailing attitude of the local gentry and tradesmen on the grand and petty juries, what the judge knew of the defendant's general reputation (for there were no adequate criminal records), all these factors might affect an offender's ultimate fate. By 1820, the movement for the reform of the capital laws led by Romilly, and then by Fowell Buxton and Mackintosh, was gaining impetus; within two decades it succeeded in completely altering public opinion on capital punishment and the penalty was removed from all but the most serious and violent crimes. One surprising kind of pressure group emerged in favour of these changes: those whom the law specially sought to protect were frequently in favour of the abolition of capital punishment for an offence. Thus many bankers favoured the abolition of hanging for forgery and their reason was the grave difficulty of finding prosecutors and securing verdicts of guilty from juries while the death penalty remained the consequence. It is also interesting to find that there were groups of jurors who by virtue of their office added to the clamour for reform.[30]

At just the same period, the administration of criminal justice was transformed by the establishment of the modern professional police forces, and by the first steps towards the present prison system. The glaring inefficiency, neglect and mismanagement that had characterized the era of parish officers and local gaols gradually disappeared. The criminal law could afford to be more humane and juries had less reason for sympathizing with defendants who became caught in its web. Certainly once the vast majority of capital offences had been removed from the statute book, juries ceased to show special sympathy for defendants on the same extensive scale.

It is, however, interesting to look at two later instances of crimes which have been unpopular with juries. One is the crime of infanticide. Until 1922 if a mother killed her newborn child while she was suffering from the after-effects of

giving birth, she committed murder and the sole punishment was death. Even by the mid-nineteenth century the
grave injustice of the law was widely recognized. Not only
did juries often refuse to convict, but doctors were prepared
to perjure themselves by refraining from giving medical
evidence of the cause of death which would demonstrate
the mother's guilt, and the Home Secretary regularly exercised his power to commute the sentence to one of life
imprisonment. The introduction of a less serious criminal
offence carrying a lesser penalty in such cases was recommended in 1866. But it took another fifty-six years to achieve
the reform, and then it was the judges who constituted the
principal pressure group.

Their complaint was not that juries would not convict, but
rather that when they did the judge faced the unpleasant
task of pronouncing the death sentence on a woman who
might not know, as he did, that the likelihood of her
suffering it was remote.[31]

The other example is concerned with the criminal consequences of causing death on the roads. Once motor
accidents became a regular problem, those who caused the
death by dangerous driving had to be prosecuted for manslaughter. It was soon recognized that juries often refused to
convict bad drivers of so serious an offence. Lord Goddard
stated that as early as 1933 he made representations to the
Ministry of Transport that the law should be changed to
prevent these acquittals occurring. He was not afraid to
label such verdicts perverse.[32] However, no reform was
achieved until 1956, when Parliament created a special
offence – causing death by dangerous driving – which carried
a lesser maximum penalty than that for manslaughter. 'Motor
manslaughter' cases are now normally dealt with under this
head, and it is recognized that juries have been readier to
convict in consequence.

It is interesting to notice that the Chicago study indicated
that there were a number of crimes which were generally
unpopular with American juries.[33] The charge that was
most often said to result in acquittals from dislike of the
law was 'drunken driving'; in England, the same frequently
applies. But in the Chicago study other examples were noticed
by the judges involved in the research: game laws protecting

hunted animals, gambling laws and laws directed against illicit manufacture and sale of liquor. These last three are all concerned with the social regulation of leisure activities. Where similar activities are restricted by the criminal law in England it is usually by means of a summary offence, triable in a Magistrates' Court. If in England it were possible for a defendant charged with this sort of crime to choose trial by jury no doubt he would be able on occasion to appeal to the ordinary man's reluctance to decide that relatively harmless conduct should be treated as criminal. But it is hard to feel that the way in which Parliament chooses to use criminal provisions to regulate these matters is likely today to become so oppressive that it is necessary to build into the system the requirement that a jury should act as supervisor. The test of the fact that Parliament itself provides an adequate forum for any complaints against the operation of game or gambling laws must be that there simply are no protests that magistrates are not the proper body for dealing with offenders. In truth an offence bearing a small maximum penalty which will be dealt with by a quick summary procedure puts the seriousness of this sort of offence in proportion; the paraphernalia of full jury trial would here be quite out of place.

One can hazard that another category of summary criminal offence might attract the resentment of the ordinary juror if such charges were to become triable on indictment: these are offences of strict liability, under which a person will be guilty of the crime even though he acted under a mistake or in ignorance of facts that make his action criminal. Since the latter nineteenth century it has become increasingly common to provide that a minor criminal offence is committed when certain facts are proved to have occurred and the defendant's knowledge or ignorance of them is irrelevant. For instance, offences relating to the sale of adulterated food, or the use of incorrect weights and measures, belong to this class. The policy behind this development is that if the prosecution had always to prove something about the defendant's state of mind when he committed the offence, it would be too easy to escape by pleading innocence, and the law could not be adequately enforced. It is easy to imagine that some juries would not appreciate the force of these wider issues in strict liability offences, and would be moved to acquit by the feeling that it was unjust to impose a penalty on a man who acted without any knowledge that he was acting criminally.

If Magistrates' Courts had not been available to try most of the strict liability offences, it may well be that juries would have constricted their development. It is certainly true that there are matters concerning strict liability offences that need careful attention. One is to ensure that the concept of strict liability is restricted to the realm of minor offences; another, that there is a strong case for allowing a person charged with such an offence to prove positively in his own defence that he made a reasonable mistake. Until recently there were few instances of indictable offences involving even a partial element of strict liability, but recently there has been some tendency to add to their number. It has for instance been held that a person is guilty of dangerous driving even if he was quite blameless in causing the dangerous situation. There has also been considerable public disquiet over decisions of the courts establishing that certain serious offences relating to dangerous drugs involve strict liability. The appeals in some of these cases only came about because a jury was prepared to convict the defendant after being instructed by the judge that the offence was committed without the defendant being at fault. Not all juries are prepared to revolt. But it would be fascinating to find out how often juries acquit in such cases, and why.[34]

A century and a half ago, the jury was a useful, if inaccurate and somewhat cumbersome, weapon for averting some of the more unjust consequences of a system of criminal law that was chaotically administered and therefore disproportionately harsh. Today the provisions of the criminal law that are likely to affront the ordinary juror's sense of morality or fair play are very much more restricted: to such matters as the regulation of leisure activities and the provision of strict liability in minor offences. At that level, the policy arguments are evenly divided, and the legislature seems the proper place for discussing what the law shall be. It is hard to see that what is there decided should be made subject to the approval of a random group of jurymen sitting to hear a particular case. The argument in favour of the jury as an arbiter of the acceptability of the criminal law no longer has much force.

THE JURY AS THE MAKER OF LAW

Where the law calls for a value judgment from the jury, someone who is trying to discover what the law is in a given fact situation will be obliged to predict how a normal jury is likely to react. If he knows the sort of verdicts which have been given in the past in similar cases, he may have a rough guide for the future. There have been situations in which it has been possible to trace changes in the overall pattern of verdicts as shifts in public attitude have taken place. Lord Justice Scrutton once pointed out[35] that when civil actions for negligence arising out of motor accidents first began to appear in the courts at the beginning of the century, motor vehicles were regarded as highly dangerous by the ordinary road user. Juries that had to find whether drivers had taken reasonable care were most reluctant to find in their favour. Gradually, as motor traffic became more common and jurors became drivers, their attitudes became much more lenient. It is unusual for a jury to try civil actions of this kind today, but similar questions arise in the criminal courts. It is now said that regular publicity of the great dangers of careless driving is causing juries once more to take a more serious view of drivers who have caused an accident. Even if one can distinguish general trends of this kind, it is unlikely that the result of a particular case will be as predictable as if the issue were tried by a judge. For out of their long experience of previous cases and regular association with other lawyers, judges may be expected to build up a more consistent set of attitudes on a particular issue.

When juries regularly tried civil actions, questions of direct evaluation were constantly being left to them. In the criminal law the instances, though less frequent, are by no means inconsiderable. Crimes such as manslaughter, obscene publication and dangerous driving are important examples. There is a clear case for insisting that, as far as possible, the criminal law should be certain and predictable in its provisions. It should be possible to ascertain in advance what conduct is liable to attract penal sanctions imposed by the state in the public interest. If conduct can be deemed criminal after it has occurred, there are obvious possibilities for abuse. This has formed the basis of the severe criticism of one aspect of the decision of the House of Lords in the *Ladies' Directory* case.[36] In that case it was decided that at the base of the criminal law there was an offence defined only as 'effecting a public mischief', or 'conspiring to corrupt public morals'. This is a 'dragnet' crime, which may be used to catch such fish as would otherwise escape. It could hardly be defined in vaguer terms. Indeed, it appeared that some members of the House of Lords did not think it mattered which of the two phrases were used, though there may well be conduct which would fall within one but not the other. The majority of the House of Lords, however, felt no fear that the existence of such offences would lead to abuse. Their principal reason was that since the crimes were indictable offences, the question of liability in each case would be left to a jury. The essential objection to this reasoning was put by Lord Reid in his lone dissenting judgment: 'You cannot tell what is criminal except by guessing what view a jury will take, and juries' views may vary and may change with the passing of time.' The discretion allowed to a jury in a case of publishing obscene literature is small by comparison. For although it is left to individual courts to decide precisely what is obscene and what is not, the offence must at least be concerned with the publication of certain kinds of literature, and the question for judgment is whether the material in issue 'tends to deprave and corrupt'. The crime of conspiracy to corrupt public morals may apparently be committed by conspiring to do *anything* which 'leads astray morally'.

Moreover there remains an unresolved difficulty about the *Ladies' Directory* decision. Did the House of Lords mean that the judge should instruct the jury to decide for themselves whether the publication of the prostitutes' guide amounted to a conspiracy to corrupt public morals, or to commit a public mischief? Or was the proper practice for the judge to direct the jurors that the crime had been committed if they found the facts proved? In earlier English cases where an offence of 'public mischief' had been included in the indictment, the judge had decided whether the conduct was criminal as a 'question of law'. But in 1955, the Privy

Council, hearing an appeal from the Windward and Leeward Islands, held that the whole question should be left to the jury.[37] One would assume from reading the speeches of the Law Lords in the *Ladies' Directory* case that they took this latter procedure to be the correct one. But in fact at the trial of the case the jury had been directed 'as a matter of law' that if they found the directory to have been published by the accused, then he was guilty of the offence, and the House of Lords did not find this to have been a misdirection. Apparently, therefore, all that the majority of the House meant by saying that juries would prevent abuse of the 'dragnet' crime was that they might revolt against a specific direction from the judge to convict if they found the facts proved, by returning a general verdict of not guilty.

A particular danger of such a 'dragnet' crime is that it will be slipped into an indictment along with more specific charges. What may happen is that the jury will acquit of the specific crimes and convict only of the 'dragnet' crime. In the Privy Council case just mentioned, the accused faced two charges of sedition arising out of political speeches made by him, and also a charge of effecting a public mischief. The jury disagreed on one charge of sedition and acquitted on the other; they only convicted on the public mischief count, and the defendant brought a successful appeal against this conviction. The point remains that in such circumstances the jury may feel that they ought to convict the defendant of something and they settled for the vaguest count in the indictment.

If the *Ladies' Directory* case really does require that in future the jury should be told to make up its own mind whether certain conduct amounts to a conspiracy to corrupt public morals, then the jury has acquired a power which is closer to 'law-making' than any power which it has previously had. It is true that a verdict is still a decision only in respect of the case being tried. However, adherents of the House of Lords' philosophy would presumably regard any verdict as showing how similar cases would be decided in future. For the basis of their view is that there is a common moral fund on which the jury would draw, and which would lead any other jury to the same conclusion. The fallacy in this argument is that conduct which is generally accepted to be wrong is declared criminal by specific provisions of the law. The conduct left to be policed by the 'dragnet' crime is morally ambiguous – the kinds of act on which there are likely to be widely differing views among different people. In consequence, verdicts will depend very much on the outlook of the members of a particular jury. The ambit of the criminal law is thus left disastrously uncertain.

In his celebrated Maccabean Lecture of 1959, Lord Devlin put forward the view that no conduct should be criminal which did not arouse strong feelings of intolerance, indignation and disgust in the ordinary man in the jury-box.[38] The lecture has been the subject of hot debate ever since, but although it was not expressly referred to in the judgments of the House of Lords in the *Ladies' Directory* case, its tenets would seem to have been in the minds of the majority of Law Lords. It is interesting therefore to notice that in a recent lecture Lord Devlin has expressly refused to accept that it should be left to a jury to decide whether a defendant's conduct is morally offensive and therefore criminal.[39] His objection is precisely that a jury should not be required to assume a positive function in law enforcement. The question of what conduct is to be treated as illegal ought to be settled by Parliament, where a forum is provided for the expression of the views of different sectors of the public.

5 · The bulwark of liberty

In 1768, William Blackstone enshrined the jury in the ordinary Englishman's heart as the palladium, the bulwark of his liberties.[1] This veneration of the jury principle has not noticeably lessened. No reference in public debate to the jury system seems complete without some echo of Blackstone's words. In 1956, Lord Devlin concluded his Hamlyn lectures on the subject by saying:

The first object of any tyrant in Whitehall would be to make Parliament utterly subservient to his will; and the next to overthrow or diminish trial by jury, for no tyrant could afford to leave a subject's freedom in the hands of twelve of his countrymen. So that trial by jury is more than an instrument of justice and more than one wheel of the constitution: it is the lamp that shows that freedom lives.[2]

In its constitutional role, the jury seems to invite accolades clothed in robust imagery. This chapter attempts to assess how far they have been and are deserved in times past and at present. Phrases such as 'the bulwark of liberty' and 'the lamp of freedom' epitomize a number of interrelated ideas about the need of impartiality in the courts, and the desire to protect against unjust deprivation of liberty or rights. We may usefully isolate and examine four of the ideas: the jury prevents the state from manipulating the strings of justice to its own ends in cases having direct political significance; the jury prevents judges from imposing the views of the class of society from which they are drawn; the jury prevents liaison between judges and the police; and the jury prevents private citizens from exerting improper influence over judges. The first two propositions can easily be made to appear much more significant than historical evidence justifies. Moreover, while juries did play a part in preventing political abuse of the courts in the late eighteenth and early nineteenth centuries, that type of abuse is not rife nowadays. The effect of the jury on the relationship of the police with the courts is today a much more serious issue. As to the danger of corruption of judges, recent allegations that jurors are being corrupted suggest that here the boot may well be on the other foot.

POLITICAL INTERFERENCE

Political pressure might be put upon the courts either through a deliberate directive from the government to the judges, or because the judges have a general sympathy with the government. Neither form of pressure is unknown in English history, though since the eighteenth century the dangers have apparently been of the latter, less direct, kind. Problems arise most obviously in connexion with criminal offences against the state and public order, such as treason, sedition, riot and unlawful assembly. Given that the state is entitled to suppress conduct which is seriously prejudicial to itself or to the peace of its citizens generally, one might still expect a jury truly concerned with protection of individual liberty to make a stand in two situations: where the state appears to be prosecuting for a political offence on a basis of unreliable evidence; and where it is necessary to extend the law so as to bring the accused within its prohibitions. In relation to the latter class, it may be observed that the precise ambit of both treason and sedition – historically two of the most important political offences – is anything but clear. The basic definition of treason is laid down in a statute of 1351 and includes such acts as compassing the king's death, levying war against him in his realm and adhering to his enemies. However, the judges have given the provisions of the statute a wide interpretation. In particular, compassing the king's death was held to have occurred once there was an 'overt act' manifesting that intention. In the seventeenth century even conversations between alleged conspirators were held to be overt acts, and so 'constructive treason' could be committed by advocating the death or the overthrow of the king. Later developments extended the definition still further, so as to impose new and important limits on the right of free speech. Sedition, too, has never had a clear meaning in law. It imposes further limits on the right of free speech and free expression. For instance a speech is seditious if made with intention of exciting disaffection against the monarch, the government, the Constitution, either House of Parliament or the administration of justice. The crime also includes inciting others unlawfully to attempt 'the alteration of any matter in Church or State established' or even promoting ill-will and hostility between different classes, if a breach of the peace is likely to occur in consequence.[3]

Before Blackstone

An historical search of political trials for treason and sedition will not reveal much to the jury's advantage before the eighteenth century. Accounts of treason trials in Tudor times afford ample evidence that the judges showed the strongest bias in the Crown's favour in many political cases: prosecutors were permitted to rant, abuse and browbeat witnesses. Prisoners were not permitted to have counsel. They could not give evidence and might find that the court refused to hear their own witnesses. The juries who bore the ultimate burden of deciding guilt seem to have been too corrupt, or too cowed by the judges, to afford more than occasional protection. Not only were jurors carefully selected and bribed, but the judges – first in the Star Chamber, and then in the other courts – also assumed a power to fine and imprison them if they were found to have returned a verdict which in the judges' view was 'false'.[4] In practice the judges used their power only against juries which refused to convict. The jurors who found the Bishop of Rochester guilty of treason in 1535 said afterwards that their verdict was 'full sore against their conscience', but they feared 'for the safety of their goods and lives which they were all well assured to lose, in case they acquitted him'.[5] Isolated exceptions do emerge. In 1554, Sir Nicholas Throckmorton was acquitted of high treason for his part in Wyatt's anti-Catholic rebellion; and a century later no jury could be found to convict Sir John Lilburne, a popular leader of the Levellers. These were not cases which mark themselves out as being based on weak evidence or strained law. The verdicts were manifestations of tides of strong anti-Government feeling among the populace of London at the time when the trials took place.[6]

The end of the judges' power to coerce juries to convict, by threatening to punish them if they did not do so, came in 1670 in *Bushell's Case*.[7] In that case, the Quakers, Penn and Mead, were acquitted of taking part in an unlawful assembly and the trial judge promptly imprisoned the jury. But thereafter the whole body of judges determined that as a matter of law he lacked any power to do this. The case is often hailed as a triumph for the independence of juries, and indeed without the courage of foreman Bushell and his fellows the issue would never have come to a head. But it is just as important to notice that their action came only at a time when they were supported by a strong tide of public opinion, for in the previous year the Commons had passed a resolution in favour of limiting the judges' power in this way. In the face of all this pressure it was the judges themselves who decided that they had no power.

After *Bushell's Case* political trials began to occur in which juries showed greater independence. In 1688, James II required a declaration of indulgence for liberty of conscience to be read in the churches, and the seven bishops who petitioned him to withdraw the order were indicted for sedition. Their acquittal suggests that juries were becoming readier to defy the government. But so were the judges: despite all James II's manipulations to secure a loyal bench of judges, his position was so precarious by the date of the trial of the seven bishops that only two of the four judges who sat urged the jury to convict the bishops.[8] But by the time Blackstone was writing in 1750 there was still little positive evidence that juries could be counted on to take an anti-Government view of dubious political prosecutions. Blackstone made no attempt at an historical justification of his image of the jury as the 'bulwark of liberty'. He contented himself with general comparisons of the conduct of trials in continental countries that lacked juries.

After Blackstone

It is only when one looks to the period of the French Revolution that more positive evidence is found. By that time the judges had had nearly a century of formal independence from the state, since they could be removed from office only by the address of both Houses of Parliament. Nevertheless they had strong affiliations with the landed aristocracy, whose hands held the reins of government. So too had the justices of the peace, and they were beginning to acquire extensive judicial as well as administrative duties.

As the flame of revolution in France sparked off new ardour in the movements for radical Parliamentary reform, Pitt's government became increasingly nervous and sought to silence the leading dissidents in a wave of 'government by indictment'. Some judges, notably Chief Justice Kenyon, showed keen sympathy with this policy in their instructions to juries. In 1793 the heavy charge of high treason was laid against a number of the leading members of the London Corresponding Society, which was in the forefront in propagating radical ideas among manual workers. The Government had sent agents to meetings of the Society, and they gave evidence that the defendants had not only spoken of revolution but had started active preparations for an insurrection. However, the Crown reckoned without the arresting advocacy of Thomas Erskine for the defence. With brilliant, forceful oratory he left the juries in no doubt about the flimsiness of the prosecution case, and their duty as champions of the liberty of the subject. In the first three cases – Hardy, Horne Tooke and Thelwell – the juries acquitted, and then the Crown offered no evidence against the other defendants. Each verdict was greeted with fervent public approval.[9]

Juries were much more frequently dealing with cases of sedition than of treason. At the end of the seventeenth century, when the judges no longer retained the power to control verdicts by punishing jurors, they took it upon themselves to decide the vital question in this vague crime: was the character of the words used seditious or not? This was kept as a 'question of law'.[10] The jurors were instructed to find the accused 'guilty' once they were satisfied that the defendants had published the words, and that the words bore the meaning that the prosecution sought to put on them. Only after such a 'conviction' was the accused permitted to move the court in arrest of judgment, if he could persuade the judges that the words were not seditious. As early as 1770, juries were registering their resentment at being coerced into convicting the accused upon the assumption that his conduct was seditious, by returning such verdicts as 'guilty of publishing only'.[11] To their efforts the championing voice of Erskine was soon added in the *Dean of St Asaph's Case*,[12] and eventually Pitt was forced to concede that juries should have the right restored to them to pronounce upon the whole question. This was done in Fox's Libel Act 1792. Even after this, the judges insisted on expounding to the jury their own opinion as to whether the words were seditious, often in forceful terms. But once the new power was conceded juries only intermittently displayed any inclination to uphold the right of free expression against which the crime of sedition was directed. Erskine appeared for many of the defendants and often his ardour won the day, but there were occasions on which a verdict of guilty was returned in circumstances which were not noticeably different from those where the jury acquitted.[13] With a Lord Chief Justice prepared to describe a mild reformatory pamphlet as 'little short of high treason', these fluctuations were perhaps inevitable. In Scotland, too, the Lord Justice Clerk, Braxfield, tried a number of cases of sedition with unexampled bigotry; meeting no Erskine in opposition he was able to carry the juries with him to conviction.[14]

There is no doubt the Crown wrung what advantages it could from the selection of jurors. Sedition was a misdemeanour, and after the judges gave up the power to punish jurors for returning false verdicts in *Bushell's Case*, they began to permit special juries to be called in cases of misdemeanour, though they never dared to extend the right to the more serious categories of treason and felony. The qualification of special jurors at the time was extraordinarily loose: everything turned on the discretion of the summoning officer. Broadly speaking, only the upper ranks of society were involved, and so a special jury was more likely to be favourable to the Government than a common jury. Moreover there is little doubt that special handpicking went on, a court official collaborating with the Crown Solicitor for the purpose. 'Guinea-men' – regular special jurors who lived off the guinea which each case brought, and who knew that con-

tinuance of this stipend depended on bringing in a verdict
for the Crown – were by no means unknown. What is more,
the social position of the 'guinea-men' was often very much
lower than that of the usual special juror.[15]

In the years of unrest that followed Waterloo one finds the
same fluctuation in the results of sedition cases brought against
radical publishers. In 1817, when the government were in a
trough of unpopularity, they were defeated in a host of
cases. William Hone, an antiquarian bookseller and impish
parodist, defended himself on a number of such charges. He
secured three acquittals in three days and had the Attorney-
General laughed out of court. Yet in 1819 a fresh spurt of
prosecutions of very much the same sort of publications
began up and down the country, and this time it was only
in Yorkshire, always a radical county, that juries showed any
resistance to the Government. A Birmingham bookseller
was successfully prosecuted for selling one of Hone's paro-
dies, and Sidmouth, the Home Secretary, was able to write
after the trial: 'The result will, I trust, operate as an encouragement to magistrates in every part of the Kingdom to show
their confidence in the intelligence and integrity of British
juries on similar occasions.' Soon afterwards the tide turned
yet again. The Constitutional Association, which took upon
itself to prosecute the purveyors of radical literature privately,
ran into opposition not only from trial juries, but in some
instances even from grand juries, which threw out bills of
indictment presented by the Association.[16]

Something of the same pattern is to be found in the treason trials of the period. Sidmouth, in his anxiety to demonstrate the Government's repressive strength, employed spies
as *agents provocateurs*. He secured convictions among a band
of Derbyshire men who had been hopelessly misled by a
Government agent, and set out to support what they supposed
to be a general uprising of workers, only to fall into the hands
of the army. Thirty-five were indicted for high treason and
twenty-three convicted; four were hanged. A similar band
from Huddersfield were acquitted only because the activities
of the Government spy were uncovered by the press just
before the trials began.[17]

In the late 1830s the Chartist movement became an increasing anxiety to the Government as its demands for work-

ing-class political representation began to be supported by violent demonstrations, organized for armed resistance and attacks on employers. The Home Secretary, Lord John Russell, was unwilling to copy the tactics of Pitt and Sidmouth and rush into prosecuting the leaders of the movement before they could be shown unequivocally to have been acting dangerously or violently. When eventually the course of events did lead to serious criminal trials, the cases were based on substantial evidence. The Government indeed faced a serious problem from the corruption and intimidation of jurors and witnesses because support for the Chartist defendants was so widespread. As the methods of the agitators became more violent, the reluctance of jurors to convict seemed to disappear. Certainly after the 1839 uprising, all the known leaders were in prison or had been transported. After the Manchester strike of 1841, large numbers were convicted and seventy-nine men were transported. In 1848 the Government did once more resort to using an agent to spy on radical leaders and to provide evidence of an insurrectionary plot, much of which the spy himself had apparently concocted. The jury which tried the leaders of this final upsurge of militant Chartism accepted the spy's story and convicted.[18]

However, this reversion to old tactics was an isolated event. In fact the Chartist period marks a watershed in the jury's role in political cases, because the movement did much to speed the development of the new professional police forces, and with them it became possible for the Government to keep itself informed about the activities of political groups and to control demonstrations and other occasions on which outbreaks of violence might occur. Earlier Governments had no ready means of discovering the strength of a radical movement and might out of fear launch prosecutions for serious criminal offences in the hope that the deterrent effect of harsh sentences would be an effective check. With the new police in action, it was no longer necessary to resort to flimsy prosecutions so readily. The police were able to attend political and other demonstrations and keep order. If they felt it necessary to lay charges, they concentrated on persons who were involved in fights and other breaches of the peace, or in obstructions of the highway. These were minor charges which could be tried before magistrates, a procedure which clearly suited the police. It avoided the high emotions of a full trial and allowed offenders to be dealt with quickly and effectively. The Magistrates' Courts have become the forum in which most political offenders are dealt with, though statutes which have created new public-order offences have often preserved the defendant's right to opt for a jury by making the maximum sentence of imprisonment greater than three months (see p. 56).[19]

In the later Victorian period, other pressures also developed which helped to restrain the Government from preferring serious charges against its political opponents without adequate evidence or legal justification. The right to vote continued to be extended and brought working-class representation in Parliament; the public became better informed about Government activity with the growth of newspapers and other forms of mass communication. Today there are a wide variety of channels through which public opinion can make itself felt. Over the last century, serious criminal charges of a political nature have only occasionally gone to juries. When they have there has been no regular refusal to convict. One isolated exception occurred in 1886, when Burns, Hyndman and two other members of the Social Democratic Federation were indicted for sedition after having addressed a Trafalgar Square meeting of the unemployed which degenerated into mob looting. The jury however responded to Burns' personal appeal to them not to convict. But mostly juries have not shown sympathy for defendants facing dubious charges. During the First World War, a jury expressed a widespread patriotic fervour against conscientious objectors by convicting a group of them for conspiring to murder two members of the War Cabinet by the unlikely means of pricking the victims with a needle dipped in a rare South American poison. The prosecution's case rested entirely on the evidence of a single Government agent who had posed as a sympathizer and thus learnt of the 'plot'. In 1912 and again in 1925 the Incitement to Mutiny Act 1797 was used to prosecute men who had produced literature addressed to soldiers calling on them to disobey if they were ordered to fire on strikers. The cases were concerned only with expressions of opinion, but both juries convicted. Certainly in the first case the jury did not represent one sector of public opinion; for after the convictions, outraged sympathizers made such a stir that the Home Secretary released the accused from prison.[20]

In other cases where there has been real doubt it has concerned the ambit of the law, and juries have not shown much propensity to react against extensions of the law made to bring a particular defendant within the net. In 1936 that undesirably vague crime, 'public mischief', was used to secure the conviction of the publishers of an anti-Semitic paper. Likewise the conviction for treason of Sir Roger Casement during the First World War, and of William Joyce ('Lord Haw-Haw') after the Second World War, are well-known cases where it was necessary to settle that the definition of treason had a wide rather than a narrow meaning in a particular respect in order to convict the defendant. In 1962 a demonstration by members of the Campaign for Nuclear Disarmament at Weathersfield Airbase resulted in several convictions under the Official Secrets Act for entering a prohibited place 'for a purpose prejudicial to the State', even though there was a strong argument for reading that vague phrase to refer only to spying activities.[21]

The truth seems to be that for more than a century juries have played a very minor role in the prosecution of political offenders. In the delicate area of the right to express political opinions, the activities of salvationists, suffragettes, Irish Home Rulers, Fascists, Communists and others have kept the courts busy when disturbances have been created; but nearly always it is the magistrates who have heard the cases, with points of law being settled by the Queen's Bench Divisional Court and occasionally (since 1960) by the House of Lords.

Yet there are powerful voices that warn against complacency. It is said that to do away with the jury would be a first step towards a police state; after all, the abolition of juries did occur in Fascist Italy (1931) and war-time Japan (1943). But it is not easy to know what is meant by 'the first step towards a police state'. If it means that first of all unpopular minority voices will be suppressed, it is clear that this can happen even now when a jury sits. The Weathersfield Airbase trial is a case in point. If it means that the way will be open

for the introduction of the full armoury of political oppres-
sion, then the whole matter is highly speculative. It is
extremely unlikely that an oppressive Government would
attain such power in Britain without wide popular backing.
If it did, it could no doubt find compelling reasons for sus-
pending *habeas corpus* and introducing all the modern appara-
tus of confinements without trial, house arrests, ninety-day
orders and so on, 'in the public interest'. If it chose to stage
trials of its opponents it could, by selecting juries from the
class which supported it, or by handpicking individual
jurors, secure the desired result. This seems to have been a
method to which Pitt and Sidmouth were not averse; and
there is still nothing in the rules for the selection of jurors
which guarantees a disinterested choice. The Morris Committee did not see it as a problem against which it was now
necessary to take strong measures, although it did propose
making juries more generally representative. Yet if the jury
system is really to protect against future oppressors, the rules
ought to provide a procedure by which Government
officials are prevented from making an unsupervised selection of jurors. For special capital can be made out of a jury
trial in which the prosecution is successful. It has the appearance of being an act of the people, and the verdict may be
used as the foundation on which to lay a particularly harsh
sentence. But Jeremy Bentham seems to have been the last
person who argued vigorously that there ought to be real
protection against biased choice of jurors. The present attitude points to the true significance of the jury as a bulwark of
liberty: a reasonable Government which feels obliged to
resort to serious criminal charges rather than summary
offences for dealing with political opponents will have
to consider whether it can carry a jury to conviction – here a
jury could have its nuisance value; against a determined
oppressor, the system as currently operated would offer
enough alternatives and means of manipulation to be
valueless.

SOCIAL PREJUDICE

The constitutional role of the jury cannot of course be confined to those criminal offences that have a direct political
complexion. There have been other important areas of social

conflict in which governments and certain classes of citizens have tried to use the criminal law to curb opponents. Here too the jury, if it is really a bulwark of liberty, should have played its part in preventing unjustifiable prosecutions.

The industrial revolution and the disturbed economic conditions of the early nineteenth century brought about agitation not only for political reform but also for improved wages and conditions of work. The struggle by workers for freedom to organize trade unions and to use combined strike action as a weapon to enforce their demands was continuously fought out in the criminal courts from the time of Pitt's Combination Acts of 1799 and 1800 to the reforms of the 1870s. The Combination Acts made it a criminal act to join any sort of association having the purpose of altering terms of employment. The Acts were repealed in 1824, but a statute was passed in the next year which had the effect of making illegal many of the activities of strikers.[22]

Only very occasionally did juries refuse to convict combiners or strikers. Sometimes the authorities feared that they would meet damaging opposition from juries, but this did not occur. For instance, the Luddite disturbances in 1812 produced so great a wave of popular sympathy that there was talk of abandoning the forthcoming Nottingham assizes at which a number of persons were charged with loom-breaking. But contrary to expectation, when the time came the juries were prepared to convict.

Usually the judges were able to rely on juries to apply the law to the facts according to the way in which they were instructed. In 1830 widespread agricultural disturbances resulted from the exceptional hardship and distress of that year. Special commissions of judges were sent out to deal with those charged with offences, and convictions followed proof of even minor acts of insubordination. A lad of nineteen was hanged for having knocked the hat from the head of a member of the Baring family during an altercation.[23] The celebrated conviction in 1834 of the unfortunate labourers of Tolpuddle under the Illegal Oaths Act 1797 is also instructive. Their 'crime' consisted of administering a secret oath to a new member of a trade union. The jury was prepared to accept the judge's direction that this fell under a statute which plainly had not been passed with such acts in mind; the preamble to the Act referred to mutinous and seditious societies and it had been passed immediately after the Nore mutiny. On the return of a verdict of guilty the judge felt justified in passing savage sentences of seven years' transportation.

In subsequent years there were many prosecutions of strikers for offences which were vaguely described as 'obstruction' or 'molestation'. These were prime examples of offences where much was left to the particular court to decide how the law should apply the facts. For the most part, the judges took upon themselves the task of determining whether particular fact situations were to be described as 'molestation' or 'obstruction'. Many were prepared to widen the law so as to catch participants who did very little in furtherance of a strike. Juries were apparently not offended by these developments in the law, for they rarely refused to convict the defendants. Changes in the law were achieved not by resistance from juries, but by the acquisition of political power by urban workers in 1867. The Conspiracy and Protection of Property Act 1875 provided that strike action should not result in a criminal prosecution except where there had been some form of aggressive picketing or physical danger or annoyance to the public.

Since then the opportunities for juries to play any part in the legal regulation of industrial action have been much less frequent. Much of the subsequent litigation over the legality of strikes and boycotts has taken place in the civil courts; either the case has been tried by judge alone, or the contentious issue has been one of law – and as we have seen (p. 107) the judges have greater power to prevent civil juries returning a verdict not in accordance with the law. The fear that juries selected by a property qualification would exhibit a class bias continued to linger. In 1906, Parliament considered amending legislation designed to protect peaceful picketers. One proposal was to give protection where the number of pickets was 'reasonable'. This was attacked on the basis that both juries and magistrates might take an undesirably restricted view of the number of pickets who constituted a 'reasonable' body. The Mersey Committee in 1913 received evidence that juries were apt to discriminate against workers, and in consequence they recommended that the property qualification for jury service be relaxed (though not abandoned entirely). Something of the old attitude appeared in a case resulting from the General Strike. A civil action was brought by a manufacturer against the Electricity Supply Committee of Stepney Borough Council, claiming damages for cutting supplies during the strike. The Committee members were only liable in law if it could be shown that they had acted out of a desire to cause the plaintiff harm. The jury found for the plaintiff, but the Court of Appeal upset the verdict, being unable to find any shred of evidence that the Committee really did desire to injure the plaintiff.[24]

If juries were rarely prone to take a liberal view of a strike action during the period when most strike action was criminal, nor were they so obviously prejudiced against it as the judges or the magistracy. The magistrates were rightly detested, particularly during the Combination Act period, for they were sometimes employers themselves and at least belonged to the employing class. They were known to use their powers in grossly unjust ways, employing their own spies and informers to lead others into forming combinations, and visiting harsh punishments upon those who were ensnared. Cobbett recorded the remarkable case of Ryding (1823), who deliberately attacked his master with a weapon rather than with his fists so as to make his crime too serious to be within the jurisdiction of the magistrates.[25] This widespread mistrust directed toward the magistracy by humble people has gradually abated during this century. Justices of the peace are now appointed from a much wider sector of the community than before. However, the method of appointment by recommendation from each county's Lord Lieutenant and a private committee to the Lord Chancellor produces distinct variations in the class structure of different magistracies – witness the recent allegations that working people were not appointed to the bench at Bournemouth. As with political demonstrators, criminal offences arising out of industrial disturbances are now almost invariably tried in Magistrates' Courts. There is little demand that there should be a right to jury trial. This reflects not only the greater trust now shown in magistrates but also the feeling that juries have not in the past done much to keep a check on dubious prosecutions.

The principal conflict between groups which has arisen in England since the industrial revolution has been a class conflict in which the major struggle has been for the recognition of the political and industrial rights of workers. The tensions produced by immigrant groups have only sporadically resulted in criminal prosecutions, though the activities of anti-Semites before the Second World War and in the early 1960s, and the occasional post-war racial disturbances, led to many summary trials and a few jury cases. In 1965, new powers were enacted for dealing with racial extremists, by making it a criminal offence punishable on indictment or summarily (but with a right to opt for a jury) to incite to racial hatred. This places a limit on free speech which does not depend on there being a likelihood of any resultant breach of the peace. The Government indicated that it intended to reserve the new offence for serious cases and there have so far been few prosecutions. Where they have been before juries, there has so far been no reluctance to convict.[26]

The steps so far taken to prevent racial discrimination in various situations have not involved use of the criminal law. Instead, the Race Relations Boards have been created to act primarily as conciliators, with the possibility of applying for an injunction from a civil court where the Boards' efforts are unavailing.[27] Before the Government decided on this policy there was much discussion of whether the criminal law ought not to have a role in preventing racial discrimination; in the future it may become necessary to introduce criminal sanctions, especially now that the requirement not to discriminate is being extended to housing and jobs. If it is left to juries to administer new criminal offences in this area it may well be that they will refuse to convict, and the law will be left to stagnate. Possibly, any new law would be restricted to summary trials without the option of a jury in order to avoid this danger.

As with other forms of prejudice, racial attitudes may infect many aspects of the work of the courts apart from these direct issues of discrimination and racialist opinions. In other countries with longer experience of widespread racial tension there is plenty of evidence that group prejudices may infect so many matters that juries are often obviously partial.

Racial prejudice was a principal reason for curtailing the use of juries in the countries of British West Africa. In South Africa trial by jury has always been reserved for Europeans, and where a crime is alleged to have been committed against an African or an Asian by a European it is extremely difficult to secure a conviction from a jury. In the United States, juries freely express the prejudices of the white community by their verdicts:

Of the thousands of cases of murder of blacks by whites since emancipation there has been scarcely a legal execution, and comparatively few prison sentences. The offender usually escapes with the sterotyped verdict, 'Justifiable homicide', or at best with a nominal fine. If the relations were reversed, whatever the provocative circumstances, the Negro would almost certainly be sentenced to death or to life imprisonment, if indeed the mob allowed the case to reach a judicial hearing.[28]

At least until recently the qualification rules and methods of selection ensured that Negroes did not sit as jurors on such cases.

Of the English jurors whom I interviewed some had tried cases in which there had been coloured defendants. My impression from their reports was that there was a pretty general desire to lean over backwards to be fair. But none of them had been concerned with cases which are most likely to raise deep prejudice, such as homicide, sexual assault or some form of mob violence. Cases of this kind are inevitable, and it is most desirable, at a time when great concern is being shown over the best ways to use legal sanctions in the fight to prevent various forms of racial discrimination, that a study should be undertaken to discover whether racial prejudice is leading juries to reach unjustifiable verdicts, especially of guilt in criminal cases.

If racial prejudice were to become a serious problem on English juries it would simply reflect more widespread communal feelings. This makes it difficult to know what precautions should be taken in advance. Certainly the Morris Committee's recommendation to extend the qualification for service to all adults is a move towards a more rational position, for juries restricted to certain classes within the community are more likely to have some common prejudice. From this point of view it may be undesirable to preclude those who have less than five years' residence in this country from jury service. At the same time the move away from unanimous verdicts may be undesirable. No doubt the problem is not one to be solved by handing over power to professional judges, but it may be that a court which combined lay and legal experience would be more effectual. For the kind of experience which a lawyer may bring to the question for decision should include the ability to stand back from the purely emotional elements of the case and judge it upon the weight of the evidence.

THE JURY AND THE POLICE

In 1960 the Central Office of Information undertook a social survey for the Royal Commission on the Police. It showed that 42·4 per cent of the public thought that some policemen took bribes, 34·7 per cent that the police used unfair methods to get information, 32 per cent that they might distort evidence in court, and 17·8 per cent that on occasions they used too much force.[29] Among the jurors I interviewed it was not uncommon to find that someone on the jury had expressed this sort of mistrust of the police. One juror reported that when trying a case of stolen goods against a junk-yard merchant, several of his fellow jurymen believed that it was a case in which the police had decided to prosecute simply because they had not received protection money – a fact of which there was no evidence. Another thought that the police were out to 'get' an accused because he was coloured. Others again considered that police evidence was 'too pat' and seized upon certain small differences between the evidence of different constables which had been underlined in cross-examination. Current scandals in various police forces were discussed. It is not possible to tell from interviews how far these suspicions really affected the results of the cases tried, but it seems that a jury is in some degree a barometer of the public image of the police force, and the extent to which this is so deserves careful investigation.

American experience runs on similar lines. The Chicago Project referred to a number of cases where a jury refused to convict a man accused of assaulting a police officer while resisting arrest. In some of them it seems that it was mistrust of the police in general that affected the verdict. But there were also cases in which the methods of interrogation used by police, particularly when their object is to secure confessions, resulted in protest verdicts, and others again which express the jury's dislike of police traps for catching suspected wrongdoers.[30]

On the police side, there is widespread distrust of the results which juries reach. Willett, in his study of motoring offenders, reported that while in general there was hardly any criticism by police officers of magistrates in their handling of cases, they were particularly critical of juries and their over-readiness to acquit. In 1965, three Chief Constables expressed their exasperation at the acquittal of 'ten-pint motorists', criticisms which are not lightly made by persons in their position. More generally, there have been the complaints to the Morris Committee from the Commissioner of Police for the Metropolis that there had been a marked deterioration in the quality of juries. This was supported by the Association of Chief Police Officers in respect of urban juries. The fact that professional people were tending to move out of towns into the surrounding countryside was offered as a possible explanation. One Chief Constable was recently stung into writing of 'the growing belief of many police officers that the present ineffectual system of criminal justice, of which the jury system in its present form is the weakest part, affords considerable encouragement to the professional criminal'.[31]

On the other hand the police have few complaints to make about the handling of cases by magistrates. Solicitors and others who regularly appear in Magistrates' Courts often comment on the tendency of some benches to accept police evidence without demur. This seems to arise in part from the trust which arises from seeing the same officers successfully prosecuting offenders day after day in their court, and in part from over-familiarity with a line of defence which is commonly offered to a particular kind of charge. And where the magistrates act as overseers of the local police force the feeling that the police deserve support from the bench may be specially strong.[32]

In a democracy it is obviously desirable that there should be a measure of protection against undue readiness to assume that the police version of the facts of a case is correct. With the growth of police forces, and the number of prosecutions instituted by them, it has fallen more and more upon the jury to provide some check, in serious cases, that the police do not have it all their own way. The significance of their contribution ought to have increased as jurors have come to be more representative of different classes of the community because of rating revaluations. There is a difficult balance to be maintained here. It is right that the police view that an accused person is guilty should not be too readily accepted. It is also fair that the prosecution case should be judged on its merits and not in a spirit of indiscriminate antipathy. If this happens regularly there is likely to be a general lowering of police morale and officers will be encouraged to feel that the scales are so unfairly weighted against the prosecution that they are justified in touching up evidence, and in conducting investigations and extracting confessions by methods which are thoroughly undesirable. A proper balance can only be maintained by trying to secure that those who decide issues of fact in the courts are prepared to make a dispassionate evaluation of the police evidence in a prosecution. For that reason we ought to know how far distrust of the police is in itself the reason for the occurrence of doubtful acquittals. It will be necessary to try to ascertain how far distrust of the police is an attempt genuinely to weigh conflicts between police and defence evidence, and how far it is the result of general antipathy to the police, based on opinions and beliefs which have nothing directly to do with the case in hand.

For the moment one can only conclude that of the various aspects of the jury's function as a bulwark of liberty the most important today is its role in preventing police influence in the courts from becoming dominant. For this reason alone, it is desirable that independent laymen should continue to have some voice in deciding the outcome of serious criminal cases. Whether the jury system is the soundest way of achieving a fair balance between mistrust and over-ready acceptance of police witnesses must remain in doubt so long as jury-rooms remain closed to observers.

CORRUPTION BY PRIVATE INDIVIDUALS

For the proper administration of justice, those who exercise judicial functions should be free from deliberate interference by private individuals as well as the Government. It may be that the presence of juries has assisted in preventing the improper influencing of judges by bribes or threats. Certainly the general reputation of English judges in this respect has been untarnished for a long time. But many other factors have contributed to this state of affairs: for the most part, their security in office is a great assurance of probity, since they are not open to the kinds of pressure which can be exerted in a system where re-election from time to time is necessary. Pay and pension rights are considerable, so they are able to maintain a position of some aloofness. Part-time judges do not have the same degree of security but they are drawn from the same professional background and rooted in the same traditions as full-time judges. It is customary now to permit single judges to sit alone in a wide variety of courts, the High Court and County Courts, stipendiary magistrates in Magistrates' Courts and Recorders at Borough Quarter Sessions appeals. Complaints of corruption against any of them are unknown.

A much greater danger is that jurors and not judges will be influenced by fear, friendship or bribery. The common law originally dealt with this by requiring the jury to remain *incommunicado* – having no contact with the outside world from the moment that it was sworn until the verdict was returned. This rule caused great inconvenience and expense, and it came to be seen in most cases as an unnecessary precaution, especially as witnesses were allowed to leave court each day and were not under surveillance while at court. In 1897, it was eventually decided to take the risk of some mishap resulting from jurors being allowed to separate each day. The old rule was maintained for murder cases until 1940, though they were perhaps not the cases in which determined interference with jurors was most likely to occur.[33] The only survival of the rule is that nowadays a jury must not separate for any reason – not even to have a meal – once it has been instructed by the judge and has retired to the jury room to reach its verdict. The change did not lead to regular abuse, but the courts had to maintain a careful watch against the occurrence of untoward events. A juror may speak to a witness, a defendant, a police officer or some other person known to be involved in the case or concerned about its outcome; this encounter may be entirely innocent, even accidental, but it inevitably looks suspicious, and if the court is not satisfied with the explanation offered it may discharge the juror or abandon the trial. If the trial is over, and the accused convicted before he discovers what has taken place, he may be successful in getting his conviction quashed by the Court of Appeal.

As has already been pointed out (see p. 51) the courts could and should do more to make it clear to all jurors that the whole trial may be jeopardized if they discuss the case with anyone other than their fellows, or have any contact at all with those involved in the case, although oral or written instructions will never entirely eliminate the risk among inexperienced people in unfamiliar surroundings. In addition, limits should be placed on the availability of the jury panel: before the trial the panel of names should be available only to counsel and solicitors, with the parties having the right to see it immediately before the ballot. Cases in which attempts have been made to 'nobble' jurors have come to light from time to time. In 1965, events surrounding a trial of five men charged at the Old Bailey with attempted robbery aroused considerable public agitation because of repeated attempts to interfere with jurors. At the first trial, the court was told that approaches had been made to two of the jurors and thereupon the trial was abandoned. At the second trial, after sixteen jurors had been challenged directly by the prisoners (not through their counsel), another juror informed the court that an attempt had been made to bribe him, and this juror was immediately discharged. Then another said that he had been offered £600 and threatened with violence. Finally a third juror reported that he had been offered £100 to say not guilty. The court trusted the honesty of these two jurors and the trial proceeded without their being dismissed. In the end four of the five men were acquitted.[34]

Other instances of attempts to interfere with jurors did come to light, though they did not generally show the same degree of persistence and were very largely confined to London. Even there, the number of known cases was small – over a period of seven months in 1966, when the problem was constantly in the public eye, the Metropolitan Police reported that they had been notified of only three cases of alleged interference. Remedial steps were taken by giving publicity to the issue, prosecuting those who had attempted to interfere with jurors or witnesses, and providing extensive police protection of the jurors serving on cases where interference was expected. But the Home Secretary decided that these measures did not go far enough, and introduced the hotly debated proposal to permit majority verdicts by ten votes to two in criminal cases (see p. 69).

The majority verdict system inevitably weakens the certainty of result that was an important feature of the unanimity principle, and the proposal was vehemently opposed as a step taken in haste without due regard to what was being sacrificed. It was abundantly clear that nothing reliable was known of how juries reached their verdicts, and what kinds of minority voice would be quelled by the majority system. Never before was opinion so widespread that there should be no alteration without investigation. A general discussion of the desirability and consequences of the change must be left until the final chapter (see p. 258). Here we must concentrate on the question of whether the majority system will achieve its direct and overt purpose of preventing approaches being made to jurors to secure a disagreement or an acquittal. The person intent on interference must now secure the cooperation of three of the jurors, or else of one juror whose personality is sufficiently strong to sway others to his view. These new hurdles ought to be sufficiently serious to deter all but the most determined.[35] It must not be forgotten that trials have taken place during which approaches have been made to jurors despite the most careful protection. During the recent 'Torture' trial at the Old Bailey, which was held while arguments on the majority system were at their height, the jurors were given constant police escort and were provided with special telephone lines to report any suspicious occurrences. Nevertheless threats were still made to the mother of one of them. It cannot be assumed that the majority system will completely eliminate interference with jurors. If trouble continues then the only solution will be to revert to the old system of holding the jurors *incommunicado* in cases involving crimes that have been carried out in a highly organized fashion. Indeed, there was much to be said for taking this step rather than introducing majority verdicts, for it was a surer way of preventing interference with jurors, and it does not have the disadvantage of lessening the degree of protection which the unanimity principle ensured.

6 · Crime: the judges of fact

This chapter raises a number of questions about how juries decide serious criminal cases, where no special factors of the kind discussed in the last chapter are present. It is concerned with the ability of amateur jurymen to act as judges of 'fact', and the ways in which their judgment may differ from that of professional lawyers. We saw in Chapter 1 (p. 21) that the Chicago Project has recently demonstrated that judge and jury differed in 25 per cent of the cases examined, on the question as to whether a defendant should be convicted, the jury usually showing a tendency to be more lenient. How far such differences exist in England remains to be tested. It was for long thought that the proportion of cases in which juries acquitted was not in itself very great. The only indication available in the criminal statistics, published annually by the Home Office, was that between 10 and 15 per cent of all cases sent to the higher courts for trial resulted in an acquittal. But as this figure included those cases in which the defendant pleaded guilty, and as it was not known how frequently this occurred the information proved very little about the proportion of cases actually tried by jury which resulted in acquittal, though claims were sometimes made that the figures showed how low the acquittal rate was.

This obvious impediment to any proper appreciation of the situation was removed by a recent study conducted for the Association of Chief Police Officers.[1] This analyzed the charges upon indictment, other than for motoring offences, which were prosecuted in the higher courts in 1965, and demonstrated that the proportion of those who pleaded guilty at the trial was 64 per cent. Of those who pleaded not guilty, 39 per cent were acquitted. The revelation that the

149

acquittal rate was as high as 39 per cent produced some over-hasty assertions that juries were acquitting too frequently. Yet the figure alone cannot justify such a conclusion. It must be remembered that some 85 per cent of prosecutions for indictable offences are siphoned off into Magistrates' Courts, and of the rest, nearly two-thirds end in pleas of guilty. Juries are left to deal with the remaining small pro-portion, and it would be not unreasonable to expect those that remain to include many of the cases in which there is some real element of doubt concerning the accused's guilt.

Nonetheless, since the acquittal rate is two cases in every five, it is no longer possible to brush aside the complaints of some police officers and judges, made on the basis of their experience in court rather than on statistics, that juries are too lenient. The Lord Chief Justice, for instance, has stated that on his reckoning only about one case in ten of those tried by juries should result in acquittal.[2] If this figure is accurate, it would mean that judges and juries would disagree on the results of criminal cases even more frequently than in the United States, on the Chicago evidence. This would be a reversal of expectation, for by and large English judges have greater freedom to indicate their views to juries than have their American counterparts. The Chicago study shows that, at least where the evidence is clear one way or the other in the judge's view, the jury very rarely comes to a different conclusion in those states where the judge is permitted to summarize and comment on the evidence, and does so; whereas variations between judge and jury do occur even in clear cases, if there is no summary and comment by the judge. But there are many imponderables which might affect the position in England: different methods of selecting jurors, different methods of challenge, different rights to elect for trial by judge alone, differences in the length and frequency of jury service. The matter should not be left to speculation. It ought to be investigated.

A somewhat different factor, which must be taken into account in discussing these statistics, is the practice govern-ing the institution of prosecutions. It has recently been stated that whereas 39 per cent of cases tried by an English jury result in acquittal, in Scotland the proportion is only 22 per cent.[3] But in Scotland it is the Crown's practice to prosecute only in cases where there appears to be a substantial chance of conviction. In England, some police forces are not so strict, and they have only to demonstrate to the magistrates at committal proceedings that there is a *prima facie* case for the accused to answer. The proportion of cases in which the case is not sent by the magistrates for trial is very small. Differences in prosecution practice must affect the number of weak cases which get before a jury, and hence the acquittal rate.

Given that there is a measurable difference in the way that professional lawyers and lay juries would decide the same case, we can explore in some detail a number of factors which contribute to the special character of a jury's verdict.

JUDGEMENT BY OVERALL IMPRESSION

It is part of the daily experience of any lawyer concerned with litigation to have to weigh the strength of a case by the various items of evidence available. By the time he is appointed a judge a lawyer will therefore have had a good deal of experience in analyzing the different pieces of evidence in a case, relating them one to another, and weighing up the merits of different witnesses. In this he will be in a very different position from most jurors, who are unlikely to have much experience of judging issues of fact between conflicting sides. The procedure followed at the trial is in some ways ill-adapted to help the jury over the unfamiliar task of inter-relating the various items of evidence. Witnesses are not collected together and asked to give their evidence on a particular point one after another. Instead, each is taken through the whole of his evidence by his own side, usually in chronological order. Then he is cross-examined on any portion of it which the other side considers may yield advantageous results. The jury is continually expected to remember back and carry forward. The overall picture of the case has to be gathered from the addresses by counsel in opening their cases and in their final speeches and the judge's summing-up.

The structure of the trial thus emphasizes that what is required of the jury is a judgment by general impression on the evidence as a whole.[4] This is confirmed by the attitude which has long existed towards the jury taking notes. It has rarely been the practice to provide jury-boxes with proper note-taking facilities, though in modern times this is done in complex cases. In the Great Train Robbery case, for example, the judge took care to see that notebooks were provided and that the jurors' attention was drawn to the desirability of keeping some record of the trial. The traditional argument has been that the jury will do best if its members sit back and observe the general demeanour of witnesses and defendants. Note-taking is only likely to be distracting both in court and in the jury-room, because most jurors will be untrained in the art of taking notes and of distinguishing relevant from irrelevant evidence. But equally it may be argued that people untrained in remembering evidence as it is given will be best assisted by some encouragement to jot down points as they go along, in order to fix what is being said in their minds. I was certainly informed by several jurors whom I interviewed that discussion in the jury-room tended to pass into the hands of those who did take notes, simply because they proved to be the members best able to recall what had been said.

In the normal case everything will depend on the collective memory of the jury when the jury-room is reached, for transcripts of the evidence are not provided. In the *Hanratty* murder trial, the jury asked to be provided with a transcript, but the request was refused by the judge[5]; this also emphasizes that a judgment by overall impression is sought.

Similarly, juries are not expected to adduce reasons for their verdict. Except where a special verdict is requested – and in a criminal case this is most unusual – nothing is done to ensure that the jury has satisfied itself that each fact has been proved which is necessary to constitute the crime in question. It is now accepted practice that a judge gives reasons for any decision he reaches on a question of law or of fact. In the latter case, he will outline the evidence and state which parts he did and did not accept, and what he found significant in reaching his final conclusions. Lord Denning once insisted that it is a basic principle of the sound administration of justice that a judge should give reasons for his judgment.[6] This widely held view led to the requirement laid down in 1958 that many administrative tribunals should give reasons for their decisions if requested.[7] Yet Lord Denning ignores the fact that the traditional common-law tribunal for determining questions of fact does not conform to this principle, and indeed many of the special advantages of the jury are thought to arise precisely because it does not do so. As a practical matter, quite apart from the loss of these advantages, there could never be any question of requiring juries to produce full reasons for their verdicts. It would be highly unlikely that juries could regularly give a consistent account of their reasoning, which would be proof against the scrutiny of lawyers searching for grounds upon which to base an appeal. But the point serves to emphasize once more the very different kinds of decision expected of a jury and a judge.

THE EFFECT OF ADVOCACY

The gradual extension of the legal aid system is bringing us closer to a situation, at least in relation to serious criminal cases, where large numbers of defendants are no longer prevented by the cost from having professional advocates to present their case. The provision of legal representation will remove the obvious disparity which exists when one side is not represented, but it cannot always eliminate the inequality which results from a difference in abilities between the advocates on each side. Such a difference is often said to have great influence on juries, while it is assumed that professional judges, having been advocates themselves, are less likely to be influenced by the way in which a case is presented.

The style of advocacy practised in English courts until the early years of the present century has left behind it a legendary aura of high drama and histrionic rhetoric. In the nineteenth century it was not uncommon to find prosecutions conducted – especially against unrepresented defendants – in a sneering hectoring manner, with witnesses mercilessly browbeaten and bullied if the occasion warranted. Defence counsel relied heavily on emotional pleas to the jury's sense of mercy and fair play. Marshall Hall was one of the last of a line of great advocates of this school. Lord Birkett wrote of him in one case:

When he came to his peroration and depicted the figure of Justice holding the scales until the presumption of innocence was put there to turn the scale in favour of the prisoner, not only were the jury manifestly impressed, but they, and indeed the whole court, were under a kind of spell. The intensity and passion of Marshall Hall in moments like these had to be seen to be believed. It was simply overpowering and juries were swept off their feet.

Conan Doyle, when remarking on the performance of a Scots advocate, said: 'My friend Marshall Hall was a very great counsel. But he could not have argued a case without a jury and before a bench of judges as this man has done.'[8]

Today the general style of advocacy is more measured and less flamboyant. Impassioned pleas have lost popularity, perhaps because in a more level-headed, better-educated age the danger that they will not be treated seriously is too great. The change no doubt serves the cause of objective and rational assessment of the evidence, but it would be wrong to suppose that jurors do not take a lively interest in the presentation of the case and the performance of counsel.

In interviewing jurors I was struck by the frequency with which they commented upon counsel; barristers are perhaps not fully aware of the keenly critical eyes which scrutinize their performance from the jury-box. Some were full of praise: for the clarity of presentation, skilful use of language or the perceptivity of cross-examination. Others were quick to compare different performances. Others again condemned poor or unpractised counsel: hesitancy, obscurity and unsuccessful attempts to introduce red herrings were frequently criticized. Some singled out an experienced man for special praise, as did a juror, writing in *The Times*, of a Q.C. who had been briefed for the defence: 'The timing, the carefully pitched voice, the studied gestures, the calculated histrionics never overdone, the suave references to the pretty girl in wig and gown beside him as ''me learned junior'', the generous sharing in the one laugh that someone else managed to snatch, all was such an artist's performance that when the jury were directed to find the defendant not guilty, I found it difficult not to applaud.'[9]

At least where the defendant has chosen not to give evidence himself his counsel is often better remembered and more fully described by jurors than the man he is defending. It is easy to imagine that trial by jury sometimes develops into trial of the lawyers. How important a factor it is, and whether it has a regularly predictable effect, is less easy to estimate.

In one American experiment, jurors were asked to say which of the attorneys who had appeared before them they would prefer to have if they needed one. Seventy-five per cent chose the attorney for the side for which they had voted, characterizing him in such phrases as 'very convincing' and a 'good actor', while the others were 'convincing, but not good enough', and 'boring'.[10]

The Chicago Project has provided a deeper analysis. In their study of judge-jury differences, the investigators asked the judges concerned to indicate cases in which either prosecution or defence counsel was superior. It emerged that the judge considered that counsel did not differ in quality in 76 per cent of the cases; but with the remainder, defence counsel was superior in 11 per cent and prosecution counsel in 13 per cent. At the same time it appeared that the disparity of counsel was given as one reason (often in conjunction with other reasons) for disagreements between judge and jury in 9 per cent of the cases in which a disagreement occurred. In particular there was material available to consider what effect the presence of superior defence counsel had on the cases in which the judge but not the jury was willing to convict. It was estimated that this superiority accounted for 3·4 per cent of all such disagreements. If a defendant did secure the services of better counsel his chances of this preventing a conviction where the judge would have convicted him was about once in every nine cases where defence counsel was superior, though it might have some effect in as often as one case in four. Where the judge would have acquitted, but the jury convicted, it appeared that the superiority of prosecution counsel could account for 2·5 per cent of the cases.[11]

In recording instances of differences between the advocates for the two sides, the judges gave a wide variety of reasons: some went to the general impression created by the advocate, skilful, congenial, likeable, or too eager, antagonistic; other reasons were based on the conduct of the case: skill in cross-examination or the address to the jury, or failure to follow up a line of attack. In a few cases, the judge thought that some of the jurors were probably indebted in some way to a well-known local lawyer. Occasionally, too, the lack of ability or experience in his advocate was thought by the judge to have worked in favour of the defendant. The jury felt a special sympathy for a man under such a disadvantage.

UNDERSTANDING THE EVIDENCE

There are three important questions to be answered about the ability and characteristics of juries in handling the questions of fact: do they understand the evidence put before them? Upon what general experience do they rely in evaluating evidence? How far do they allow factors not strictly part of the evidence to influence their judgment? These matters will be explored in turn.

The first aim of any general investigation of jury-room processes would be to measure how far jurors understand the evidence put to them. In other words, how much substance is there in the view that since juries are not in any way selected for their ability or experience there will be occasions on which they fail properly to understand what a case is about?

There is as yet no statistical information which accurately measures basic facts about criminal prosecutions in England, such as variations in the length of trial, the number of prosecutions and defence witnesses, the kinds of witnesses called or the frequency with which a defendant refrains from giving evidence himself. Nevertheless, a large number of all cases are concerned with relatively straightforward subject matter and do not take more than a day to try. There are certain categories of case which do regularly prove complicated either because of the amount of evidence or its technicality; for example, cases where there are a number of defendants, or where medical or accounting evidence has to be given. These special cases are separately considered in the next chapter. Were criminal cases regularly concerned with specialized subject matter, the jury would no doubt have been the subject of much heavier criticism. We shall see that it was for this reason that, even in an age when special juries could be requested, trial by jury was generally acknowledged to be quite inadequate to deal with commercial disputes in the civil courts. Soon after it became possible to request trial by judge alone, it became standard practice to do so in commercial cases (see p. 237).

Jurors often comment on the simplicity and relative unimportance of the cases which they have been called upon to try. They arrive at court expecting to adjudicate upon a plot of detective novel ingenuity, or a serious offence of the kind that attracts considerable press publicity. Instead, they may be faced with a case of small-scale shop-lifting or theft or assault in which there are only a few easily understood points of conflict in the evidence. Reactions then vary from relief at not having to assume heavy responsibility to boredom and inattentiveness.

The Chicago Project found that a similar pattern emerged. They asked the judges to classify the degree of difficulty in understanding the subject matter of a case. The answers showed that 86 per cent of the cases were (in the judge's opinion) easy to comprehend, 12 per cent somewhat difficult and 2 per cent very difficult. The investigators were struck by the very considerable infrequency with which, if a judge disagreed with a jury's verdict, he offered the explanation that the jury had not understood the evidence. They also showed that the average length of time taken by the jury to reach a verdict was roughly proportionate to the length of the whole trial, but that it was considerably greater in those cases which were difficult to understand than in those which were easy. All these points led to the conclusion that 'for the law's practical purposes the jury does understand the case'.[12]

But though this is a valuable indication of the scale of the problem of understanding the evidence, it would be dangerous to accept this optimistic conclusion without looking further for direct confirmation of the matter. The Chicago Project's findings are only a record of the judge's explanation of how juries reached their verdicts, and of his estimate of the difficulty of the case. It must weigh heavily against the jury system if it is true that even in a small proportion of all cases verdicts are being reached after failure to comprehend the evidence – and even the judges were prepared to classify one case in fifty as being 'very difficult'. The Chicago study itself shows that there are a wide variety of other factors which may be present to explain differences between judge and jury. It thus does not take one a great deal further to demonstrate that juries deliberate longer in more protracted and difficult cases, or that they seldom differ from judges when the matter is complicated. Moreover, the idea of 'understanding' the evidence involves a great many differences of degree: at one end of the scale the jury may be quite unable to grasp any part of what the witnesses are saying; at the other there may be a failure to appreciate the significance of one small but nonetheless vital piece of evidence. There are nuances here that cannot be adequately investigated otherwise than by direct observation of juries, actual or experimental.

EVALUATING THE EVIDENCE

In all the functions which jurors perform – judging whether a witness is speaking the truth or is mistaken or lying, deciding whether proof of one fact leads to the inference that another occurred, deciding how the law should apply to the facts – they will be obliged to fall back on their personal experience, for it will be unusual for them to have the knowledge of other cases which would play a part in decisions made by judges and lawyers. One of the Chicago experiments measured the amount of time given over in the jury-room to different kinds of discussion, and it emerged that on average the jurors spent about as much time discussing individual experiences of their own as they gave to the judge's instructions and the testimony: 22–23 per cent on each.[13]

Only rarely will a juror have any knowledge or experience which particularly concerns the case he is trying. Since the eighteenth century the principle has been that jurors should judge a case only on the evidence presented in court. The judges have done much to prevent press reports spreading prejudicial information about a defendant before his trial is complete (see p. 208). If a juror has personal knowledge of a litigant or the circumstances of the matter before the court, then he ought not to sit, and may be challenged for cause (see p. 45). Occasionally he will prove to have some piece of objective information about which a defendant cannot reasonably complain. In a recent prosecution the accused said, as part of his defence, that he had visited a certain public lavatory. One of the jurors lived in the vicinity and was able to inform the judge that it had been closed for repair at the time in question.[14] At least in large cities such a coincidence must be most infrequent. Of much wider import is the general experience which any person forming conclusions from evidence will use as background reference.

A juror whom I interviewed related the following instance. A man was charged with receiving a coat knowing it to have been stolen. His story was that he had innocently bought it from a stranger who knocked on his door and offered it at a cheap price. The middle-class members of the jury were inclined to believe the story, thinking him entitled to jump at a good bargain if he could. But the working-class jurors, some of whom lived on the same kind of housing estate as the accused, treated the tale with the utmost suspicion, having learned never to trust such a caller themselves. Their view ultimately prevailed, because it was felt to be better informed. Many criminal cases involve issues of this kind, and juries must frequently be involved in similar speculations. The instance just given may be contrasted with the experience of the juror who found himself on a wholly middle-class jury in Manchester. The jurors had to decide whether a defendant charged with receiving a stolen wireless set was likely to have bought it in all innocence from a man in a pub. None of them had any direct experience of whether such transactions did ordinarily take place, and so were obliged to make an uninformed guess.[15] It is an important part of the argument for extending the qualifications for jury service that a jury should include persons of widely different backgrounds in order to provide varied day-to-day social experience upon which the jury may call.

Professional judges, and to a large extent justices of the peace, are drawn from a comparatively narrow social group and thus cannot be expected to have the same breadth of ordinary experience as that of a jury selected from the whole of the adult community. The kind of experience which they will have, but which juries will lack, will be the knowledge gained through taking part in other trials. Regular acquaintance with the vagaries of conduct that provide the daily fare of the criminal courts is unlikely to be experience leading to an optimistic or trusting view of human nature. The nub of the case against having regular judges in the criminal courts is simply that familiarity breeds certain attitudes and prejudices, and with time these may become deeply ingrained. First there is the bias towards believing the police, which may grow out of the knowledge that they have been right before. This we have already discussed. Then there may be an over-readiness to discount a defence, just because it is one that is regularly offered. The danger of an experienced judge responding 'I've heard that one before' to a case of genuine innocence is one of the very real problems of any system of criminal justice. A criminal court in which a professional lawyer sits alone as the judge must in principle be objectionable on this score, though a right of appeal can to some extent dissipate the objection. It is notable that in the one instance where a single judge can sit alone in a criminal court in England – the stipendiary magistrate in a Magistrates' Court – there is a right of appeal by way of full rehearing of the case at Quarter Sessions.

Judges may become cynical with time, but at least their experience will have carried them past the reaction often experienced by persons who are gaining a first acquaintance with the criminal courts. Jurors are apt to find out that tales of injured innocence put up by defendants cannot always be taken at face value. They often report how this was brought home to them by hearing the previous convictions of a defendant whom they have found guilty read out in court. Then it may be that they will swing the other way and display an unnecessary degree of scepticism towards subsequent defendants.[16] A judge will at least be long past such painful disillusionments.

Concern over professional cynicism should not allow one to be blind to the fact that long experience of disputes will inevitably equip a lawyer with a great deal of experience which would enable him to make a discriminating judgment about the issues before the court. He will, for instance, learn to recognize small signs which may indicate that a man is lying, and if he has a flexible cast of mind he will learn that such signs can be misleading. He will also come to know the indications that a witness is less sure of what he is saying than appears at first glance. Much of this knowledge will be passed on by an experienced advocate to a jury, in particular through cross-examination. The judge also has the opportunity to give the jury the benefit of his experienced judgment in his summing-up, so that the gap between the knowledge of the lawyers in court and the lack of experience among the jurors may be reduced. Nonetheless it is there, and no amount of careful instruction can invariably implant the significance of some matter in the minds of people who are not trained in advance to see its relevance. There is no neater illustration of this than one of Professor Devons' examples from his own experiences as a juror in Manchester. A man was charged with breaking and entering a private house. A woman had disturbed an intruder in her house but had not seen his face; fingerprints found at the place were shown to correspond with the accused's in a large number of points, and therefore provided strong evidence that he was the intruder.

In summing-up the judge drew special attention to the evidence of the finger-print expert, pointing out the significance of the certainty given by the number of identical characteristics he had found and indicating that in view of this, the fact that the woman was not able to identify the intruder did not really matter.

However, the jury was unable to reach a verdict because half its number were sceptical of the finger-print evidence without the support of identification by the woman.[17] Most lawyers would take exactly the opposite attitude, just as did the judge in the case, because they know not only that there is little chance of clear finger-print evidence being wrong, but also that identification evidence is open to a great many defects, and has sometimes caused innocent people to be convicted.

Different attitudes produced by familiarity with the criminal courts may be measurable. In the analysis of reasons given for disagreements between judge and jury, the Chicago investigators isolated the cases in which no factor other than the evaluation of the evidence was stated to be the reason for the difference of opinion. Among them, only two factors seemed to recur with sufficient regularity to have the predictable effect of making the jury more lenient: one was the fact that a defendant without previous convictions gave evidence himself, the other, that in looking for proof beyond reasonable doubt, the jury required a higher standard than the judge.[18]

The importance of both these factors was confirmed to me in the course of interviews with jurors. Time and again, a juror would comment on the great reluctance which either he or one of his fellows had felt about assuming the responsibility of convicting a defendant, either because of the state of the evidence, or because the defendant had gone into the witness-box to explain himself. One indication that English judges have felt that juries adopt too severe a standard of proof was the search conducted in the 1950s to find a substitute test for 'proof beyond reasonable doubt' (see p. 96). This seemed to be concerned to find a formula which would not suggest so stringent a standard to jurors. As we have already seen, it may well be that the precise terms in which a judge sums up on the burden of proof mean little to jurors: they are more concerned with satisfying themselves that they can live with the responsibility of having convicted a defendant.

SCIENTIFIC AND OTHER TECHNICAL EVIDENCE

Although the courts have received evidence from experts on non-legal subjects for some four centuries, the problem of providing a court which is equipped to understand and evaluate expert witnesses is essentially a modern one. The immense advances in fields such as medicine, psychiatry, biology, chemistry and engineering are reflected in the increasing complexity of expert evidence which from time to time comes before the courts. In criminal law the number of different experts who are able to assist in the process of detection has grown steadily since the professional police forces were first established. Handwriting experts were first admitted in the criminal courts in 1865 (1854 in civil cases); chemists were permitted to test the writing on a will to prove a forgery for the first time in 1910; the 1940s saw the introduction of electro-encephalogram test results to demonstrate the likelihood of an accused man being an epileptic.[19] Such examples could be multiplied many times.

The English courts have stuck firmly to the ordinary accusatorial procedure in dealing with scientific and other expert evidence. The parties provide their own experts as witnesses. If there is a conflict between experts called by either side, the jury will have to decide which to believe. If there are cases in which a jury does not understand evidence of any kind, or lacks adequate experience to judge a question, it is likely to be one involving the evidence of experts. The example given above of the jurors who distrusted the fingerprint evidence is a good one. The extent of the problem is hard to gauge; there is not even any accurate information about the frequency with which different types of expert witnesses are called in English courts.

There is American evidence of the greatest interest concerning the way in which jurors pool any specialist knowledge that they happen to possess. In one investigation a number of trials were observed and the jurors were afterwards interviewed to discover how the verdict was reached. Several cases were concerned with accidents involving a motor vehicle (they were civil cases, but the subject matter might equally well have arisen in a criminal prosecution), and expert evidence had been called. In one case an engineer on the jury used knowledge of engineering, mathematics and design to demonstrate a number of conclusions about the cause of an accident. In another, a tool designer gave his own opinion as to how and why the tie-rod on the defendant's tractor had come out of the socket. In another again, a doctor's wife 'was the acknowledged jury-room doctor, testifying as to the costs of office visits, knee operations, patients' reluctance to undergo surgery and similar matters disputed during the trial'. The same woman used social contacts to find out the opinion of local doctors about one of the expert witnesses. There were instances of mistakes arising from jury-room expertise: for instance, an accountant wrongly informed his fellows that an award of damages would be subject to tax.[20]

The full report of these investigations is still to be made. The fascination of these brief glimpses suggests that interest in the findings of any investigation will be considerable. In the end, however, it does no more than confirm and quantify what one would suppose to be a natural way for a group of persons who have no previous experience to set about solving a problem requiring expert judgment.

NON-EVIDENTIAL FACTORS AFFECTING GUILT

We have already considered three important factors which, quite apart from the evidence, may cause a jury to refuse to convict. One is dislike of a particular rule of law, the second a general bias against the police, and the third, the differences in ability between counsel. A fourth factor is the element which has been usefully called 'jury equity' – circumstances in which the jury is swayed by some sympathetic or other emotional response, which leads it to the view that, *despite* the evidence, the defendant should not be convicted. This the jury may rationalize by saying that the evidence did not show proof beyond reasonable doubt, for doubts about the evidence and special grounds for sympathy are often present together in the same case. Perhaps the most striking part of the analysis provided by the Chicago Project has been evidence of the variety of categories into which 'jury equity' may be subdivided.[21] They can only be indicated in summary form here.

In the first place, a defendant may be acquitted if he has some personal attribute which attracts sympathy or admiration. This does not cover just the legendary reaction of an all-male jury to a beautiful young woman defendant. A wider range of other characteristics seems to produce similar results: the youth of a defendant or his age, a difficult family background, or the presence of a number of trying circumstances beyond his control, such as past illness or unemployment or a physical disability. Indications of remorse or repentance, especially by defendants who broke down and cried in court, also played their part. So also did the fact that the defendant's family were prepared to stand by him – the judges commented on the effect of a wife or mother being present throughout the trial. A defendant who had heavy family responsibilities was in a similar position. The fact that the defendant was able to indicate his record as a serviceman – in some cases by the crude method of wearing his medals to court – also told in his favour.

On the material before them the Chicago investigators were able to suggest that the fact that the defendant attracted special sympathy was the explanation of why the jury acquitted where the judge would have convicted in some 11–14 per cent of all the disagreements of this kind. Moreover it could be predicted that this sort of sympathy would be the operative factor in swaying the jury to acquit once in every five of the cases in which it was an element noted by the judge.

There were also converse cases in which juries convicted when the judge would have acquitted, and in some of them a lack of sympathy for the defendant was offered as an explanation. Glibness, insolence, false piety and bad language all seemed to lead to a refusal to accept the story put forward by the defendant. In some cases he was a coloured man involved in sexual offences with whites, in others he had indulged in perverted or immoral sexual conduct. In others again, his treatment of his family or children was neglectful or harmful. Perhaps most interesting of all were cases in which the jury appeared to be influenced by the callous conduct of the defendant in leaving an injured victim without giving or calling for help. These were all cases in which the judge thought that the evidence was not strong enough to justify conviction upon the charge which the jury found proved.

THE JURY AND PUNISHMENT

Any attempt to assess how far judges would differ from juries in their decisions on guilt is likely to be affected in some measure by the fact that juries know that they have no direct power to settle the punishment, whereas judges are accustomed to do so and would no doubt take their power into account if they were to decide the question of guilt. The various special characteristics of a defendant which may lead a jury to acquit despite the evidence against him are just the factors which judges at present consider relevant, after conviction, in settling the punishment. The basic questions are whether judges and juries feel the same facts to be deserving of sympathy, and whether it is more desirable to let such defendants off completely, or with some appropriately light or nominal punishment. It must be remembered that while guilt is determined on the facts immediately surrounding the case itself, sentencing involves a much wider consideration of the accused's background and record.

There are undoubtedly cases in which jurors become concerned not so much with whether the accused committed the crime, as with whether he deserves to be punished for it. Apart from the cases when the defendant is acquitted because the jury feels that in all the circumstances it would be unfair to convict, there are those in which a verdict of guilty is returned but with a rider recommending that mercy be shown, or that the punishment be limited in some way. The judges have not encouraged recommendations for mercy. They do not inform the jury that it may add qualifications to the verdict. Counsel for the defence is not permitted to allude to the jury's right directly, and the practice of making some indirect reference to it, although apparently approved by the Bar Council in 1928, has subsequently been deprecated by the Court of Criminal Appeal.[22] This attitude of reluctant permissiveness may well produce the unsatisfactory result that the jury will only make a recommendation of mercy if it happens to know that it has the right to do so. The cautious attitude taken by the judges has much in common with the attitude of limited trust implicit in their reluctance to encourage jurors to take notes or ask questions. But there is a particular reason for not encouraging juries to add riders to their verdicts. Jurors who are arguing for a conviction may induce a reluctant juror to swallow his doubts and agree to a verdict of guilty by the proposal that a recommendation for mercy be added. The fear that this would happen frequently if the practice were changed, and juries were instructed of their power, must be enough to prevent introduction of such a change.

One of the important problems raised is how far jurors act out of ignorance or misinformation as to what punishment will be imposed. English law has few fixed penalties. Most serious offences leave the matter to the discretion of the judge, with or without some prescribed maximum. It is unusual to provide even a required minimum sentence. Conformity between sentences is policed through the supervisory powers of the Court of Appeal. Unless a jury contains a member who has some previous experience of the criminal courts, it will have little knowledge of the customary levels of sentencing, of the extent to which special factors lead to variations from the mean, of the effect of a previous criminal record, and so on. The jurors may have only a slight idea of the wide variety of punishments available. These may vary from absolute or conditional discharge at one end of the scale, through punishment aimed at helping to reform the defendant such as probation, to fines and imprisonment at the other. The knowledge of jurors about available and likely punishments could usefully be investigated, together with the influence of their views about punishment on the question of guilt.

Professor Devons has reported his experience of a Manchester jury on which two women expressed reluctance to convict a man of drunken driving because it had been indicated in evidence that he would be in great difficulty with his job if he lost his licence to drive. In the jury-room they were persuaded to convict, but agreed only on condition that the judge would not take away his licence. How they expected to impose this limitation was not clear. The case turned out to be one in which the judge was obliged to take away the licence for a period, and one of the women was stopped from protesting only because she was held back by the foreman.[23] Such attitudes are apparently not untypical: my interviews revealed a number of similar instances. The judges reporting to the Chicago Project showed a similar awareness. In particular, some of them suggested that juries feel a punishment to be too harsh if it puts the defendant's job in jeopardy. The Project was also able to show that special facts in a case might for a different reason make punishment undesirable. Thus, if the crime had led to the defendant himself being injured, or caused him to suffer special remorse, he might be regarded as having been punished enough already. The same applied where the jurors knew that an accomplice had already been dealt with because he had pleaded guilty, and had been treated leniently because he had owned up; they felt that preferential treatment should not be shown to the accomplice as against the defendant whom they tried.[24]

Should juries be given some indication of the penalties which may be imposed if the accused is found guilty? At its most general, this could consist of a brief outline of the varieties of punishment which are awarded in English courts. This information could be included in the proposed handbooks for jurors. At its most particular, the judge could include some reference in his summing-up to the range of penalties appropriate to the offence and the kind of qualifying factors which would be taken into account in relation to the particular offender. There are dangers in either course: for instance, that fears could be aroused through incomplete understanding of what is being said. It would be possible to take another, more radical, step and allow the jury to deliberate on the question of punishment together with the judge, after a finding of guilt. This would provide a channel by which jurors could express their feelings about aspects of the case calling for special sympathy or other consideration while allowing the judge to correct misapprehensions and mistakes.

In certain other countries where the jury system has been introduced the jury has been given power to consider the punishment. In Denmark, for example, it was found that juries were acquitting too readily in certain cases, and it appeared that the reason was a dislike of judicial sentencing policy in relation to those offences. As a result, the law was changed from the English approach so that the three judges who sit in a criminal trial there now retire with the jury after a conviction has been recorded for the purpose of deciding the sentence. Each judge has four votes to every one of a juror. Voting strength between judges and jurors is thus equal. But there are serious objections to this procedure. One is that a juror may be tempted into agreeing to a conviction by the bait that he will afterwards be able to argue for a light punishment. The other is that sentencing is now recognized to be a complex matter, in which considerations of equality between case and case and the need to select the most appropriate sentence for the offender in the light of his whole background have to be delicately balanced. This requires considerable knowledge and experience. It cannot be expected to exist as a matter of common moral feeling or divine inspiration among complete amateurs. As long as the system continues, we are likely to be left with juries which acquit because they feel that the accused ought not to be punished even though he has committed the crime. The matter that deserves investigation is how often this becomes an important practical issue. The judgment that then has to be made is how far it is dangerous. It is surely wrong in principle that a person who has in fact committed a crime should leave court upon a finding that he did not commit it, if there is adequate evidence against him: it may be suggested that he does not deserve to have a conviction recorded against him, because of the consequent moral or social stigma. But can these often be greater than a conviction followed by an absolute discharge? We no longer live in an age where mere conviction involves loss of civic or property rights as a matter of course. Moreover, as a practical matter, the grounds for sympathy are often not what they seem at first sight. The jury's only acquaintance with a defendant will be in the dock or on the witness-stand. In the strange circumstances of a court-room a defendant can often appear to be only the poor victim of fate. If he is convicted, a good deal more will be known about him before he is sentenced. Hard information about previous convictions often compels a jury to view a meek and well-mannered defendant in a rather different light.

SCIENTIFIC CRITICISM OF EVIDENCE

Over the last century forensic science has transformed the processes of detection. It may well be that the next century will see a development by psychologists, psychiatrists and others of more scientific methods and techniques for the evaluation of evidence. It is worth speculating briefly on such possibilities for the future, with special thought to its effects on jury trial. The attempt in a court trial to reconstruct a series of events which are, at the very least, some weeks old is inevitably an imperfect affair. The court has to depend very largely on the perception and recollection of witnesses and these may be faulty, misleadingly incomplete or deliberately false. What the findings of psychologists are able to demonstrate are the sources and extent of errors of perception and memory of witnesses who are genuinely trying to speak the truth.[25]

For instance, a good deal has been shown about the factors which impair the ability to recollect. Lapse of time, age and intervening intellectual effort are factors which are known to have a pronounced effect on memory. Indeed they suggest that English courts should place greater reliance on statements taken from witnesses shortly after the events concerned, whenever this is possible.

Another tendency that has frequently been demonstrated is the way in which an observer, in recalling past events, will subconsciously incorporate into what he actually perceived imaginary details representing what he would have expected to happen. In one reported experiment, it was arranged that a student should unexpectedly interrupt a class, saying that he was looking for some escaped white rats. The members of the class were asked to recollect afterwards what they remembered of the incident. One fifth of the class stated that the student was wearing a maroon-coloured sweater. In fact he had on a coat of a quite different colour – but maroon was a common colour at the university. A majority said that he had searched diligently in the corners of the room, though he was in fact under specific instructions not to do so.[26]

Related experiments have demonstrated that statements made by a person in a highly excited or disturbed emotional state – because, for example, he has just been attacked or involved in an accident – are particularly likely to contain inaccuracies. The legal doctrine which allows hearsay evidence to be given of the dying declarations of the victim in a homicide case runs counter to this finding. It is based on the unwarranted assumption that a person will speak the truth *in extremis*, and ignores the fact that the person's powers of perception may have been seriously dulled by the circumstances. It has also been shown that memory of events is affected by the fact that they were observed when the witness was in a highly emotional state. This is no doubt one of the principal explanations why identification evidence by persons who have been robbed or assaulted is sometimes demonstrably wrong.

A good deal of medical and psychological knowledge about illusions and defects in perception, particularly in seeing and hearing, is now becoming available. For instance, it has been demonstrated that in judging heights most people tend to overestimate, whereas horizontal distances are generally underestimated. A moving object such as a car will appear to be going faster than it is if it is also making considerable noise; so, too, if it is small rather than large. Judgments of colour may be affected by colour blindness, and by the relative intensities of different colours in different lights. Deafness tends first to exclude the higher frequencies of vibration so that those going deaf may not hear whistles and screams, but will hear clicks and thuds. Many other examples could be given. It is also known that observers can be trained to improve their judgment by learning to counteract or take account of natural distortions, so that trained witnesses may be more readily trusted than the inexperienced.

The question which has to be posed is whether the ability of those who act as judges in the courts can be enhanced by being given some formal instruction in this sort of matter. As far as lawyers are concerned, the academic side of English legal education provides no training in the ways and means of proving facts. It is not even accepted, as it is in Scotland, that a course in forensic medicine should form part of a lawyer's training. Instruction in scientific methods of investigation or in the evaluation of evidence does not generally form part of courses on the criminal law or the law of evidence. What a lawyer learns about these matters comes from his practical experience of cases in which he is concerned or which he hears about. The danger of this sort of knowledge, if it is not supplemented by generalized information collected under controlled conditions, is that it is likely to be distorted by the experience of particular cases.

The process of estimating what reliance should be placed upon a witness's evidence depends upon a variety of general assumptions. One consideration is the inherent likelihood that a witness's perception or memory is faulty. Knowledge of the physiology and psychology of perception may ensure more informed assessments of this sort of probability. From this point of view, a layman, unless he has some special training, is likely to be even less well informed, since he lacks even the background of court experience to which a lawyer may turn. And if he is only to serve in court for a relatively short period of time, as on a jury, it is clearly impractical to consider giving him formal instruction. In the nature of things, jurors must remain amateurs. It may well be that the gap between the professional and the amateur judge of fact is about to start widening perceptibly.

We have already seen that much of the law of evidence is concerned with precluding suspect evidence or with directing juries as to how to deal with it, and that one of the problems of reforming the law is to ascertain how far other tribunals can be trusted to evaluate such evidence. In large degree the present rules of evidence are the result of observations of human prejudices and imperfections which psychologists are now measuring. Thus the rationale of the rule against hearsay is supported by the findings of Professor Bartlett in his classic work on memory, that if information is transmitted from person to person it becomes increasingly subject to omissions, rationalizations, transformations of information concerning one person to another, and transpositions of the order of events. The need for corroboration of the victim's evidence in cases of sexual assault reflects not only the fact that the intense emotions generated may be a source of confusion, but that there is a special danger that personality problems may have led to false accusations for which there is no apparent motive.[27] Yet these are relatively crude attempts to limit and direct different kinds of evidence and the conclusions to be drawn from it. What is now required is a careful study of the extent to which judges and justices can be given effective general training in the assessment of all kinds of evidence in the light of modern techniques for measuring and assessing defects in perception. This is the type of innovation that should eventually provide an answer to the question of how far judges with experience and training can be left to decide a case on the whole of the evidence, without the intervention of formal rules of exclusion and instruction.

The Lord Chancellor has recently remarked of the 'general feeling among those used to our criminal courts that the proportion of obviously guilty people who are acquitted has risen a good deal in the last few years'.[28] We have now seen that for this circumstance there are several explanations. One important consequence of the inexperience of jurors is that the sudden and unexpected responsibility placed upon them will make them reluctant to convict a man unless they feel sure of his guilt. They require a high degree of proof from the prosecution. Moreover, they lack the sort of experience which might lead them to consider police evidence particularly trustworthy and deserving of support. But a verdict of acquittal may be an expression of general dislike of the police, unconnected with the case and therefore palpably misguided.

To some extent, the difference between the views of judges and juries may be explained by the fact that the judge has considerably more knowledge of circumstances surrounding the case or the defendant. The judge will, for instance, know the previous record of the accused, and he may have tried him before or have dealt already with others concerned in the same crime. The difference may also reflect the fact that the jury has some sympathy for the defendant, which a judge might regard as worth taking into account when fixing the penalty. All other things being equal, it is right that these factors should affect not the verdict but the question of punishment. In a few cases, the jury's verdict may express a simple dislike of the provisions of the law in general, not merely in its application to the case in issue. Such verdicts were usually related in the past to the sentencing policy contained in the law. Where the same feeling is operative today, the restriction which the law seeks to impose may well be unpopular, but is usually justifiable and ought not to be circumvented by particular juries.

We still do not know how far the jury's inexperience, and possible lack of education, intellectual ability or familiarity with the judicial process and legal language prevents a full understanding of the evidence in a case. The point has already been stressed that some issues will best be decided by reference to general knowledge based on years of day-to-day experience, and here a jury drawn from every sector of society may as a tribunal be superior in some respects to either judges or justices of the peace. But on other issues, especially where technical evidence is given, or where evidence which is apparently convincing to the lay mind would be treated with suspicion by a professional, the jury must represent a special risk.

This risk may well be tolerable in so far as it leads only to acquittals. The real danger is that precisely the same kinds of mistake or ignorance will lead to unjustifiable convictions. As we have seen, the Chicago Project found that their judges would have acquitted entirely or convicted on some lesser charge in 3 per cent of the cases examined. This did not destroy the reporters' faith in the jury system as a whole. If it were to be found by research in England that this difference occurred with equal frequency, it is to be hoped that the situation would not be accepted with equanimity, but that further investigation of the reasons why juries convict in such cases would be set in motion immediately.

Certainly, the history of English criminal trials is not entirely free of cases in which it has been demonstrated conclusively that the accused was entirely innocent of the crime, not merely convicted on insufficient evidence. Some of them fall into particular categories. There have been a number of cases in which a mentally disturbed woman has fabricated evidence to suggest that another person has written 'poison-pen' letters, and the other person has been convicted and imprisoned.[29] Another class concerns mistaken identity. One of these cases, that of Adolf Beck, led eventually to the setting-up of the Court of Criminal Appeal in 1907.[30]

Since these miscarriages of justice have been shown to be possible, we must consider whether a new rule of evidence should be introduced to warn courts of the danger that a particular kind of evidence presents. Even with this safeguard, there are other cases which do not fall into any predictable category. At least the present virtual abolition of the death penalty has meant that the risk of a mistaken verdict in a murder case does not involve the loss of a life. It is not easy to forget the tragic case of Timothy Evans, executed for murdering his daughter while living in the house of John Christie who was afterwards found guilty of killing a number of women in furtherance of sexual assault upon them. In 1966, an inquiry conducted by Mr Justice Brabin produced the finding that the evidence against Evans on the charge of killing the baby was not strong enough to justify his conviction, although there was sufficient evidence of a crime with which he was not charged, the murder of his wife![31]

The significant question to ask about such a case is whether a different tribunal would have reached a verdict of acquittal. Certainly in any murder case in which the judge had serious doubt about the correctness of the verdict, it would have been surprising if he did not recommend, in the report which he was customarily asked to provide to the Home Secretary, that the death sentence be commuted to life imprisonment. Similarly the accusations against innocent persons charged as a result of mistaken evidence of identity were apparently acceptable to the judges who tried them. Likewise the disastrous series of unfounded prosecutions brought by Detective Sergeant Challenor before his mental illness was discovered managed to convince judges and stipendiary magistrates as well as juries.

The truth is that there is no workable system of criminal justice that can be guaranteed never to involve the conviction of an innocent man. The most that can be hoped for is that a vigilant watch will be kept at all times so that unnecessary errors may as far as possible be avoided; and that techniques for detecting them will be improved – for instance by introducing restrictive rules to protect against the wrong construction being put upon dubious evidence. Part of this process must now include research to measure the extent to which the various factors discussed in this chapter do in fact influence juries in reaching their verdicts. Only then will it be possible to make an informed judgment of the special values and pitfalls of jury trial and the true extent to which it differs from trial by professional lawyers alone. The vigorous outcry which followed the Government's announcement that it intended to introduce the new system of majority verdicts proceeded from a very real feeling that the change was being made from a position of complete ignorance, and that a safeguard of real value might well be disappearing. Lack of knowledge as to how juries reach their decisions meant that no proper information could be put forward. Suggested reforms in the system will no doubt be mooted in the future. It cannot be right that they should all be met by the hopeless argument that the *status quo* must be preserved because otherwise some inestimable value will disappear for ever. The way to improve the administration of criminal justice must lie in part through a proper understanding of how well its present institutions work; and such knowledge must not be garnered at a time when some serious problem, such as the intimidation of jurors, makes hasty action necessary.

7 · Crime: some special problems

Clearly the jury system's unique combination of inexperience and freedom from the need to give a reasoned decision will not work equally well in all cases. This chapter explores specific areas of the criminal law, in which trial by jury either creates special problems or provides a particular advantage. As far as the problem areas are concerned, we have already considered in general terms the conditions that may create difficulties: the length or complexity of a case, the introduction of expert evidence, or the presence of some emotional factor which blurs the true issue at stake. Difficulties in comprehending the evidence may be particularly acute where there is a multiple trial, or where the case concerns a commercial fraud, or raises a defence of insanity or of diminished responsibility. These are discussed before we pass on to two situations in which emotional responses are likely to be strong: sexual and motoring offences. The two final sections are concerned with the other side of the coin – cases in which the representative view of the community as provided by the jury has some special justification: these are the censorship of obscene literature and criminal contempt of court.

JOINT TRIALS AND MULTIPLE CHARGES

A criminal court deals with several charges at once in cases where two or more defendants are charged with the same offence, or where a single offender is charged with a number of different offences, or where these circumstances occur together. It is obvious that an increase in the number of charges will produce an increase in complexity. Yet there are strong reasons of expediency for trying together a number of persons said to be concerned in the same event or series of events, or a number of charges against a man alleged to have committed several similar crimes. Trials are time-consuming and expensive. It is clearly desirable to keep to a reasonable minimum the amount of time which must be devoted to the trial of charges arising out of any one set of circumstances where this can be done without creating unfair conditions. Yet the trial of more than one charge at a time creates possibilities of prejudice against the accused of the kind which the law of evidence otherwise seeks to avoid by the careful exclusion of general evidence of the accused's bad character and past record. We have already noted in Chapter 3 that these are probably the most easily justifiable of the whole class of rules excluding evidence on the ground that juries may give it disproportionate weight. In a joint trial, where it appears to the jury that one man is guilty, the fact that others are associated with him at all may be enough to damn them as guilty, too. In a trial upon multiple charges, the fact that a man has been shown to have committed one crime may lead the jury to think that he must be guilty of others in respect of which the evidence is by no means so strong. It may even be that when so many different charges are alleged against a man the jury is bound to think that he must be guilty of something.

Yet the courts have shown little willingness to order separate trials of different charges because of the suggestion that the jury may be affected by this kind of prejudice.[1] The pressures of expediency have been strong. It is precisely these multiple cases, where directions are given which require the jury to treat evidence as admissible for one purpose but inadmissible for another (see p. 94), that are most frequent. In general it is for the judge to decide whether the different charges should be tried together. Only where a number of persons have been charged in different indictments is it necessary to obtain their consent before they may be tried together. Where they are initially charged together in one indictment (the more usual case) the judge alone has power to order separate trials. This he will do only with reluctance, and only if he is persuaded that without such an order there is a chance of very strong prejudice arising against one or more of the accused. The same applies to the trial of a single defendant upon charges arising out of different events.

The dangers of multiple trials are thus twofold: the jury may be confused by the evidence, and may succumb to special inducements to entertain prejudice. How far these are real dangers has yet to be discovered. There can be little doubt that at the start of cases in which there are a number of defendants many jurors are considerably bewildered. Already the strangeness of the surroundings and the intricacies of procedure may well impair a juror's concentration; then he is confronted with an indictment consisting of a string of charges and a row of individuals in the dock, each one of whom has to be associated with the charges against him and the counsel who is defending him. A number of jurors whom I interviewed spoke of the confusion which they experienced during the early stages of a trial of this nature. One of them sat on a jury which in desperation asked for a diagram showing the position of each defendant in the dock, and of his counsel. These jurors were on the whole of the opinion that the case against each accused became clear in their minds as the trial wore on. In particular, they commented on the considerable degree of repetition inevitable in a joint trial where each defendant was separately represented.

Yet it is clear that cases still occur in which confusions arise, and remain undispelled when time comes for the jury to return its verdict. There have been recent cases in which the Court of Criminal Appeal has considered that the jury must have been unable to appreciate that evidence concerning some of the defendants did not affect one of the others. Of one convicted defendant, the Court said: 'We think that he is really a typical example of a man who was sunk by means of a mass of evidence about frauds of different kinds, with the great majority of which he had no connexion either direct or indirect, and in which he took no part whatever, and in which his name was never even mentioned.'[2] As this quotation shows, the case concerned a commercial fraud of the kind dealt with in the next section (p. 179). But a similar danger must exist in other types of case. I was told by a juror of a case in which a man was charged with receiving four different lots of goods. The jury was agreed that sound evidence against him existed on three of the counts, but not on the fourth. Most of the jury were nonetheless ready to convict on this count as well, without distinguishing clearly which parts of the evidence were relevant to each count, on the basis that if he had committed one crime he had done the lot. It took some forcible argument by a minority group to convince them otherwise. According to the juror's report, in this case the rational view of the evidence was finally accepted by the whole jury. One is left fearing, without any more definite knowledge, that other cases must have been decided as the majority would first have settled this case.

One kind of multiple charge deserves mention on its own: that is the case where a person is charged with a number of offences of varying degrees of gravity in connexion with one event. If, for instance, the Crown instigates proceedings in connexion with a robbery, the charges against a defendant may range from robbery with violence, through robbery and assault with intent to rob, to carrying an offensive weapon in a public place. Part of the purpose of including a range of charges in the indictment is to leave room for negotiations between the police and the defence for a plea of guilty on one of the less serious charges. But if the defendant continues to assert his innocence, and the case is tried, the jury has a choice before it in the verdict it returns.[3] In a rough way it will be able for once to indicate how serious it considers that the offence was, and so provide a standard by which the judge must calculate the punishment. But the choice may also provide room for manoeuvre in the process of reaching an agreed verdict. I was informed of several cases in which jurors who at first were not prepared to convict at all were persuaded to find a man guilty of a lesser charge on condition that others on the jury agreed not to convict on a more serious charge. One effect of the introduction of ten-to-two majority verdicts may be that compromises of this kind may now be struck further up or down the scale. In any investigation which aims to discover what differences majority verdicts are bringing about, special attention should be given to cases of this kind.

COMMERCIAL FRAUDS

During this century, the number of complex cases of financial fraud has increased steadily. The 'long firm' fraud, where a company is formed to obtain goods on credit without any intention of paying for them, has made regular appearances, and is likely to involve lengthy unravelling of the state of the company's accounts. Modern instances often involve a network of interrelated companies of inordinate intricacy. High rates of taxation and substantial government subsidies have also added to the attractiveness of creating elaborate business systems for dishonest ends. If criminal proceedings eventually result from operations of this kind there is likely to be lengthy expert evidence from accountants and other businessmen. Such cases are cumbersome and costly to mount. They tax to the utmost the patience and perspicacity of all those involved, but the jurors face a particularly difficult task if they lack business experience of the kinds of transactions and records involved.

Certainly lawyers are conscious that such cases should be presented to a jury with meticulous care. Efforts at clarification and simplification have to be made at all stages, and this must create dangers that some omission or mistake will occur which will lead to a successful appeal. One recent example was the *Lime Fraud* case.[4] The Ministry of Agriculture has a scheme whereby a government subsidy is paid to farmers who purchase lime as a fertilizer. A lime supplier, his accountant and nine farmers with whom he had dealt were charged with having obtained subsidy moneys on the basis of prices which were too high for the amount of lime supplied. There were twenty-four counts in the indictment charging the supplier, the accountant and each farmer in turn with perpetrating different frauds. But in addition there was one omnibus count charging all eleven of them with conspiring together to defraud the Ministry. The prosecution persisted with this charge even when it emerged in evidence that none of the farmers knew of the transactions taking place with any of the others. All the accused were tried together. The jury had to hear 95 witnesses, look at 263 exhibits including accounts and schedules, and return 78 different verdicts. The trial spread over ten weeks. All the accused were convicted and either fined or imprisoned. However, the verdicts were upset on appeal. The Court of Criminal Appeal considered that the whole case had become so elaborate in its presentation that the manful struggles of the judge to keep his summing-up as brief and clear as possible had resulted in his leaving out a great deal of what might have been said in favour of one or other of the defendants.

The Court stated: 'We do not believe that most juries can ever really understand the subtleties of the situation.' This remark was prompted by the fact that it had been necessary to explain to them that certain evidence which had been given was inadmissible against the farmer to whom it referred in relation to the specific charge against him, but could be considered in relation to the omnibus conspiracy charge, once he had been shown to be a conspirator. The Court went on to express the view that general conspiracy charges should not in future be included unless there really was some evidence outside the specific acts charged that a more general fraudulent plan had been made by the alleged conspirators. In the case under appeal each defendant should have been tried separately for the specific fraud alleged against him.

One juror whom I interviewed had been on a fraud case. He happened to be an accountant, and had had to open proceedings in the jury-room by giving his own explanation of the sheets of figures provided in evidence. He considered that nine of his fellows had been unable to follow this crucial information in any adequate fashion. Perhaps his presence on the jury for that particular case was accidental, but it may have been arranged. For, as the Morris Committee on Jury Service recognized, it has been a practice at certain courts to see that in appropriate cases some jurors belonged to a profession that gave them some general knowledge of financial matters. The Committee recommended that any informal system of strengthening the fibre of juries should cease, because it was capable of being misunderstood, however well-intentioned. In any case it is a system capable of being defeated by the defence, for they may peremptorily challenge the jurors whom they know to be capable of understanding the figures – a practice which is by no means unknown.

The Morris Committee was against any return to a system of specially chosen jurors because it discerned a trend of opinion among witnesses against doing so: 'Witnesses who have been able to speak with experience have expressed the view that the average jury today is able to cope even with long and difficult cases.'[5] One wonders how far those witnesses spoke in the knowledge that juries have to some extent been handpicked by judicious stage-management. In any case, the evidence before the Committee was by no means unanimous. For instance, it was the view of 'Justice' that so long as juries continued to try financial fraud cases there ought to be a special panel of potential jurors who had experience in matters of accountancy, and that some of each jury trying a fraud case should be drawn from this panel. Moreover, it must be remembered that the Morris Committee was recommending a general reform of the qualification rules which would have the principal effect of markedly increasing the proportion of women and young people eligible for service. This is likely to increase the number of jurors lacking the sort of business experience which would provide a useful background to the understanding of a fraud case.

It is hard to accept with equanimity the Morris Committee's views that ordinary juries are an adequate instrument for dealing with these cases. It is here that the case against juries on grounds of lack of qualification and experience is strongest. It is notable that in Canada the Commissioners for Uniformity of Legislation have recognized that juries are inadequate for fraud cases involving companies' shares and securities. They have accordingly recommended that it should be possible for a judge to order that a case likely to be too complicated and long drawn out for a jury to tackle should be tried by judge alone.[6]

For many years, it has been the rule in England that a civil case is tried by judge alone if it involves 'prolonged examination of documents or accounts or any scientific or local investigation'.[7] However, the undesirability of having one man decide questions of criminal guilt has already been commented upon, and it is likely that in England such an expedient would not be considered a desirable reform. A more satisfactory tribunal might perhaps be composed of lawyers and accountants or other businessmen; a less radical proposal might be the revival of special juries in this field. In the early years of this century, criminal prosecutions for fraud were still being tried in this manner in the King's Bench Division.[8] In the United States a similar system has been fostered in some areas. Jury commissioners draw up lists of jurors specially qualified by their profession to sit on 'blue ribbon' juries, and the system is thought to work well in both civil and criminal cases.[9]

One particular problem which has dogged commercial fraud cases in England has been the failure of the jury to reach a verdict at the end of a long trial. In June 1965, five men and two companies were charged with conspiring to evade purchase tax on toilet and household goods and plastic toys to a total of £132,462. The first trial lasted forty-four days, and the jury, having examined a considerable array of documents and heard 116 witnesses, was unable to reach a unanimous verdict. One newspaper estimated costs at £125,000. A second trial had to be held, which took fifty-three days. In the end the defendants were convicted. The trial judge said afterwards that the jury at the first trial of this case was prevented from reaching a unanimous verdict because a single juror held out against it.[10] This could have been the result of bribery and corruption; certainly the frauds alleged in such cases are on a big enough scale to make attempts to interfere with jurors more likely than in most other prosecutions. This danger was specifically advanced as a reason for introducing majority verdicts. Yet it is in just these intricate cases that juries will be most likely not to understand the evidence. At least under the unanimity rule there was the reassurance that all twelve jurors were prepared to agree on one result. Now it is possible that the one or two members of the jury who have grasped the issue will find themselves in a minority and unable to convince the majority.

THE MENTAL STATE OF THE ACCUSED

In the previous chapter, we discussed in general terms how the development of modern science had led to an increase in the variety and complexity of expert evidence which may now be in issue in court proceedings, and questioned how far juries were able to deal with it. Nowhere has the advance of scientific knowledge presented greater difficulties than in the realm of medical and psychiatric evidence on the mental state of an accused person who pleads insanity or diminished responsibility. Historically, the defence of insanity has played its most important part in murder cases, for if it was successful the defendant would not be hanged, even though he would be detained 'at her Majesty's pleasure'. The test in law of whether a man was insane at the time of committing a crime has been extremely cautious and difficult to satisfy. It was laid down in the *M'Naghten* rules of 1843.[11] In practice, the test in the rules that is usually in issue is: was the accused suffering from a disease of the mind at the time of committing the crime so that he did not know that what he was doing was wrong in law? Or to put it more simply: could he tell right from wrong? The Rules are particularly restrictive in that they deal only with intellectual under-standing and ignore the fact that mental processes may be seriously disturbed by emotional stress and personality factors. Psychiatric knowledge has advanced a long way since 1843, and most psychiatrists now find that the question in the *M'Naghten* test is artificial and outmoded. All the same, it is not easy to devise a new legal criterion. Medical classifica-tions of mental abnormality and ill-health provide no con-venient dividing line which the law could adopt in order to distinguish between those who are responsible for their conduct and those who are not. The differences are of degree only, and medical opinions about the mental condition of a defendant at the time of his criminal act must often be specu-lative and imprecise; yet the law requires a decision one way or the other. The result has been that in England the *M'Nagh-ten* rules have remained the basis of the law, and the issue has been left in the hands of a jury to settle as best it can on the basis that it is not obliged to give reasons for its verdict.

The judges have shown considerable reluctance to inter-fere with the jury's verdict. In 1950 the Court of Criminal Appeal went so far as to insist that the jury might convict even in the face of unanimous medical evidence that the accused was insane, because the jurors were entitled to look at the evidence in the case as a whole. Lord Goddard said:

It is for the jury and not for medical men of whatever eminence to determine the issue. Unless and until Parliament ordains that this question is to be determined by a panel of medical men, it is to a jury, after proper direction by a judge, that by the law of this country the decision is to be entrusted.[12]

More recently the Court has been rather more careful to look for substantiating evidence from which the jury might con-

clude that the defendant is sane before allowing a conviction
to stand in the face of uncontradicted evidence of insanity
or diminished responsibility from the defence psychiatrists.[13]

There has been much discussion of a new formula to
replace the *M'Naghten* rules. The Royal Commission on
Capital Punishment heard much detailed evidence from
medical and legal witnesses on whether further categories of
insanity could usefully be added to the rules in the light of
modern medical knowledge. But that is only one side of the
question. The other is how far a jury is capable of appreciating
the significance of any instructions given them on the law,
and of absorbing the evidence given by expert witnesses.
The secrecy of the jury-room left the Royal Commission
with practically no information about this aspect of the
matter. The Lord Chief Justice, Lord Goddard, in giving
evidence to the Commission took the view that 'a jury can
always be trusted to do justice, where it might be impossible
to bring the case strictly within the *M'Naghten* rules, but
everybody would say that the man's acts were the acts of a
lunatic'.[14] On general impressions of this kind a majority
of the Royal Commission was satisfied that the better course
was not to add to the old rules but to replace them entirely
with a direction to the jury that indicated more compre-
hensibly what was expected of them. The judge should put
the direct question: Was the accused suffering from a disease
of the mind or mental deficiency to such a degree that he
ought not to be held responsible for his act? The Commission's
report contained a number of recommendations which required extensions of the powers of juries and which would
depend on their good sense and judgment, but this proposed
method of dealing with the question of insanity was perhaps
the most striking part of the Commission's testament of
faith in the system.[15]

However, there were critics whose trust did not extend
so far as to think it right that the jury should be left without
guidance to decide the whole question of whether the accused
ought to be held responsible. When the Homicide Act 1957
was passed, the Commission's recommendation was not
included. Instead, a special defence of diminished responsibility, available only in murder cases, was introduced. It

has the effect of reducing the defendant's crime to manslaughter where the jury is satisfied that the accused was
suffering from such abnormality of mind 'as substantially
impaired his mental responsibility' for the crime.[16] Though
more limited in scope this leaves the jury to make its own
broad judgment about responsibility.

The Chicago Project has collected information of just
the kind which was lacking to the Royal Commission.
Using the technique of playing recorded trials to 'jurors'
selected on the same basis as real jurors, the researchers have
amassed a considerable body of evidence about how juries
handled the issue of insanity in two cases, one a minor housebreaking charge in which the accused had a long history of
mental illness, and the other a charge of incest with his
daughters against a man who otherwise led an apparently
normal life.[17] In both the plea of insanity was supported by
evidence from two psychiatrists, and in both the direction
from the judge as to what amounted in law to insanity as a
defence to crime was varied: one third of the juries were
instructed to apply the *M'Naghten* 'right-from-wrong' test;
one third were directed to find whether the defendant's act
was the product of a mental disease or defect (the so-called
Durham test, after the United States case in which this
formula was introduced as an alternative to the *M'Naghten*
rules); and one third were given no legal criterion of mental
responsibility, thus putting them in a similar position to that
which the Royal Commission on Capital Punishment suggested for England.

The psychiatric evidence was varied to correspond with
the legal test that was being applied. In the housebreaking
case, the psychiatrists gave no clear answer when asked
whether the accused knew right from wrong (in the *M'Naghten* trials) or when asked whether his behaviour was the product of his mental condition (in the *Durham* trials), so
the juries had no firm evidence to follow when applying the
tests. In the incest trial, however, the psychiatrists in the
M'Naghten version said that in their opinion the defendant
could distinguish right from wrong, whereas those in the
Durham version said that his behaviour was a manifestation
of his psychic condition. In neither case was there equivalent
evidence where the jury were being given no legal formula

to apply.[18] From this it can be seen that the Chicago study did not test two situations: that where psychiatrists could reasonably conclude that the defendant was insane under either of the legal tests; and – most difficult of all – that where there are prosecution and defence experts both of whom give strong but irreconcilable evidence as to the accused's mental condition at the time of the crime. It would be most interesting to pursue the experiments further by dealing with these other conditions.

In the housebreaking case, only thirty experiments were conducted and the final verdicts reached by juries did not vary significantly according to the way in which the law was formulated. The researchers therefore turned their attention to the incest trial, which they repeated to sixty-eight different juries. Here the difference in the psychiatric evidence and the legal tests together produced a significant variation. In the *M'Naghten* trials all the juries finally agreed to convict the defendant save one which was unable to agree. In the *Durham* version, a fifth of the juries were prepared to find the accused insane and a similar proportion were unable to agree.

When the juries were uninstructed, they reacted very much like the *Durham* juries. This result is interesting because the researchers anticipated that the ordinary juror, left without legal guidance, would be concerned with the accused's ability to comprehend the quality of his act, and that in the particular case it was difficult to think that he did not know that what he was doing was wrong. Certainly in all three versions jurors spent much time discussing this question, and many of them expressed their mistrust of modern psychological theories and their effect in eroding clear moral values. In addition juries carefully reviewed all the evidence concerning the defendant's conduct in order to decide if he knew what he was about. In particular they were impressed by the steps he took to provide contraceptive devices. Cool calculation was looked upon as the antithesis of madness. It was clear to the researchers that most jurors were well aware of the distinction between the clinical diagnosis of which the psychiatrists gave evidence and the question of legal responsibility for crime. Indeed many of them felt that because the psychiatrists were not asked whether the accused should be held responsible, their evidence was not directly relevant.[19]

These findings suggest that under a less restrictive test of insanity than the *M'Naghten* rules juries are likely to find an accused person insane about as often as they would if left uninstructed. But even if psychiatrists are prepared to say that the accused's act was a manifestation of his mental illness (in relation to a *Durham* direction), still juries are no more likely to find the accused is insane than if they are left to follow their own unguided instinct. To refer back to the evidence before the Royal Commission on Capital Punishment, it seems that there are cases in which under the *M'Naghten* rules juries feel obliged to convict where if left to themselves they would have held the accused irresponsible in law. If the Royal Commission's suggestion had been adopted, more people could have expected to plead insanity successfully, but the results would have reflected more accurately the views of ordinary citizens about when a man should be entitled to say that he is insane.

This in turn raises the question of whether a jury is the right body to decide questions of mental responsibility for crime. One issue is certainty of the result. The Chicago juries produced differing results because of their individual composition. The study found that there were few general characteristics among the jurors which could be used to predict their likely opinion. There was some evidence that jurors of low-social-economic status tended more readily than others to find the accused insane. So did those under thirty-five compared with those over that age; and so also did Negroes compared with those of other ethnic backgrounds. Religion, income and sex produced no discernable trends, save that housewives (as opposed to other women, as well as men) showed a special tendency to convict the defendant in the incest case.[20] The question of whether jury trial is undesirably uncertain cannot be properly discussed until information is collected about how lawyers and psychiatrists would judge the same cases, and the likelihood of differences of opinion emerging could be assessed.

In criminal cases, the predictability of the result is only one desirable aim. The matter of crucial importance is to ensure that those who decide the issue should understand the evidence and be able to reach a detached and sensible view in applying the law to the facts. The most interesting part of this Chicago study is its review of how the various juries deliberated. As has already been mentioned much of the discussion centred on parts of the evidence which were relevant to deciding whether the accused knew what he was doing. But a good deal was also said about how the insane were thought or expected to behave. This led jurors to dredge up whatever experience they had had of mentally sick persons. Some spoke of intimate experiences involving friends or relatives, and the researchers noted that the process sometimes led to the juror concerned taking a more sympathetic view of the defendant.[21] Time and again, the views expressed about insanity and mental illness show how unfamiliar the jurors were with any learning on the matter, the concepts for describing mental conditions and the general medico-legal problems. One has only to study the reproduced transcript of one of the jury deliberations[22] to see that many of the jurors had naïve and limited views on the question at issue and that the actual experience of one juror, despite its marginal relevance, might be listened to with attention and discussed at length. It is hard to imagine a group of doctors or lawyers discussing the case and their views upon mental responsibility in so hesitant and limited a manner. The only apparent advantages of a jury are that a large number of people have to agree on any verdict, that a difficult issue can be resolved in secret behind closed doors, and that the jury is to answer to the inevitable fear that if the matter is left to experts they may abuse their power. It is difficult to read the Chicago evidence and not wonder seriously whether these advantages are not rather tenuous. Experiments need to be done in this country to see whether similar patterns emerge here. In particular it would be interesting to know how juries work when they have to resolve conflicting psychiatric evidence. If there is broad confirmation of the American evidence the time has come to give questions of mental responsibility over to another body such as a joint bench of legal and medical experts.

The Chicago study made a number of other findings of which two in particular deserve mention.[23] The fact that the juries took only very general notice of the evidence of the psychiatrists is reflected by the discovery that it apparently made no difference whether the psychiatrist gave evidence in rather involved, technical language, or in a 'model' form that had been specifically designed to put the evidence as lucidly as possible to a lay audience. Nor did it matter whether or not the jury was actually instructed that the consequence of finding the accused guilty would be imprisonment, and that of finding him insane would be commitment to a mental hospital. Most of the jurors knew this without being told (93 per cent), and, even when they were told, exactly the same proportion (7 per cent) thought afterwards that the accused would, if found insane, be sent to prison, put on probation or set free!

Finally, one special problem of insanity and diminished responsibility cases deserves to be mentioned. Suppose that an accused person has evidence available that establishes an alibi for him, and there are also doctors who consider that if he did commit the crime he must have been insane at the time. Legal practitioners recognize that in the eyes of a jury the alibi may be irremediably weakened by a plea of insanity.[24] The idea of relying on alternate pleas is one to which a person with legal training becomes accustomed, but to do so often seems alien and unrealistic to the layman. The advisers may well consider, or the defendant may decide, that he should only raise the alibi, and hope to get off completely. If he is then convicted by the jury, the Court of Appeal is unlikely to allow him a new trial in which to raise the defence of insanity.[25] An immediate advantage of introducing an expert panel to decide questions of insanity and diminished responsibility would be that if there is doubt about whether the accused committed the crime at all that issue could be put to a jury; then, if necessary, the experts could decide the question of mental responsibility.

MOTORING OFFENCES

It is in motoring cases that juries are most frequently criticized for acquitting too readily. Many lawyers who are otherwise strong believers in the jury system have expressed their dissatisfaction at the apparent irresponsibility of some verdicts in these cases. Such criticisms cannot be lightly dismissed, for juries do not sit to hear minor charges of illegal parking, obstruction or even careless driving. They deal with the top end of the scale. In particular, dangerous driving, driving while unfit through drink or drugs, being in charge of a vehicle while unfit, driving while disqualified and driving without compulsory insurance are all offences for which the accused has the right to elect to be tried by jury. Dangerous driving and driving while unfit are the two crimes which most frequently produce allegations that juries are acquitting without justification. Some lawyers now consider that the extensive national campaigns for road safety which have given so much publicity to the causes and consequences of accidents have led jurors to show greater readiness to convict. Others think there has been little change. Their views often reflect their recent experience in practice, and it is clear that there has been no universal alteration of attitude.

No figures are as yet available to show accurately the proportion of those charged with motoring offences who are acquitted by juries. The Criminal Statistics, it will be remembered, show that of all those who come before the higher courts for trial, including those who plead guilty, between 10 and 15 per cent are acquitted; they also indicate that the rate is much higher for the offences of dangerous driving and driving under the influence of drink and drugs – between 30 and 45 per cent.[26] Of course one does not know whether the proportion pleading guilty is lower or higher in driving than in other cases. Persons charged with dangerous or drunken driving are generally sent to be tried on indictment because they opt for a jury, though sometimes it is because the magistrates think the case too serious to try it themselves. One suspects, without knowing, that fewer of them are ready to plead guilty in the higher court than occurs among defendants sent to Assizes and Quarter Sessions, taken as a whole. The Association of Chief Police Officers demonstrated that in non-motoring cases some 82 per cent of those stated to have been convicted in the higher courts pleaded guilty or were there merely to be sentenced. Professors Elliott and Street have shown that if one applies this figure to statistics for dangerous and drunken driving charges the proportion of those acquitted after a jury trial may be as high as 78 per cent.[27] But this can only indicate the order of magnitude of the acquittal rate in these cases; accurate national figures have yet to appear.

A variety of explanations may exist for the apparent over-readiness of juries to acquit. The first is that, as with 'motor manslaughter', juries are expressing disapproval of the law itself or the methods by which it is enforced. The Chicago Project's judges most frequently offered this sort of explanation for jury acquittals in drunken driving cases with which they did not agree.[28] Crimes such as dangerous or drunken driving rarely involve premeditated conduct, as in a planned robbery or murder. In the case of dangerous driving the defendant has not usually acted intentionally at all but has been thoughtless or careless. Indeed, the law now is that no matter how cautious he is, if he brings about a dangerous situation, he is liable. It may be that juries are expressing the view that such conduct ought not to be criminal, or at any rate a crime triable in a higher court with a serious maximum penalty. If such feelings are at work it isl ikely that they will operate in combination with some special sympathy for the defendant in all the circumstances of the case. Many jurors will be road users who have themselves been in similar situations. Defendants in motoring cases may well have an appearance of respectability and a class background which is closer to that of many jurors than are those of persons on other charges. Willett, in his study of motoring offenders, found that a high proportion of those who elected to be tried by jury were middle-class.[29] We have also noticed that this is an area in which jurors may have special fears about the penalty because they will know or suspect that conviction involves disqualification from driving for a period. It is a well-known advocates' ploy to slip into evidence the fact that the defendant has to drive for a living. All these factors may be compounded in an emotional reaction often summed up in the view that jurors are too prone to say: 'There but for the grace of God go I.'

But it must be realized that juries may be reluctant to convict for quite different reasons. The evidence in many motoring cases is provided by persons who have been in-volved or who have observed events which have happened quickly and which may have caused them fear or shock. It is situations such as these which produce the kinds of error of perception and memory which have been demonstrated so significantly by psychologists. The law recognizes the danger in connexion with speeding offences by requiring corroboration of evidence of the speed at which a vehicle was travelling. Lady Wootton, from her experience as a J.P., has written of

the extraordinary difficulty of finding out just what did occur and who is to blame for what. In the case of a theft or burglary, it is generally clear enough what has been done by someone, and the only problem is to catch the right man. Nor is the complainant likely to have had a hand in the matter: people do not usually burgle their own houses. But in the case of motoring crimes, where the only evidence available relates to the consequences of the offence, not to the offence itself, it can be extraordinarily difficult to disentangle the true facts.[30]

Prosecutions for serious motoring offences arising out of accidents are brought by the police on the basis of the evidence that they have been able to collect from the observable consequences such as damage to vehicles and skid marks, and from what they can gather from the drivers involved and other eye-witnesses. They will be hampered by each driver's freedom not to answer questions if he chooses, both before and at court, and by the fact that if they charge both drivers involved in a collision they cannot call either as a prosecution witness unless there are two separate trials. In such cases, the police often guess which driver was more likely to have been in the wrong and charge him. When they get to court, they may well have the irritating experience of seeing a witness who was most positive when he gave his statement start to flounder and contradict himself, especially under cross-examination. Difficulties of proof in many motoring cases are considerable.

There is an urgent need to test how far it is a matter of sympathy and how far a matter of difficulty of proof when juries acquit in motoring offences for which lawyers would expect a conviction. The only really valuable research that can be done will involve real juries and actual verdicts, because one of the matters in issue is how jurors respond emotionally to the defendant. In the first instance, a series of interviews with jurors who have tried particular motoring cases should be carried out, and any conclusions suggested by the interviews should be tested by recording the course of deliberations in further cases. If it emerges that considerations of sympathy or disapproval of the law are predominant, then consideration will have to be given to finding some other tribunal to replace the jury in motoring cases. For it cannot be seriously doubted that dangerous and drunken driving should be crimes, and that drivers who ought to be convicted hope to escape the consequences of their acts by electing to be tried by a higher court. But if juries acquit mainly because they find that the evidence does not establish the accused's guilt beyond reasonable doubt, then the case for change is different. It is a common complaint that magistrates show an unwarranted tendency to prefer police evidence most frequently in motoring cases. It would indeed be impossible to expect stipendiaries and justices who sit at all regularly on traffic cases to discount their previous experience in dealing with defendants who each present some variation from a standard set of excuses. A jury's freshness of mind may here have some very real advantages.

In their recent book, *Road Accidents*, Professors Elliott and Street have explored in detail the desirability of setting up special courts to deal with all grades of traffic offences requiring a judicial hearing.[31] They point out that if Traffic Courts are to be more than a change of name for one division of the Magistrates' Courts, it would be necessary to train specialist full-time magistrates for the job, so that they could carry in their heads accurate information about such matters as road conditions in their district and the performance of different vehicles. In addition they would need to be advised by specialist experts in construction and highway engineering, acting either as assessors or court experts, and it would be desirable to create court procurators to conduct investigations into the causes of accidents before deciding who, if anybody, should be charged with a criminal offence. In the end the authors reject the possibility of Traffic Courts as being too expensive for the potential advantages. They favour abolishing jury trial and training special panels of magistrates to deal with the lists of traffic cases. To accept this is to accept the risk of prosecution-minded magistrates who may too easily be satisfied that an offence has been proved beyond reasonable doubt. The jury's advantage remains that it is much more likely to treat the case that it tries as one of first impression. If upon investigation it appears that most juries are troubled by questions of proof as much as by sympathy or prejudice, it would be wrong to take serious motoring cases entirely out of the hands of lay judges without regular court experience. It may well be that the jury is no longer the best way of keeping the lay judge within the framework of the court: for the effect of requiring ten out of twelve quite inexperienced laymen to agree to a conviction is often to put on the prosecution very high burden of proof indeed. The independent lay element could be preserved in a less extreme form by substituting a court in which regular magistrates sit together with ordinary laymen who do only occasional service in the courts.

Where serious motoring offences turn on issues of hard fact, such as whether the accused had forged his driving licence or was driving without compulsory insurance, complaints about the over-readiness of juries to acquit are rare. It is in dangerous and drunken driving cases, where the law requires an evaluative judgment, that it has been hard to get convictions. Juries have been reluctant to find it proved beyond reasonable doubt that a driver was 'unfit through drink' or drove 'in a manner *dangerous* to the public'. The introduction of an objective factual basis for the law is therefore likely to make juries less reluctant to convict and so to make the law more definite in its operation. This is one important advantage of the recent creation of the crimes of driving or being in charge of a vehicle while having more than a prescribed proportion of alcohol in the bloodstream, ascertained, after a preliminary breathalyser test, by compulsory blood and urine tests.[32] The new crimes are additional to the old offences of driving or being in charge while unfit, but it is now regular practice to bring a charge based only on the blood-alcohol content. The case then depends on evidence from scientific tests, which can be queried only on the ground that they were inaccurately carried out. Subjective factors, previously much beloved of defence counsel, such as the variation between different persons' abilities to drive after drink, are not relevant to the requirements of the new law. During the passing of the legislation in 1966 and 1967, the lobby against it protested that the elimination of these personal factors made the law unfair to drivers who had 'good heads' for alcohol – an argument which ignores the fact that every person's responses are to some extent slowed down by alcohol.

It is still too soon to discover how juries generally are treating defendants charged under the new law. They ought to be readier to convict than they were of the old drunken driving charges. But some of them may want to express a feeling that the new law is unfair, or allows the police to get evidence against a driver too easily. Certainly the Chicago Project found that dislike of compulsory tests involving the use of 'drunkometers' was given by the judges as a reason for unexpected acquittals in drunken driving cases.[33] One suspects that if spot check breathalyser tests for all drivers, whether suspected of unfitness or not, had been introduced as the Minister of Transport first proposed, there might have been quite a strong reaction from juries. If this reaction does appear in England, it would be wrong to allow juries to circumvent a policy approved by Parliament for attacking a serious and persistent social problem. It is not the sort of measure which should have to receive the popular approval of jurymen before it can in practice be enforced.

SEXUAL OFFENCES

Sexual offences are the other type of case in which it is often said that juries may be affected by an unusual degree of emotional prejudice. The survey of Queen's Bench judges conducted by the Lord Chief Justice showed that among the 'very rare' cases in which it was thought that juries convicted where the judge would have acquitted, only sexual offences were specifically named as a possible category. This was explained on the basis that juries might be more ready to ignore the corroboration warning which must be given in all such cases.[34] One is left wondering whether this is indeed the only explanation.

The practice of challenging to get an all-male jury is common in sex cases. This emphasizes the belief that women may be specially prejudiced against a defendant in a sordid case. The power given to the trial judge in 1919 to order a jury to be composed entirely of the members of one sex[35] seems designed to give the same protection, as well as providing a means for shielding women from the unpleasant facts of certain cases and from the embarrassment of having to discuss the evidence with members of the opposite sex in the jury-room. But these indications do no more than add to a natural suspicion that as a class sex cases are likely to produce emotional reactions from jurors; and since these are likely to be feelings of abhorrence, they may give rise to prejudices against the accused and lead to a conviction not justified by the evidence. This is a class of crime which deserves early attention from investigators.

As with motoring offences, sex cases also give rise to particularly difficult questions of fact. Thus some of the less serious offences leave no physical marks on the victim, so that it may not be clear whether any offence was committed by anyone. Some offences, such as rape, depend on the absence of consent by the other partner. This can lead to conflicting evidence which it is difficult to sort out. It is certainly not unknown for a person who appears perfectly well balanced to make an allegation that he or she has been sexually assaulted, and this later proves to be mistaken, imagined or invented, the product of serious emotional or mental disturbance. It was the danger of false accusations which led to the requirement that juries receive the corroboration warning (see p. 97). In addition there is the absolute rule that a child's unsworn evidence must as a matter of law be corroborated before it can be acted on.[36] This reflects the general anxiety that a child will indulge in fantasies or be drilled to give false evidence by an adult.

Some aspects of these rules are open to criticism on the ground that they have become unnecessarily formal and technical. Thus it is at present the law that if a person is accused of quite separate attacks on different victims at different times, the victims do not corroborate each other by their evidence. So, too, a child giving unsworn evidence cannot be corroborated by another child whose evidence is also unsworn.[37] Yet it is certainly desirable that the jury should be most carefully warned of the danger that a wrong accusation has been made, even if there is no apparent motive for doing so. Indeed there is one class of case, prosecutions for sending poison-pen letters, which, since they often have sexual overtones, ought to be added to the list of offences as requiring a corroboration warning. Cases have come to light in which mentally disturbed persons have written such letters, often filled with obscenities and sexual references, and have deliberately fabricated evidence to lead to the prosecution and conviction of someone else.

The question raised by sexual offences which cannot at present be answered is whether the likelihood of prejudice combined with the difficulties of the evidence leads in-experienced juries to decisions, particularly in favour of conviction,[38] with which lawyers would not agree, or whether the present protection – general guidance from the judge and the requirements laid down in the rules of evidence – provide a sufficient guarantee against mistakes. This is another area calling for special consideration.

It has been suggested that there is a particular reason for removing to a less formal court any sexual case which in-volves a child victim.[39] The atmosphere of sessions or assizes will be likely to frighten the child, since it is necessary for him to remember the evidence and repeat it once more to a large number of strangers. This may be both damaging to the child and to the court, for the circumstances are not con-ducive to the giving of accurate evidence. Prosecutors recognize this problem and sometimes proceed for a lesser offence, which can only be heard by magistrates, so as to lessen strain on the child. It is probably undesirable in principle to start distinguishing the modes of trial available to the defendant solely because of the age of the victim, but it is one reason why all sexual cases should be transferred from the higher tribunals to some special form of court in which jurors do not sit.

OBSCENE LITERATURE: CENSORSHIP

The last two sections of this chapter deal with two areas in which the jury may have a special role because of the import-ance of obtaining a representative view of ordinary members of the community. The first of these concerns the place of the jury as censor of obscene literature.

In England there is no pre-censorship in the form of a licensing authority whose permission a publisher must seek before producing a work. This is in contrast with the production of plays, which until 1968 has required the Lord Chamberlain's licence, and the showing of films, which requires local authority approval. For literature the only medium of control is the criminal law, and the duty of deciding what is obscene is divided between juries and magistrates. There are two ways in which proceedings may be launched.[40] The first is by prosecuting for publishing obscene literature. This charge will be dealt with either by judge and jury or by magistrates, the defendant having the right to demand jury trial if he wants it. Secondly, there is a quite different kind of procedure aimed at preventing literature ever coming into the hands of those whom it may corrupt; a magistrate may issue a warrant to the police to search and seize articles which they 'have reason to believe to be obscene articles and to be kept for publication for gain'; the articles will be forfeited and destroyed unless in court proceedings the justices are satisfied that the matter is not obscene. A jury has no part in this forfeiture procedure. Until recently it was left entirely to the prosecutor to decide which course he would follow (see p. 203). Under the forfeiture procedure it is not uncommon for different copies of the same book to be seized in different parts of the country and brought before local magistrates; the results of the cases may vary – the first decision does not legally bind any later court to reach the same conclusion. It is not yet clear in law whether a publisher may be prosecuted before different juries for publishing different copies of the same book. In practice the cost of mounting full prosecutions and the seriousness and formality implied in putting the case to a jury make it unlikely that the result of the first jury trial will be challenged in a second case.

The test of whether an article is obscene is: will its effect, if taken as a whole, be such as to tend to deprave and corrupt persons who are likely to read, see or hear it?[41] There is nowhere any precise specification of what may and may not be published: no list of words not to be used, acts not to be described, or things not to be shown in illustrations or photographs. Each case is left to be considered on its own merits, in the light of the general test.

Two factors in particular make it difficult to decide whether a publication is obscene. An obscenity charge does not turn upon harm being done or contemplated to a specific person or group. The law is satisfied if there is a *tendency* to deprave or corrupt persons whose minds are open to immoral influences. No actual victims make their appearance in court; 'It is always someone else; it is never ourselves,' as counsel for the defence put it in the *Lady Chatterley's Lover* case. Secondly, there is very little knowledge of the effects of apparently corruptive literature on the 'consumers' who read or look at it. A significant departure was recently made in a prosecution of a firm that manufactures sweets for including obscene cards in their bubble-gum packets. The cards showed battle scenes, and were alleged to be likely to deprave and corrupt children for whom they were primarily intended. The magistrates refused to allow the prosecution to call child psychiatrists to give their opinion of the likely effects of the cards on children of different ages. But the Divisional Court held this to be wrong: the psychiatrists ought to have been permitted to say what they thought children might do as a result of looking at the cards, and even (since the case concerned children and was being judged by a body of adults) whether they thought that the children would be depraved or corrupted by doing so.[42]

Nonetheless the day when there is enough sociological and psychiatric information available to draw a scientific distinction between what is obscene and what may be published is still a long way off. In the meantime, the law will continue to call for a rough guess on a broad, common-sense basis. This lack of precision is reflected in the fact that it has never been settled whether a person is depraved and corrupted simply if he is induced to think immoral thoughts, or whether his thoughts must be followed by action. These circumstances combine to suggest that twelve ordinary citizens may be the most satisfactory tribunal to decide the issue. The law against obscene publication has, after all, the sole purpose of protecting the general public from direct inducements to immorality, and representatives of the public may be the body best able to decide whether a particular book is corruptive.

The difficult borderline cases do not arise in connexion with the considerable trade in books, magazines and photographs of which the one purpose is erotic titillation. A great volume of traffic in this kind of publication is dealt with each year under the forfeiture procedure before magistrates. The problems arise over books which have some claim to literary value, or which are intended as a serious description of facts or expression of views, but which are thought objectionable or dangerous by the police or some private citizen. Prosecutions concerning this kind of book have occurred in spasmodic bursts throughout the last fifty years, and have given impetus to the movement for reform which would give serious works greater protection against being found obscene. In 1955, prosecutions were brought against five publishers of novels, all of which had some claim to literary merit but which nevertheless contained frank descriptions of sexual activity. One pleaded guilty and the others were tried by jury. Of the latter, in one case the judge summed up strongly for the prosecution, and the jury convicted. But two of the other publishers were acquitted and the fifth discharged after the jury could not agree either at the trial or the retrial.[43] A reaction set in against the prosecution of books of this sort which was enough to achieve the limited reforms of the Obscene Publications Act 1959. This Act provides important new protections for serious publishers, by requiring the jury or magistrates, in deciding whether a book is obscene, to consider it as a whole – this obviates the undesirable practice whereby the prosecution could confine attention to the 'juicy bits'; and by introducing a new defence that, even if the book is obscene, its publication may be 'justified as being for the public good on the ground that it is in the interests of science, literature, art or learning, or other objects of general concern' – upon this issue the evidence of literary, artistic, scientific or other experts is to be admitted. The 1959 Act left it in the discretion of the prosecution to decide whether to take the case before a jury or to follow the destruction order procedure.

The way in which juries react to the prosecution of a work having literary merit under the new law was first tested in the prosecution of Penguin Books for publishing *Lady Chatterley's Lover*.[44] The jury was required to read the whole book through at an early stage of the trial, and to hear evidence of thirty-five expert witnesses on literary and ethical matters, all called by the defence. The ultimate verdict of acquittal did not reveal whether the jury thought the book was not obscene, or obscene but of sufficient merit to justify publication. The verdict was widely regarded as setting a commendable atmosphere of moderation for the future, but it left open the question of how a jury might act when faced with conflicting evidence from prosecution and defence literary experts.

Subsequently, there was distinct reluctance to use the procedure of full trial before a jury. When Cleland's *Fanny Hill* was produced in a modern cheap edition, the Director of Public Prosecutions decided to proceed by means of a forfeiture order before magistrates. When the publishers heard that search warrants were out they stopped further deliveries in order that there could be a test case, and asked the Director if he would proceed by way of a prosecution which could be tried on indictment. The Director somewhat disingenuously replied that because of the responsible manner in which the publishers had acted the case only merited the lesser proceedings for forfeiture. The Director was accused in the House of Commons of acting out of spleen towards juries as the result of the *Chatterley* case. However that may be, *Fanny Hill* continued to be dealt with by a series of proceedings for forfeiture before magistrates in different parts of the country where copies were found on sale. In London, the proceedings were heard by a single stipendiary magistrate, in other places before a bench of justices. All agreed that the book was obscene and the copies should be forfeited.[45]

The most recent developments have surrounded the publication in this country of Selby's *Last Exit to Brooklyn*. In 1966, Sir Cyril Black, M.P., obtained an order for seizure of copies of the book. A stipendiary magistrate afterwards found the book to be obscene and to lack the saving grace of literary merit, and he ordered the copies to be forfeited. The Government feared that this demonstration of the private citizen's rights to seek a forfeiture order might lead to a spate of annoying and costly proceedings by officious do-gooders. It was therefore provided in the Criminal Justice Act 1967 that a warrant for search and seizure could be issued only on an information laid by the Director of Public Prosecutions or a constable.[46]

The publishers of *Last Exit to Brooklyn* informed the authorities that they would not withdraw the book from circulation. The Director of Public Prosecutions eventually decided to launch a full-scale trial on indictment. The jury was faced with experts from both sides who gave conflicting views as to the literary and social value of the novel. It reached the same conclusion as the magistrate had earlier done; the publishers were fined £100 with £500 costs and the whole affair was estimated to have cost some £15,000. The publishers thereafter wrote to *The Times* pointing out that the book was 'written largely in demotic American and used expressions completely unfamiliar even to most British book reviewers. Some members of the jury claimed to have read it in a little over an hour and only one juror took more than five hours. We know that most people who have read it for review or to help the defence took considerably longer than that and they are highly literate people.'[47] The publishers went on to suggest that the verdict might lead to the prosecution of more books of an intellectual nature, dealing with controversial subject matter, and that jurors ought to be selected with A-levels as a minimum educational qualification.

There are separate questions here. The issue of the work's literary merit necessarily involves expert judgment, and it raises the question of a jury's ability to understand and judge the opinions of expert witnesses in an unfamiliar field. No one expects jurors necessarily to have any knowledge of the art of literary criticism. The experts may find themselves addressing twelve persons whose only regular reading consists of scanning tabloid newspapers. If the jurors succeed in understanding what the experts are saying, it is unlikely that they will properly appreciate, let alone have any sympathy for, the many values which lie behind the experts' judgments. In any case, where there is a conflict of evidence on the issue of literary or other merit, the unskilled nature of the jury must make it as unpredictable and as unsatisfactory a tribunal as almost any that could be devised. The law has accepted that literary merit is a defence. The issues raised by the defence ought to be dealt with separately before a tribunal that is adequately qualified to have some real understanding of the evidence and to be able to reach a conclusion that does not seem to be wholly the result of chance medley.

The tribunal could be a jury of twelve having a minimum standard of general education. But a smaller group drawn from a panel of acknowledged literary experts would be less cumbersome and at the same time better informed.

As the law now stands, literary merit is only a secondary question arising by way of defence once the material has been found to be obscene as tending to deprave and corrupt. This first issue has to be decided differently because it is not yet usually a question on which experts can provide evidence. As long as the criminal law continues to be used to control the publication of obscene literature (and this book is not the place to consider the broad question of whether such control is needed), the question whether a book is obscene is likely to be better settled by a jury than any other body. The one justification of the law is that it may protect members of the public against themselves, and to do this it has to make a very rough guess about the likely effects of a piece of literature on potential consumers. There will be some books for which the potential consumers are not ordinary members of the public, but are for instance children or a special group of readers. But mostly it is a question of the ordinary public's reaction to the work. A jury is perhaps more likely than any other tribunal to ask itself the unaskable question: are *you* likely to be depraved and corrupted by this book? Magistrates and judges, concerned with their position of public responsibility and having perhaps a less well-informed view of who is likely to get hold of the book and read it, may too readily assume that if it gets into the hands of others less intelligent or informed than themselves it is likely to do harm.

It is not the English practice to divide the issues in a criminal case so that they come before different tribunals, but nor is it usual for there to be a special defence which has to be proved by the defendant. Having separate tribunals to deal with the issues of obscenity and literary merit would mean that both would have to read the material before them; but this would only arise if the jury found against the defendant on obscenity. There would be no need to indulge in the costly and lengthy process of calling literary experts at all if the book was not obscene. The practical advantages of dividing the issues between an ordinary jury and a group of experts might be considerable.

The number of obscenity cases is likely to increase in the immediate future with the abolition of the office of Lord Chamberlain as pre-censor of plays. Since the eighteenth century it has not been possible to put on a play in public without the consent of this official of the Queen's House-hold. He and his staff have had absolute control over what may be said and done in a play, and if a performance was put on which was not under his licence those concerned might face prosecution for failing to obtain a licence. The grounds on which he has objected to proposed scripts in the past have been much wider than just indecency and obscenity and have included invidious representation of a living person or a person recently dead, violence to the sentiment of religious reverence, and interference with friendly relations with a foreign power.

As long ago as 1909, a Parliamentary Committee recommended that the Lord Chamberlain's licensing powers should cease to be compulsory, and in 1967 a Joint Select Committee favoured abolishing his functions altogether and leaving the promoters and performers of plays to the chances of the criminal law of obscenity after performance.[48] These recommendations have now become law. The Obscene Publications Act has in effect been extended to the theatre, the only basis for a prosecution being obscenity and the defence of literary and other merit being available. There is no limited procedure equivalent to the forfeiture provisions for publications, which means that in any prosecution the defence will have the right to opt for trial by jury. There is, it should be noted, protection against frivolous prosecutions by private individuals – it is necessary to obtain the Attorney-General's consent for a prosecution to be brought.[49] But it looks as though there will be more obscenity cases in the courts and the ability of juries to handle them will be more regularly under scrutiny. The pressure to remove the question of literary merit from them may well grow swiftly if there are more cases of the *Last Exit* type in which the jury is expected to resolve a conflict of expert testimony.

CONTEMPT OF COURT

If there really is a strong belief in the efficacy of the jury as the guardian of individual liberty against abuse of the criminal process, then there is one area of law in which it is surprising to find that the jury has been almost entirely superseded. It is the power of the courts to punish for contempt. The ambit of contempt is wide: it covers any conduct which brings the authority and the administration of law into disregard, or interferes with litigation.[50] As well as failure to obey the orders of a court, and direct interference with the proper conduct of proceedings (for example suborning witnesses and jurors), the superior courts may punish so-called 'constructive contempt'. This, in particular, includes expressing critical opinions of judges and publishing information or criticisms which would prejudice the fair hearing of a trial that is pending or in progress. Constructive contempts are nowadays tried summarily by a High Court judge, who has unlimited powers to fine or to imprison for a definite or an indefinite period. In some cases involving the press, judges have not hesitated to use this disciplinary power sternly as a general deterrent. In consequence the interference with liberty can be serious and the issue as to whether the power should rest in the hands of the judges alone is an important one.

Trial by jury was in fact the medieval method of dealing with contempt. But the Court of Star Chamber assumed power to commit for contempt without reference to a jury, and after its abolition in 1641 the common-law judges began to follow the same practice. In the result, the power to try contempts on indictment before a jury has fallen into disuse, and the accused has no right to demand it.[51] There are, however, other indictable offences which cover some of the same ground as contempt and which can be dealt with only by the ordinary procedures of the criminal law. For instance, it is a common-law misdemeanour to tamper with witnesses. Attempts to bribe or influence jurors constitute the ancient crime of embracery, and editors who print prejudicial information about trials may be convicted of attempting to pervert the course of justice. But in practice cases concerned with published reports of court proceedings or matters *sub judice* are dealt with as contempts of court.

In a number of questionable instances, newspapers have been found to be in contempt of court for publishing criticisms of a judge. Perhaps the most extreme example occurred in 1931, when the editor of *Truth* was fined £100 for casting wry aspersions on Lord Justice Slesser. The remarks suggested no more than that the judge was unconsciously affected by his political and social convictions. The matter is one on which judges' views will vary from generation to generation. Three members of the present Court of Appeal recently refused to hold Mr Quintin Hogg in contempt for inaccurate criticisms of the court that were much more trenchant than in the *Truth* case.[52]

The basis of this rule of contempt cannot be the private injury to the judge's reputation. For that, the law of defamation is available, although one supposes that a judge may be reluctant to use it. The justification is rather that the public may conceive a general distrust of the administration of justice. This is reflected in the law's classic test: in order that an attack on a judge be contempt, it must 'excite in the minds of the people a general dissatisfaction with all judicial determinations'.[53] It is surely unlikely that a judge is the best person to form an objective judgment of the effect on the public of a criticism of one of his fellows. It would be only natural for some judges to be ready to treat such criticisms as undermining the whole position of the judiciary. Here again the law calls for a judgment about public reaction – the best judges of the 'minds of the people' ought to be the members of a jury. It is not necessary to have a judge decide the question in order that a precedent may be laid down, for the strength and effect of each criticism will depend very much on the particular words used, the surrounding circumstances and the state of public opinion at the time. It would indeed be a measure of the maturity and wisdom of the judiciary that they should be prepared to give over to a jury the power of deciding what criticisms of them should be allowed.

The other aspect of the contempt power which deserves special mention concerns publications likely to prejudice the fair trial of a civil or criminal case. We saw in Chapter 3 how the fear that juries might be prejudiced by reports of committal proceedings led to limitations on the right to publish reports concerning them. For the same reason, it has been held to be contempt of court for a newspaper to publish information concerning matters which will be inadmissible in evidence at the trial, such as an accused person's criminal record or past history. In addition material which may cause a judge or juror to prejudge a pending or current case is published under risk of punishment for contempt. In a criminal case this prohibition begins with the arrest of the accused. It is clear that the judges have had the lack of experience of jurors very much in mind in developing the law so strictly. There is a rule that the law of contempt will not be applied so stringently where the hearing which may be prejudiced will take place before judges alone.[54]

In the United States, much greater freedom is allowed to the press to comment on pending trials. Newspapers conduct their own investigations, and interview parties and witnesses. Prosecutors allow publicity to be given to their examination of accused persons. In one recent case a sheriff had interviewed the accused on television and had extracted a confession from him. Because some jurors had seen the programme his conviction was quashed by the Supreme Court.[55] Such hazards do not arise in this country, and it is hard to avoid feeling that the administration of criminal justice proceeds in a calmer and more judicious way as a result.

The danger of the English approach is that the press will be unduly constricted in its ordinary reporting of court proceedings and matters over which litigation may arise, because of the way in which the judges are free to expand the law of contempt. One direction in which they began to do so in the late 1950s was to make publishers liable for contempt even though they did not know and could not reasonably have found out circumstances which rendered the publication wrongful.[56] Special statutory protection was given in 1960 to two situations: (i) where a person publishes information without appreciating that judicial proceedings are pending or imminent, and (ii) where a person distributes a publication without suspecting that its contents contain material that is in contempt of court. However, a person raising either defence must have taken all reasonable care to see that no contempt occurred.[57] In the same statute a right of appeal was given to a person found guilty of contempt. It is remarkable that until 1960 a single judge's unlimited power to punish a contempt was not even qualified by the basic safeguard of a right to appeal.

The question of whether trial by jury should be available in the area of publication which prejudices a fair trial has been made less important by these recent changes. The law is not here concerned to estimate public distrust in the administration of justice resulting from general criticisms of it, but to take steps to prevent specific proceedings being prejudged, especially by jurors who cannot be forewarned of the danger. This is something which a judge is likely to be in a better position to appreciate than a jury.

Moreover, it is important here that the law should be developed so that the press may be guided in what it may and may not do. A newspaper wants, for instance, to know what steps it must take in order to demonstrate that it did what was reasonable to ensure that no contempt occurred in the publication of a report; without this knowledge it cannot avail itself of the defence created in 1960. For instance, it is established that the press may report that a man is suspected of crime up to the moment of his arrest. Thereafter only the charges against him may be stated. If a newspaper mistakenly believes that a man has not yet been arrested, and publishes the wrong kind of report, what must it do to show that it took reasonable steps to ascertain the true position? It is right that the law should lay down an acceptable procedure which a newspaper may direct its editors and reporters to follow. This sort of law can be developed by the decision of judges in particular cases. A jury's verdict carries no equivalent promise that a subsequent jury in another case will come to the same conclusion. There is thus a special argument here for leaving the contempt issue to the judges, with correction by the legislature, if it is felt that they have taken a wrong turning.

8 · Civil actions

Juries are now used in only a small number of High Court cases each year, and very rarely indeed in the County Courts. So this chapter has two principal concerns: on the one hand, whether juries are worth preserving for the few cases that they now try; and on the other, whether they deserve to be given a more extensive role in the civil courts once more. It will be remembered that there are eight kinds of action where, unless there are unusual complications, a party may demand a jury (p. 74). Of these, defamation actions (libel and slander) are the most frequent, and false imprisonment and malicious prosecution occur with some regularity. Together they form a very small part of the business of the civil courts, though they attract a disproportionate amount of public attention. The right to demand a jury in such cases is still frequently exercised. The first part of this chapter accordingly explores the reasons for this continuing demand.

In contrast, there are three major areas of civil litigation – personal injuries, divorce and commercial cases – which have all at one time involved the use of juries, but are now almost invariably tried by judge alone. In the case of personal injury litigation, where the eclipse of the jury has been most recent, there are special questions concerning the assessment of damages which call for extended discussion. The other areas will be referred to more briefly. Finally, some consideration must be given to the future of juries in the civil courts as a whole, and the adequacy of the methods of trial which have replaced them.

DEFAMATION

The law of defamation affords protection against an unjustified attack on a person's reputation, and it is therefore an important limitation upon freedom of speech.[1] Attacks on reputation arise in innumerable ways, and an assortment of defamation cases is likely to be as variegated as it is colourful. It is a favourite fighting ground of the noted and the notorious, and it also serves to sort out small grudges between neighbours. But the ever-increasing scope and extent of press publications and broadcasting in this century has made it clear that the prime social function of the action for defamation has been and will continue to be as a control of the misuse of the power of mass media. The press, publishers of books and magazines, producers of plays, films and radio and television programmes for the most part watch warily to see that they do not transgress the defamation laws, often employing legal experts to read their copy in advance. Some go so far as to take insurance cover against liability, in which event the broker and his solicitors will play an important part in deciding whether potentially defamatory material shall be published or performed. The regular use of juries has had much to do with the impact of this branch of the law as a deterrent. On the issue of liability, that is the question whether the defendant has unjustifiably defamed the plaintiff, either side, or even both, may see a distinct advantage in having a jury. A plaintiff's advisers may consider that his case will best be made by a broad appeal to the sense of ordinary courtesy and decency of a jury, rather than by a technical assessment of the different issues specified by the law. Or it may be felt that a borderline case will be strengthened by relying on some special sympathy for the plaintiff, for instance, because he will appear as a lone David fighting the Goliath of the press. A defendant, on the other hand, may also see advantages in seeking the broad non-technical approach of a jury. Many statements alleged to be defamatory are damaging to a person only if a certain construction, or innuendo, is put upon them. It may be thought that a jury is more likely to discount ingenious innuendoes suggested by counsel for the plaintiff.

On the issue of damages, however, it is almost always the plaintiff who wants a jury, and the defendant who fears one. For one thing, juries are likely to assume that actual losses suffered by a plaintiff – for instance to his business or credit – are the result of the defamatory statement, whereas a judge will be more scrupulous in looking for evidence that there is in fact a connexion between the two. For another, it has been demonstrated over and over again that juries, when it comes to defamation damages, think in generous terms.

Liability

A statement is defamatory in law if it tends to lower the plaintiff in the eyes of right-thinking members of the community. The law has assumed this form just because the judges have traditionally been instructing juries and have assumed that they are addressing twelve 'right-thinkers'. In these broad terms, the burden of evaluating whether the plaintiff's reputation has suffered is placed firmly on the jury's shoulders. There are obvious reasons why a jury ought to be a satisfactory tribunal for the task. It is neither possible nor desirable that more specific rules of law should be developed for the purpose of determining whether a statement was defamatory or not. Words depend for their effect on their immediate context, on the meaning attached to them at the time, and on wider issues of social and moral attitudes and public knowledge. Moreover it is frequently not a question on which it is easy to achieve unanimity of opinion. Many statements, for instance, only appear injurious if looked at in one sense and not in another, or in the light of certain additional facts. The advantages of a jury are, first, its sheer number – for a verdict arrived at on the basis of many opinions is likely to be more acceptable than that of one or two persons; and secondly, that the opinions are drawn from representatives of the whole community and not simply from one sector of it. Here is yet another advantage to be derived from removing the property qualification for jury service.

Despite this, the record of juries in defamation cases is far from satisfactory. Much of the difficulty has sprung from the considerable complexity of many actions. An action about the import and effect of words can involve the trained mind in an orgy of speculation about possible meanings and inferences to be drawn from them. Add to this the fact that fashionable and expensive counsel are often involved, and the result is that finesse of pleading and argument have become a by-word of this branch of the law. This expertise will be devoted not only to the question of whether the statement was defamatory but also to the question of whether a defence, such as justification, fair comment or qualified privilege, applies.

It would be surprising if juries were not sometimes bemused by the proceedings. In some respects their presence may be salutary in that they will ignore unnecessary subtlety, but the results are not always so happy. Because it is the custom for the judge to ask for a special verdict on each of the different issues being tried, the jurors' sense of confusion becomes apparent from time to time when inconsistent answers are given to the various questions posed to them.

The difficulties experienced by defamation juries are recognized by the judges in the introduction of rules designed to prevent unreasonable verdicts. In the eighteenth century, it will be remembered (p. 83), judges for a time successfully asserted a right to settle the question of the libellous nature of a statement themselves; since 'libel' included seditious, blasphemous and obscene, as well as defamatory, libels, it had great political significance. This situation was eventually reversed by Fox's Libel Act 1792. But the judges did not lose their general right to refuse to accept an insupportable verdict. Indeed, in civil libel actions, unlike criminal prosecutions for libel, it was probably never the law that the judge, rather than the jury, decided whether the statement was defamatory. In the nineteenth century it became established practice for the judge to rule as to whether the statement was 'capable in law' of being defamatory before leaving the issue to the jury.[2] In other words, the judge had power to prevent the jury from judging the character of a statement when in his opinion it clearly could not be defamatory (see p. 108). But the cases show that there can be differences of opinion between judges even over this preliminary issue. In *Sim* v. *Stretch*[3] two ladies had indulged in lengthy domestic warfare over which of them should retain the services of one particular housemaid. The eventual victor sent the vanquished a telegram requesting her to send on certain articles belonging to the housemaid, including the money that she had borrowed from the housemaid. As the recipient of the telegram had not borrowed any money from the servant, she claimed that such an untruth injured her reputation. The trial judge held that the statement was 'capable in law' of being defamatory, and the jury found that it was 'in fact' defamatory. An appeal was lodged on the ground that the judge was wrong to hold that the telegram was 'capable in law' of being defamatory. Two out of three members of the Court of Appeal thought that the trial judge was right. But three members out of five of the House of Lords disagreed, and so the defendant eventually won, although, taking all three decisions into account, there was a larger number of judges who considered that the preliminary question ought to have gone against her.

This case, one of the silliest actions ever to be taken to the House of Lords, demonstrates how easy it is for opinions to diverge about the effect of a statement on a plaintiff's reputation, and suggests how difficult it might be for a judge to say after a jury's verdict had been given that its conclusion was insupportable. At present the judge gives his ruling on whether the words are capable of bearing a defamatory meaning in the presence of the jury. It is commonly feared that the jury takes this to mean that he thinks that the statement *is* defamatory.[4] This danger could easily be avoided by asking the jury to retire while he hears arguments and gives his ruling.

One matter that has recently given rise to difficulty is the question whether the defendant was actuated by malice. In law, malice means any improper motive, not necessarily spite or ill-will.[5] If the jury finds that the defendant acts maliciously in this sense, then he will lose the benefit of the defence of fair comment (that is, that he was expressing an opinion on a matter of public interest which did not go beyond the bounds of what is reasonably acceptable), or the defence of qualified privilege (that is, he made the statement in circumstances where the law recognizes that he should be entitled to do so, however damaging to the plaintiff). For example in *Broadway* v. *Odhams Press*[6] an article in *The People* had severely criticized the methods of a firm of stamp dealers. The dealers had advertised packets of stamps for sale by post and, on receiving an order from a young boy, had also sent him on approval a much more expensive packet as well as the packet he ordered. When this was neither returned nor paid for, solicitors' letters had been sent to the boy. With considerable ingenuity, it was suggested against the newspaper that members of its staff might have been motivated by malice. The jury found that while the comments had been fair, they had been made maliciously. On the evidence the Court of Appeal were most sceptical of this finding and were able to find defects in the judge's summing-up on the question of malice which allowed them to order a new trial. In another recent case, the jury returned into court to ask not only for further help on the definition of malice, but also for a dictionary. This the judge refused, saying that the dictionary definition of malice was irrelevant. But the jury would no doubt have taken it into consideration if they could have found it out.[7]

Even more revealing were the events behind the remarkable case of *Boston* v. *Bagshaw*.[8] The defendants, an auctioneer and a television company, had made announcements about the theft of three pigs saying that the thief had described himself as 'Boston of Rugeley'. The plaintiff answered that description, but as he had not stolen the pigs he claimed that he had been defamed. The defendants claimed that they were protected by qualified privilege, and the judge, before ruling on that issue, put various questions to the jury. These included, 'Were the defendants actuated by malice?', to which the jury answered: 'No'. The judge then ruled that the occasion was privileged, so that in the absence of malice the plaintiff should not be entitled to the £11,000 damages that the jury had awarded him. This roused a sense of indignation among the jurors, and when the case reached the Court of Appeal counsel for the plaintiff was able to say that he had affidavit evidence from all twelve of them stating that they had intended to answer the question about malice 'Yes' instead of 'No'. The Court of Appeal considered that the original verdict was clearly correct on the facts, and refused to consider the affidavits from the jurors dealing with their true intentions in returning their verdict (see p. 52). Interviews with the jurors by a newspaper revealed that, at least after the appeal was over, the jurors retained little impression of the judge's direction of the legal meaning of malice. Some thought that it meant spite or ill-will. Several seem to have been concerned that a finding of malice might reflect discredit on the police, who had sanctioned the broadcast, although they were not defendants in the action. It is hard to escape the conclusion that the jurors were prepared to answer the questions about malice in any manner which they hoped would give the desired result in the end: that the plaintiff should have his damages. The case does leave a feeling of serious disquiet about the ability of juries to comprehend the judge's instructions and apply them to the evidence in this sort of case.

So long as juries continue to be used in defamation cases there are a number of things that could be done to improve their performance on questions of liability. A thorough investigation should be made of methods of pleading and raising issues, if we are to deal adequately with the increasing number of criticisms of the complexity of libel proceedings. All is clearly not well when a Lord Justice of Appeal can remark:

This is an ordinary simple case of libel. It took fifteen days to try: the summing-up lasted for a day: the jury returned thirteen special verdicts. The notice of appeal sets out seven separate grounds why the appeal should be allowed, and ten more why a new trial should be granted, the latter being split over forty sub-grounds. The respondents' notice contains fifteen separate grounds. The cost must be enormous. Lawyers should be ashamed that they have allowed the law of defamation to become so bogged down in technicalities that this should be possible.[9]

When the case will involve the consideration of complicated technical evidence, as sometimes happens when a man says that his professional reputation is ruined, the court should be given power to order that the case be tried by judge alone, or possibly by a judge and assessors who have knowledge of the field in question. In order to avoid lengthy retrials, consideration should be given to the possibility of permitting verdicts by a bare majority, at least after the jury has deliberated for a certain period. In one recent case a plastic surgeon sued a Harley Street specialist for writing an article headed 'Be wary of those smooth-tongued "plastic surgeons"'. It took no less than three trials before a jury was found which agreed unanimously.[10] The costs and the amount of court time consumed were considerable. In a field of law where so much depends on the jurors' opinions, once there is a disagreement it is unlikely that it can ever be established that one view is clearly right and the other wrong. In such circumstances is it not as sensible to take the view of the majority of the first jury, as to wait until a jury is found all of whose members can be persuaded to the same opinion?

The difficulties that juries have recently been experiencing over malice as a bar to the defences of qualified privilege and fair comment are not easily solved. Some of the cases suggest that juries do not always feel that the law should provide these defences as a protection against having made a defamatory statement. Yet if the two defences were not available the right to report and comment on numerous public affairs would be put in jeopardy. At present the defences ensure that persons who make defamatory statements in such circumstances are protected unless they acted maliciously. The case for changing the law so that it reflects the view of such juries is weak. One step which might be taken would be to give the jury written instructions on the applicable law in a defamation case. The danger of instructions not being followed because the jury does not understand or remember them would be reduced. The more radical solution, recently espoused by a Joint Committee of 'Justice' and the International Press Association, is that the question of malice should be decided by the judge, not the jury.[11] It is true that the judge decides whether the occasion on which the statement was made gave rise to qualified privilege, but this can be justified on the basis that many of the occasions giving rise to qualified privilege are likely to recur. It is desirable to have the judge settle the question of whether a recurrent situation attracts qualified privilege or not, as a matter of law. On the other hand the question of fair comment is left to the jury. This is an issue which will depend very largely on the circumstances of a particular case. The same is true in respect of the motive for the defendant's conduct. The question of malice is in many ways an appropriate one for the jury, so long as juries are retained in defamation cases.

Damages

Clearly the money value of an injured reputation cannot be set at any precise figure. It is a matter of rough judgment on which there may be the widest differences of opinion. A not unsatisfactory solution may be to put the question to a large body of people such as a jury. Their discussion will inevitably produce compromise when opinions differ. Some juries deliberately add up the figures suggested by each member and divide by twelve.[12] Where the defamatory statement has been widely circulated – in a newspaper or a broadcast – a whole host of actions stand witness to the way in which juries think in big terms. In 1934 a Russian noblewoman, Princess Yousoupoff, obtained £25,000 from M.G.M. for releasing a film in which it was suggested that she had been raped or seduced by the monk Rasputin.[13] In 1962 two newspapers carried reports that a Mr Lewis was managing director of Rubber Improvements Ltd, and that the company's affairs were being investigated by the fraud squad. This was said to suggest that the company was being fraudulently run. It was not shown that any specific financial loss resulted from the publication of the reports. However, two juries in separate actions against the newspapers awarded the company £75,000 and £100,000 and Lewis £25,000 and £17,000 – total £217,000.[14] This was quite out of proportion to the level of damages for personal injuries. Had Mr Lewis been negligently injured in a car accident the only circumstance in which he might expect a sum even approaching the £42,000 which the jury gave him for defamation would have been if he were reduced to a state of quadriplegia – paralysed from the neck down without hope of recovery.

Although judges from time to time comment outspokenly about this disparity, their general practice on appeal is to interfere with a high award of damages only in circumstances where they are prepared to say that no twelve reasonable men and women could have arrived at such a figure. Because of this, Princess Yousoupoff's damages withstood an attack in the Court of Appeal, though the remarkable figures in the *Lewis* cases were upset. One reason why the judges are loath to interfere with a jury's verdict is that if they do their only course is to order a new trial before another jury on the question of damages. The Court of Appeal has no power to substitute its own award, as it would have on an appeal from a case tried by a single judge.

However, in the last five years, the judges have launched

a new line of attack on high awards. The basic purpose for which damages are awarded in a civil action is to give compensation to the injured plaintiff, but since the eighteenth century it has been recognized that in certain cases it has been possible to include in the damages a sum intended to make an example of the defendant and punish him if his conduct has been outrageous. In *Rookes* v. *Barnard*[15] (a case well known in connexion with the law of strikes), the House of Lords found that the idea of giving damages by way of punishment, rather than as compensation, was anomalous, and must in future be confined to cases where there had been an abuse of office, or where the defendant had deliberately calculated that his wrongful act would reap him a profit greater than any damages were likely to be. Moreover, even in these exceptional cases, only a very moderate sum should be given for the purpose of punishing the defendant.

This general rule was soon applied to defamation cases, because, although a jury's verdict itself involves no disclosure of how it was reached, it is a fair assumption that one motive in awarding a high figure is often to mark a distaste for the defendant's conduct. No doubt some jurors do not clearly distinguish the idea of punishment from the notion that a large enterprise can afford heavy damages. In one case, four newspapers misreported an incident at an inquest. They suggested that the doctor concerned in a hospital accident had tried to shift the blame for the mishap from himself, and had been reproved by the coroner. In fact, the doctor had accepted responsibility. The Court of Appeal refused to allow the jury's award of £9,000 damages to stand. In the Court's view, the jury must have been trying to punish the newspapers. A new trial on the question of damages was ordered.[16]

The stamp dealers' case, already mentioned in connexion with malice (see p. 214), came in for similar treatment. An award of £15,000 was upset. Recently Mr Justice Widgery has brought the point home by asking the jury to answer the following questions in a special verdict: 'What amount of damages should be awarded to compensate the plaintiff? Is the plaintiff entitled to exemplary damages? If so, what additional amount should be awarded on this account?'[17]

Rookes v. *Barnard* establishes that there is an exception allowing exemplary damages where the object of injuring the plaintiff was to reap a profit. It was arguable that a newspaper intended this whenever it published a libellous statement. But in accordance with their new tough approach to libel damages, the judges have refused to accept this.[18] A defamatory statement in the press will only come within the exception if it is proved that the particular statements were published with a view to making some special profit, as might occur if the particular story is given advance publicity or banner headlines.

It is hard to predict the long-term consequences of the attack on exemplary damages. If it succeeds in reducing the general level of awards, then the popularity of the jury may decline. But it may be that awards will continue to remain high – it is after all a reasonable argument that damages should be high where wide dissemination has caused very considerable injury. Moreover, if there has been deliberately wrongful conduct, it is possible in law to award a greater sum of damages to compensate for the aggravation arising because the plaintiff as well as losing reputation has been injured in a hurtful way. Moreover, the Court of Appeal may be discouraged from regularly upsetting verdicts because of the danger that the jury at the retrial, not knowing what damages were originally awarded, may fix a sum which is the same or higher.[19]

Such a situation might force the adoption of new methods of trial. The Court of Appeal might be given power to refer the issue of damages for retrial by a judge alone. Alternatively, it has been suggested that the jury's power to assess damages should be taken away from it entirely, leaving it to deal only with the question of liability.[20] We have already discussed the difficulties inherent in separating the functions of finding guilt and sentencing in a criminal court; they are perhaps even greater in actions for defamation. If a jury is left only to decide whether the statement was defamatory, it may well refuse to do so because it cannot know what damages the judge will decide to award. Take a case where at present the jury returns a verdict of guilty, but awards contemptuous damages of a halfpenny, thereby finding the defamation to have been technically proved but the plaintiff's action in some respect unjustifiable. A jury which feels that this is the proper solution overall is unlikely to feel that it can give a verdict for the plaintiff which cannot be qualified in this way.

The press loses few opportunities of emphasizing its view of the injustices of very high awards of libel damages. The sensational awards in the *Lewis* cases, even though upset on appeal, seem to have struck terror in the hearts of even the most courageous. Certainly fear of the consequences in court was said to have been the reason why knowledge that John Profumo had lied to the House of Commons was kept from the public.[21] The present system may bear particularly hard on provincial newspapers, which generally speaking live modestly by publishing local news and not on sensational journalism. Moreover, the prospect of large damages may make it financially attractive to issue a writ, and gold diggers in search of a sizeable sum of money rather than compensation for truly injured reputation are certainly not unknown. The 'Justice' Committee came to the conclusion that many of the complaints received by the press were motivated solely by the hope of gain.

The Committee also considered that the press should be given new protection from the operation of the libel laws, so that the freedom to publish news should not be fettered in cases where the newspaper cannot prove the truth of the statement up to the hilt before it goes to press. The recommendation was made that there should be a new qualified privilege, where an item of news has been published in good faith on a matter of public interest, the report having been based on evidence reasonably believed to be true. The only obligation on the newspaper would be to publish upon request a reasonable letter or statement by way of explanation or contradiction and to withdraw any inaccurate statements, with an apology if necessary.[22] Already two Parliamentary bills have been promoted by private members, seeking to achieve this reform. It may be noted that by calling a new defence on these lines a 'qualified privilege' the issue would be settled by the judge, not the jury. In fact the defence would involve two questions. First, whether the newspaper had taken sufficient steps to check the story. This, like the question in contempt proceedings as to whether the press had taken reasonable steps to check whether criminal proceedings had been instituted against a person, is one which deserves to be settled as a matter of law by the judges: the press is entitled to know whether a certain routine for checking statements is sufficient to protect itself or not. Second, there is the question of good faith, which is akin to that of malice, and this should be referred to the jury so long as other questions of malice are also settled in this way.

The grievances of the press have some substance, but before accepting their validity without further question we should ask why it is that juries are so ready to impeach the press for its conduct. No doubt they consider that large organizations can afford, and will only be affected by, large damages awarded against them as compensation for harm suffered. But they may also wish to air a general complaint about reporting methods which involve unjustified intrusions into private lives. The trouble really is that the law of defamation constitutes the only regular sanction that the individual has over the activities of the press. As such it is an imperfect weapon. In some respects – where a statement has been published about a person which is both damaging and untrue – it can be wielded with great force. In others – where the statement is either true or not destructive of reputation – it is not available at all. The law affords no redress for an unjustified invasion of privacy as such. The aggrieved individual can complain to the Press Council, which will hear the case and publicize any reprimand that it may find justified, but it has no other powers. The Council's Annual Reports show that cases of abuse are by no means infrequent.

Suggestions that the law should provide a right to privacy are often met with the objection that it would be too difficult to formulate a legal test defining those invasions of privacy which would be unlawful. But general rules of law concerning privacy have been evolved in the United States by the judges, and these principles and the cases from which they developed would make a useful starting point. The deliberations of the Press Council could also provide practical examples of press conduct which in the past it has held to be improper.[23] No doubt it would be extremely difficult to achieve any such change by legislative enactment in this country, because of the powerful interests that would fight it as a restriction of 'the freedom of the press'. What should be insisted upon is that no legislation should be passed to ease the operation of the law of defamation in favour of the press without a full investigation of the possibility of establishing a right of privacy.

If substantial reforms were to be achieved on the issues of malice, qualified privilege for innocent publication of a matter in the public interest, and the level of damages, the present popularity of juries in defamation cases may well decline. Yet the broad questions of evaluation which arise in the law of defamation – whether a person's reputation had been lowered, whether a comment was fair and so forth – seem matters which, for the most part, may well be settled by the opinions of ordinary laymen. Moreover, a jury will provide a large number of opinions. In the end, it therefore remains, so far as the settling of these issues is concerned, a tribunal with much to recommend it. Is it satisfactory to offer, as the sole alternative, trial by a single High Court judge? It may be argued that there is room here for some form of composite tribunal in which the judge sits together with a number of laymen, in order that these matters of judgment should not be left to one man, who is a professional lawyer. It must be remembered that there is a right of appeal from the judgment of a single judge to the Court of Appeal. Where the question in issue on appeal is a question of fact in the narrow sense – whether events did or did not occur – the appeal court will recognize that the trial judge had a considerable advantage through having seen the witnesses in court, and will therefore be reluctant to interfere with his decision. But in respect of intermediate questions of evaluation, the Court of Appeal considers that it is equally well equipped to make up its own mind. There is thus, under our present system, an opportunity of having the second opinion of three Lords Justices of Appeal added to that of the trial judge.

Nonetheless the point remains that this is an area of the law where many of the issues require broad value judgments which ought not to be the sole prerogative of lawyers. The best interests of the law might now be served by a composite tribunal of lawyers and laymen which would decide the 'questions of fact' as a group by majority vote.

FALSE IMPRISONMENT AND MALICIOUS PROSECUTION

In actions for false imprisonment and malicious prosecution, again either party has a right to demand a jury. The defendants in these cases are likely to be members of organizations concerned in the maintenance of public order. In peacetime this means the police. False imprisonment occurs from the moment that a person is unlawfully detained against his will, so that if the police wrongfully arrest a person or detain a suspect without authority and against his will they may be sued for damages. If a police officer brings unsuccessful criminal proceedings, then the person prosecuted can sue for malicious prosecution. But the plaintiff must be able to show that the officer acted maliciously, that is, from some improper motive, and that he had no reasonable and probable cause for believing that the prosecution would succeed.[24]

We have already noted (see p. 142) the propensity of some juries to take a sceptical view of the propriety of police behaviour. Actions for false imprisonment and malicious prosecution against police officers are liable to generate an atmosphere of recrimination and ill-feeling in which even the most moderate juror may be tempted to think that the case really is one where the police have overstepped the mark. Nevertheless the circumstances are just those in which any suspicion that the judge is siding with the police will cause the most obvious dissatisfaction. The two actions are therefore specially appropriate for jury trial.

A successful action against a police officer damages the reputation of the service as a whole. The judges have been ready to prevent a case which they consider unreasonable from reaching the jury, and recent judgments have not attempted to disguise the mistrust which, in this area, the judges have of juries. In false imprisonment, the substantial question is frequently whether the policeman has the power to arrest, and this generally turns on whether he had reasonable grounds for suspecting that the man detained had committed or was about to commit an offence for which he could be arrested. The judge decides whether his suspicions were reasonable as a 'question of law'. In malicious prosecution it is for the judge to decide whether the defendant had reasonable and probable cause for believing that the prosecution would succeed. Here again the question is deemed to be one 'of law'. In both instances the judge's decision is not intended to apply beyond the facts of the particular case.[25]

The judges settled that they had this power at the end of the eighteenth century, when the climate of feeling scarcely favoured the judges' claim to characterize conduct in a way which could be all-important in deciding the result of actions so closely connected with individual liberty. They therefore decided that the jury should first return a special verdict upon any facts in dispute relating to the question of reasonable cause for thinking that the prosecution would succeed. One fact often in dispute in this connexion is whether the defendant actually thought that it would succeed, and it therefore became common practice to ask the jury: 'Did the defendant honestly believe that the plaintiff was guilty?' If they answered 'No', it might then be difficult for the judge to rule that nonetheless the officer still had reasonable cause for believing that the prosecution would succeed, although that is, strictly speaking, an objective and not a subjective question. However, in recent cases the House of Lords and the Court of Appeal have strengthened the power of the judge, by stating that unless there is 'strong positive evidence' that the policeman did not believe in the case that he prosecuted, the jury should not be asked the question about his state of mind.[26] The sort of case in which this applies is one where a man is unsuccessfully prosecuted and he then sues the police, claiming, on his word alone, that the officer concerned made some remark to him during the prosecution which showed that he did not believe that there were grounds for laying the charge. This is denied by the police officer concerned. The judge is likely to decide that there is no 'strong positive evidence' on which to leave the question of 'honest belief' to the jury. This new restriction in the law reflects the view of the judges that juries are prone to return an unsatisfactory answer to the question. Lord Denning went so far as to say that he hoped that the question about the defendant's own belief would fall into oblivion: 'it has caused a cartload of trouble'. If it were put to the jury in every case, 'it would put every police officer at the mercy of an accused who happened to be acquitted'.[27]

The role of the jury on this question is therefore circumscribed. In malicious prosecution it still settles the quite separate issue: did the defendant act maliciously? Malice means any improper motive, as it does in the law of defamation. No doubt juries are just as troubled by the term here, but in practice the issue is of little importance beside the judge's decision on reasonable and probable cause. In both false imprisonment and malicious prosecution, the jury awards damages and the plaintiff may hope that allegations of dishonesty will produce a large award. Certainly juries have shown a tendency to think in ample terms. For instance, in a recent case of false imprisonment and malicious prosecution brought by two men against two police constables who had arrested them and prosecuted them unsuccessfully for attempting to steal a motor car, the jury assessed damages at a total of £8,000.[28] What was said about exemplary damages in connexion with defamation must apply here with equal force. It is no longer correct that the damages should contain an element intended as a punishment of the defendants. There has so far been no attempt to have damages in such a case reduced because the jury must have been trying to penalize defendants. Nor would it be easy to persuade an appeal court that this was so, for there must almost always be some element of spite or wrongful motive if the case against the defendants is found proved, and the jury is permitted in assessing damages to find that the plaintiff's injury was aggravated by its deliberately hurtful nature. These aggravated damages are represented by a sum over and above that awarded for the inconvenience to the plaintiff of being detained or the injury to his reputation which the institution of criminal proceedings may have caused.

The torts of false imprisonment and malicious prosecution provide a special remedy as the private citizen's means of legal redress against the police and other bodies for abusing their powers of arrest and prosecution. For this reason it will remain desirable to retain a jury for the court that tries these cases even if juries disappear from all other civil actions. Even if one accepts that judges or magistrates are unlikely to side deliberately with the police, there is still the likelihood that their experience will condition them to accept police evidence or to feel that the police ought to be supported. The judges have already developed the law quite sufficiently to prevent the jury giving rein to anti-police feeling in an unfair or bigoted manner. The present position represents a not unreasonable compromise, but care should be taken to see that the balance of power is not shifted further in favour of the police.

PERSONAL INJURIES

Actions that are the aftermath of accidents on the road and in the factory form a substantial proportion of all civil litigation. Their volume has increased enormously with the growth of industry and the increase in the number of motor vehicles. In the last century juries were regularly used to try personal injury actions, but gradually the proportion of cases has fallen. It was in 1918 that for the first time it became the rule that a party wanting a jury had to ask the court in its discretion to order one. After a temporary return, from 1925 to 1933, to the old position where a party could normally demand a jury, it was settled that a jury should be awarded only in the discretion of the court. After 1933, the Masters of the Supreme Court, who in practice dealt with most of the applications for a jury, and the judges who supervised them, were somewhat perplexed about the best means of exercising their discretion to award a jury. It was not obvious which factors should be taken into account. There was a tendency not to allow a jury unless the case involved some unusual feature. This tendency was challenged in 1937, in *Hope* v. *G.W.R.*, and the Court of Appeal held that the discretion was 'completely untrammelled'. It was not to be fettered by any rule that there should be a jury only when there was a special cause or reason.[29]

There followed at least a temporary rise in the number of jury trials in the King's Bench Division, but then came the war-time ban on civil juries. They were restored in 1948, but subsequently it has been in only a very small proportion of all civil cases that trials by jury have been ordered. No doubt one reason for the change has been the fact that solicitors and counsel have become used to the practice of having trial by judge alone. Certainly this was the explanation given by Lord Devlin, who offered as evidence the information that in 1956 only about 2 per cent of all Queen's Bench cases involved a request by one of the parties for a jury.[30] As far as personal injury actions are concerned, however, there are undoubtedly practitioners – especially those who act regularly for plaintiffs – who have always believed that their clients will do better before a jury, both on questions of liability and of damages. To them it was not a question of their reluctance to depart from well-trodden paths, but rather that masters and judges had made it clear that a jury would be awarded only in rare instances, and that therefore there was little purpose in applying for one. The only cases in which the application was likely to be successful were those in which the plaintiff had suffered an unusually serious permanent injury. On this basis, while it was true that by 1956 juries were rarely sought in personal injury actions, the responsibility for this state of affairs lay at least as much with the courts as with practitioners.

Liability

The question of liability in personal injury actions is determined upon a legal test which leaves a great deal to the judgment of the particular tribunal. A defendant will be liable for the tort of negligence if the circumstances of the accident were such that a reasonable man would have foreseen the likelihood of harm occurring, and therefore would have taken greater care to avoid it than the defendant did. Here all depends on the attitude of the reasonable man – 'the man on the Clapham omnibus'; this means the ordinary juror, for the law was formulated by judges for the purpose of summing-up to juries. Despite this, there have been reasons why many litigants and their legal advisers have come to prefer trial by judge alone on the issue of liability. One important factor has been the desire to achieve standard results in similar cases. Road and factory accidents often follow recognized patterns: centre-of-the-road collisions between cars overtaking in opposite directions, collisions where one driver has turned out from a side road into a main road, work injuries caused to a man who has not been instructed how to use a tool properly, and so on. Lawyers and insurance companies, who handle large numbers of claims and often have to advise on settlement without trial, want to predict with reasonable accuracy what attitude the 'reasonable man' will take upon liability in regularly recurrent situations. Although judges will differ to some degree in assessing what conduct is reasonable, variations amongst them are likely to be less than amongst juries. The long professional experience of the judges will lead to a consistency of attitude which cannot be expected of juries.

The kind of case in which a plaintiff's advisers are still likely to prefer a jury on the issue of liability is one where the evidence of negligence by the defendant is weak. It may be hoped to bolster the plaintiff's case by drawing forth a sympathetic response for the plight in which his injury has left him. Formerly, there were many more who belonged to this class of plaintiff, for it was the original doctrine of the common law that if the defendant could show that the plaintiff's own negligence contributed to his injury then the defendant had a complete defence to the action. Juries were then sought in order to mitigate harsh applications of this rigorous rule, and indeed they were considered to do so with sufficient frequency to make this a well-recognized instance of a rule of law which juries refused to enforce consistently. It is interesting to note that in parts of the Commonwealth and in the United States, where juries are still used with some frequency to try personal injury cases, in many instances the strict common-law defence of contributory negligence has not been altered by statute: mitigation is left to the conscience of particular juries.[31] In England, however, a change was introduced in 1945; it was laid down that if a plaintiff was proved to have been contributorily negligent he should lose only a proportion of his damages, the proportion being a rough assessment of the extent to which his own negligence, rather than the defendant's, was the cause of his injury. This change undoubtedly reduced the demand by plaintiffs for juries to try the issue of liability.

Damages

The question of what damages a defendant should pay for personal injuries involves problems that are among the most intractable that the courts have to face. In recent years it has been this issue rather than the question of liability which has caused parties to seek juries. Damages are assessed under a number of different 'heads'. Some items under these heads represent direct compensation for financial losses incurred before the date of the trial, such as losses of earnings and outlay for medical treatment, and these rarely give rise to serious dispute. But most other parts of the total award require at least some degree of intelligent guesswork. If the injured man is likely to go on suffering loss of earnings after the trial then he is entitled to compensation for what he would have earned but for the accident. This may turn on a variety of factors: his prospects of promotion before the accident, the age at which he would have retired, events which might have caused him to stop work before that age, the chance of his finding suitable alternative employment and his prospects in it, and so on. Other heads again are even more difficult. An accident victim may qualify for damages for loss of expectation of life, pain and suffering, loss of happiness in the future, or the inconvenience of having to live without some physical or mental capacity which he previously had – 'loss of amenities' as it is called. Here it is quite impossible to measure the rightness of the sum of damages by reference to financial losses, real or prognosticated, and the amount actually awarded has simply to be one that the court settles on the basis of the vague criterion of 'fairness' or 'reasonableness' to both parties. These difficulties are inflamed by the invariable rule that damages must be a single, once-for-all lump sum. It is not possible to provide for weekly or monthly payments even when the plaintiff's condition may change in the future.[32]

When a judge sits alone he deals with the damages dilemma by trying at least to follow a consistent course from one case to another, so as to achieve relative fairness between different sets of parties. This has led to the theory that the judges award damages within certain conventional limits, a theory which has been rendered more plausible by the appearance of manuals (particularly those of Kemp and Kemp, first published in 1953) which collect together systematically a growing number of representative cases. These conventions remain broad indications of 'the kind of figure' one can expect a judge to give for a particular sort of injury. There are still 'plaintiffs' judges' and 'defendants' judges', and

Kemp and Kemp provide a convenient list of each Queen's Bench judge's awards to enable one to tell whether a particular judge is usually above or below average. The judges have been slow to allow counsel to draw attention in court to earlier awards in similar cases – so the damages manuals have remained out of sight, if not out of mind.[33] Moreover, the various conventions are meaningful only in relation to the different 'heads' of damage. Yet in cases where the assessment is made under more than one 'head' (for example for loss of earning power, pain and suffering and loss of amenities) the judges have refused, save in exceptional cases, to do more than state the total award without dividing it up under heads.[34]

In the result, it is often impossible to tell whether meaningful conventions have been followed or not. The Court of Appeal exercises a power of surveillance over the awards of damages made by judges in personal injury cases and can alter an award which it considers to be out of line with the vague conventions. The Court does whatever seems reasonable to secure a rough uniformity between similar cases.

On the other hand, if there is a jury, there is no question of conventions being observed. The jurors do not know the conventions, and neither counsel nor the judge is permitted to say anything which might enlighten them.[35] If the verdict is outside the limits of what one might expect from a judge, the Court of Appeal has no power to alter the jury's verdict itself. It has no equivalent power to that wielded by appeal courts in America, of offering the party who has lost the appeal the alternative of a new trial, or of accepting the figure which the court thinks right; it can only order a new trial.[36] And since it still pays the traditional judicial respect to a jury's verdict, it will interfere only if the sum given by the jury shows such a radical departure from normal that it is obliged to find that no twelve reasonable men could have arrived at such a verdict.

What this situation produces is the *chance* that a jury will give a verdict for a sum substantially higher than a judge would give, but which will withstand assault on appeal. This very chance puts the plaintiff's solicitor in a good bargaining position for reaching a favourable settlement out of court. Whether it is true in England to say that juries would regularly arrive at these higher awards is another matter. The evidence one way or the other is slight, because juries have been used so infrequently in the post-war period. If one looks at the twenty or so reported jury awards of the last fifteen years, it is fair to say that about a third of them are higher than could be expected of a judge; a slightly smaller proportion seem low by comparison, and the rest are not readily distinguishable. But those which are higher are in some cases markedly higher. In 1962 and 1963, two cases concerning quadriplegics (persons paralysed in all limbs) were litigated, and for the first time in a case concerning such an injury medical evidence established that progress in the treatment of quadriplegics was such that there was no calculable shortening in the life span of the patient. Juries were ordered to try both cases, and in assessing damages each arrived at figures around £50,000. The Court of Appeal considered that a judge sitting alone would have awarded between £30,000 and £35,000, but this in itself was not a ground for upsetting the awards. In one case the award stood; in the other the judge's summing-up was found to be sufficiently misleading to require a new trial on damages.[37] These awards occurred just before the judges were the subject of considerable criticism for their parsimony in awarding damages, and the two factors seem to have combined to produce a new ceiling for damages in the most serious cases, and some consequent increases at all levels of seriousness.[38]

In Commonwealth jurisdictions, where juries are still regularly used in personal injury actions, it is by no means universally the case that insurance companies, who are the usual real defendants, fear a jury trial. Many of their representatives consider that what may be lost on the swings of the most serious cases, where sympathy for the shocking plight of the plaintiff may cause a jury to make a high award, may be made up on the roundabouts of the less horrifying. An Ontario judge recently remarked:

It is my experience that it is the insurer who serves jury notices. The reasons are not hard to find. Juries unacquainted with the value of these claims generally assess damages in an amount lower than a judge, sometimes considerably lower. If a defendant must go to trial and lose, it is a good chance the verdict will be in modest proportions if the jury is composed of farmers and workmen. The exception is the occasional jury of businessmen in a metropolitan area.[39]

In the United States, a number of advocates have widely publicized their ability to wring high awards of damages from juries, and in consequence it is commonly the plaintiff who feels that he will have the advantage of trial by jury and not by judge alone. This view is confirmed by a recent finding of the Chicago Project that on average American juries award damages at a rate 20 per cent higher than judges would for the same cases.[40]

At the end of 1962, the Court of Appeal, led by Lord Denning, the Master of the Rolls, delivered the first of a series of judgments that have resulted in a change from occasional juries in cases of serious permanent injury, to trial by judge alone in virtually all cases. These decisions culminated in *Ward* v. *James*[41] when a five-judge court unanimously decided that the 1937 decision in *Hope* v. *G.W.R.* (see p. 227) did not prevent the court from now holding that the discretion to order a jury in these cases should be exercised only where there were 'exceptional circumstances'. A variety of different reasons were given by the court: jury trial is longer and more expensive and so requires a special justification; the Court of Appeal is prevented from exercising satisfactory supervision because its power to allow appeals from jury verdicts is too closely circumscribed; jurors may be improperly influenced by the knowledge that an insurance company stands behind the defendant although it is not named as such. But the basic reason given by the Court was that since most assessments of personal injury damages must be conventional, and as judges know the pattern of awards but juries do not, only the judges can properly do justice between the plaintiffs and defendants in different cases. It is surprising for the Court of Appeal so nakedly to depart from a clearly established precedent such as *Hope's* case, but in this case the judges were obviously influenced by the recent emergence of more clearly defined 'conventions' regarding damages.

Was the Court of Appeal right to take the step of virtually eliminating the jury in personal injury actions? There were two sensible courses open to them: either to increase the number of juries or to eliminate them altogether. The former course would have given fuller rein to the view that the level of awards for damages can best be settled by reference to ordinary opinion in the community, the latter to the view that judicial conventions are the proper answer. Apart from the awards in the two quadriplegic cases, which together with the reaction to *Ward* v. *James* certainly contributed to recent increases in judicial awards, it is difficult to see that the isolated jury awards under the post-war system were of advantage to anyone save the occasional plaintiff. On the whole, they were too infrequent for much notice to be taken of them.

There is much to be said for the Court of Appeal's choice of alternatives. Consistency in awards of damages is a desirable aim, and it is hopelessly euphoric to expect juries to achieve this without previous experience by calling on some mysterious communal ethos. But it is hard to accept the Court's view with unqualified approval: for that, there are too many defects in the method of assessing damages currently practised by the judges. Consistency in awards is desirable, but it is not the only virtue to be cultivated. Conventional awards can secure that like cases are treated alike, and that their seriousness in relation to one another is reflected in the comparative size of the damages. But in themselves the conventions can tell us nothing about the principles on which the various 'heads' of damages are founded, nor about the rightness of the range of awards which the conventions cover.

The size of his damages is a matter of great importance to the plaintiff, yet their ascertainment is often marked by a brevity of argument and calculation which appears to be at the least casual. Various factors contribute to this impression. As already mentioned, the judges are reluctant to do anything other than announce a cryptic total of damages. Lord Goddard once went so far as to suggest[42] that it was the total sum and not its components to which the conventions should be applied; this renders the concept of 'heads' of damages and conventions quite meaningless. The Court of Appeal has directed counsel to draw the judge's attention to other cases 'only very sparingly' because they were 'always most anxious not to put any additional burden on judges of first instance. They have quite enough to do'.[43]

This has also led to a failure to seek information which would reduce the elements of guesswork involved in the very principles which the judges say they are applying. Suppose a man has lost his power to earn in the future. The amount of damages will depend on predictions of the victim's ability to earn but for the accident. Detailed information of average life and earning expectancies for persons of different ages, occupations and sex have been built up by actuaries for life-assurance companies. The courts could well use this information, which actuaries could provide either as expert witnesses or as court experts. Yet solicitors have been given no encouragement to call actuaries as witnesses in these cases. Instead the judges make their own guesses. Professor Street has shown incontrovertibly that their assessments under this head are regularly low, sometimes ludicrously low, compared with the expectancy of earning based on actuarial calculations.[44]

In some cases the *total* award under all the heads is less than an actuarial figure for loss of earnings alone. In Australia, Canada, South Africa and the United States this kind of assistance is welcomed in the courts. There is no reason why England should lag behind. Again, the conventional figures should be adjusted to take account of falls in the value of money, but this happens only haphazardly and spasmodically. No evidence is taken of price indices or other scales which have been suggested as guides to such calculations.[45]

Awards for such matters as pain and suffering and loss of amenities cannot be precisely calculated sums, but little thought has been given even to general principles on which proper conventional figures might be settled. The construction of a scientifically worked-out scale of awards would require careful analysis of injuries and losses actually incurred in recent years, in order to predict the fund that ought to be created to meet future claims.[46] The judges have never called for such information to be produced. It may be that greater emphasis should be placed on the future happiness or security which the victim of an accident can buy with his damages rather than the monetary value of his actual loss and suffering.[47] There is evidence of a general kind that the lack of serious thought devoted to the assessment of damages has meant that the levels at which our conventions, such as they are, have settled are much lower than in some other western countries, particularly in some parts of the United States and Belgium.

The search for rational bases for the assessment of damages presents difficult problems, but it does not deserve to be shrugged off as intractable. The underlying premise of the decision of *Ward* v. *James* was that the existing system of assessment by the judges was as satisfactory as any other. The decision itself had a very small practical effect of bringing to an end the occasional jury trials. Yet it was scarcely surprising that it provoked a heated outcry against the methods followed by the judges. The extinction of trial by jury was seized upon as the only available stick with which to stir up stagnant waters. The protests included a Commons motion deploring the decision, and this led to the appointment of a Committee under the chairmanship of Lord Justice Winn to consider procedural questions, and the question of damages was taken up by the Law Commission.

The problems of providing an adequate system of compensation for personal injuries are complex, because the variety of possible solutions is considerable. The most radical proposals would abandon or seriously restrict the ambit of the common-law action for damages based on the defendant's negligence. In its place would be substituted a system of recovery on an insurance basis, in which the defendant's negligence was no longer a necessary element in the right to compensation. In principle this would resemble the rather limited National Insurance scheme which at present provides benefits for those who have received an industrial injury.[48] An insurance scheme would remove the problems of assessing liability which arise in a common-law negligence action. But some system of assessing the level of compensation would have to be devised, and this presents the same problems as do less adventurous plans to improve the existing system. One crucial question is the extent to which the system of single lump-sum payments should be abandoned in favour of periodic payments by the week or the month. Such a change, even if it were only partial or optional, would do away with many of the problems of prognostication presented by the present method. It would also provide a means for supplying immediate relief to the victims of accident at a time when they are most likely to need it. Under the present system, this might be associated with a much earlier trial of the question of liability.

Even if the guesswork involved in the assessment of damages for personal injury is reduced by being able to take account of a plaintiff's actual circumstances from time to time, there is still a need to carry out careful investigation of the costs of accident compensation systems and of the financial needs of those who are injured, in order to establish appropriate levels for awards. In moving towards a scheme under which the assessment of damages is based upon specific and complex social data, inevitably one is leaving behind the world in which the rough judgment of a random group of jurors has any useful role. A great deal remains to be discovered and discussed before an adequate new system emerges, but there can be little doubt that when it does emerge it will require the judgment of experienced professionals and not of untrained laymen.

COMMERCIAL CASES

By the eighteenth century, the common-law courts had become the forum for the litigation of many commercial matters. As a consequence, trial by jury was the established method of trying commercial disputes, until it became possible for litigants to ask for trial by judge alone. In 1895, a Commercial Court was established within the Queen's Bench Division, and very rapidly it became the practice there for litigants, on the advice of their lawyers, to request trial by judge alone. The reason seems clear: jurors, whether common or special, were quite unfitted to try such cases. The Mersey Committee in 1913 heard heavy criticism of their performance in 'actions involving questions of policies of insurance, bills of exchange, bills of lading, charter parties and customs of mercantile trades of which probably they have never heard until they go into the box'.[49] There has been no serious attempt to reintroduce them since that date. We have already seen that the City of London special jury, carefully preserved for commercial cases when special juries were otherwise abolished in 1949, has not in fact been used since 1950 (see p. 33).

But it is not simply juries that are unpopular among commercial litigants. The courts themselves have lost much of their work in the field to private arbitration. Arbitration has spread because it suits the convenience of business people. It can be cheaper, quicker and more private than court proceedings. It can be held at times suitable to the parties and the arbitrator. It can even serve as a method of keeping a dispute out of the hands of lawyers. One particular advantage, of importance from our point of view, is that it has been a means by which an expert in a non-legal field can be brought in to adjudicate in a dispute, for even a High Court judge who has practised at the commercial bar cannot be expected to have the specialized knowledge of a particular trade which has become second nature to a man whose whole professional experience has been in that one field.

The popularity of arbitration is to some extent beginning to wane, because in some spheres it is becoming expensive, time-consuming and difficult to find suitable arbitrators. It is probable that there will be new pressures to return to the forum provided by the High Court for the settlement of commercial disputes. The question must then be faced whether it should not become the practice to constitute the court in a way that will provide the kind of expert adjudicator who is available in private arbitration. There is room here for considering whether some system of trial using expert assessors should not be developed. Nautical assessors have by long-established custom been used in Admiralty cases, which deal with collisions and the like. Experts in navigation, usually Elder Brethren of Trinity House, sit with a High Court judge, and with the Court of Appeal.[50] Their function is not to adjudicate but to advise the judge, who is free not to accept their opinion if he wishes. This may seem curious; the justification given for it is that experts may judge by too high a standard in assessing, for instance, whether the master of a ship has been negligent.[51] There are rules of court which allow the assessor system in this form to be extended to other cases, though it is very rare for the practice to be adopted.[52] If it were desired to give non-legal experts a power of decision, then it would be necessary to alter the rules in order to allow this.

Even in commercial matters which do not call for trade or technical expertise, juries are no longer sought. Sometimes a judge is heard lamenting the lack of a jury when he is faced with having to resolve a direct conflict of evidence,[53] but this is infrequent. In an age when many transactions are put into documentary form, many commercial disputes are in any case concerned with the construction of written agreements, and questions of construction are traditionally treated as 'questions of law' for the judge. The modern justification for this rule is that by this means a particular verbal formula will have a consistent legal consequence. It is most important that legal practitioners should be able to advise clients with certainty on the effect of using particular forms. Hence the possible role of a jury in modern commercial disputes is in any case circumscribed.

DIVORCE

It became possible to obtain a divorce in England by means of a court order, as opposed to an Act of Parliament, in 1857. The court established to try the new divorce actions was likely to be faced with defended cases in which there was hard swearing on either side, since the basis of divorce law was proof that the defendant had committed a matrimonial offence. In consequence it was provided that either party should have the right to require trial by jury, and the practice became fairly common. By the 1900s some 50 per cent of defended cases were being tried by jury.[54]

Fifty years of experience with juries did not prove altogether happy, for in 1912 the Royal Commission on Divorce recommended that they be abolished. The grounds of objection were that a jury were sought only by a party who had a weak case – particularly by petitioners who were seeking to establish cruelty, or by a party who only wanted to delay the proceedings, or to increase the costs, or to get heavy damages from a co-respondent for seducing the petitioner's wife. However, no change was made until 1933, when it was established, in common with most other kinds of civil action, that a jury could be awarded in a divorce case only in the discretion of the court. Before that date there had in any case been a considerable decline in the proportion of contested divorce cases tried by jury. The change in 1933 continued the atrophy; since the war their appearance has been only occasional, and they now appear to have died out completely.

It is unlikely that many would support their revival. The Committee on Procedure in Matrimonial Cases which sat shortly after the war took the same attitude as the 1912 Royal Commission, giving as its reason the broad ground that in a divorce case the court had a duty to consider the public well-being, as well as the interests of the parties, and this could best be met by leaving the issue to a trained judge. But no doubt the objections raised by the 1912 Commission remain just as pertinent today. Until recently, all divorce cases, defended and undefended, have been tried in the High Court before a High Court judge or special commissioner. Now the County Courts have also been given jurisdiction to hear undefended cases, but it is unlikely that the change will spread to defended cases as well. Previously the County Courts played little part in the administration of family law generally, the one exception being the making of adoption orders, a jurisdiction which is shared with the High Court and the Magistrates' Courts. Magistrates' Courts, however, have a wide family jurisdiction, dealing with, amongst other things, matrimonial disputes such as applications for separation and maintenance. The recent extension of divorce jurisdiction to the County Courts has only served to emphasize the degree of diffusion of jurisdiction over family matters.

It is by now a much-discussed suggestion, with much to recommend it, that a single set of Family Courts should be established to deal with all the various issues, including perhaps the criminal liability of juveniles. The proper way of constituting Family Courts raises interesting problems. Is it right to place the power of decision in the hands of a single judge, as now occurs in the High Court and the County Courts? Could a legally qualified judge and two lay justices do the work? Such a court now sits in London, for London stipendiary magistrates are obliged to have two justices of the peace with them on the bench when they sit to hear matrimonial matters. It is unlikely that in this connexion much thought will be given to any possible role for juries. It is increasingly recognized that in family matters that involve legal disputes it is important to build into the administration of the law a method of settlement that leaves room for conciliation and agreement based on an investigation of all the family circumstances. A formal jury court, in which issues are fought out by opponents and the judge merely acts as 'umpire', could not provide the proper atmosphere or procedure. The development of social work as a profession, with tasks carried out for the courts by probation officers, has facilitated the emergence of an entirely new approach to legal aspects of family problems. As far as the constitution of Family Courts is concerned, the important question is to what extent trained social workers should be given places on the bench. It would clearly be unsatisfactory for the social worker involved in a case also to adjudicate upon it, and very difficult to build up and retain the family's confidence in such circumstances. But there might well be a place, once the present shortage of properly trained workers is overcome, for social workers not connected with the probation service at the court in question to sit on the bench together with trained lawyers and possibly experienced justices of the peace such as the ones who at present sit in juvenile courts.

In serious criminal cases, doubts about the manner in which juries fulfil their functions have so far not led to the abandonment of the system; but in the civil law, it is often the same objections which have led to trial by judge alone. Civil actions involving sophisticated commercial dealings were quickly taken out of the hands of juries once the parties had a choice in the matter; in criminal frauds juries still struggle with complex accounting and similar evidence. In the criminal courts where the issue is whether the defendant is proved guilty beyond reasonable doubt, many people accept that if juries go wrong it is in the accused's favour, and a measure of 'jury equity' is regarded as something valuable in itself. But failure to understand the evidence or the law, and verdicts that are produced by special sympathy or aversion, are not so acceptable when the loser is not the state but a private litigant.

THE JURY

In the last chapter it was suggested that there were parts of the criminal law, such as obscene publications and contempts of court by denigrating judges, which needed jury trial because the law turned on some reaction of the ordinary public. The same may be true of certain areas of civil law. For instance the protection of advertising and sales goodwill depends partly on the right to bring a 'passing-off' action against other traders who produce or advertise their goods in a way that might lead to their being mistaken for those of the plaintiff. An essential question is whether members of the public could be confused by such devices, and be unable to distinguish the defendant's goods or business from those of the plaintiff. A jury representing the general public may well be the proper tribunal to settle such a question. But the present disfavour into which civil juries have fallen makes it unlikely that they will acquire new roles in such cases.

In general, civil juries have not survived for cases in which there is likely to be a clash of evidence as to the facts, though judges often regard juries as being particularly good at settling such questions. Where they have been retained longest, it has been for cases in which an important issue requires a value judgment which can only be made as a matter of rough common sense – as in the assessment of damages for personal injury and defamation of character. There has been a tendency to develop processes for avoiding the need for general guesswork. It is to be hoped that the method of assessing personal injury damages is about to go through this transformatory stage. When this occurs, the questions to be settled by a court require background knowledge and special experience. The jury's only future role in the civil courts can only lie in a kind of case where there is special reason for wanting a broad judgment from a random group of representative laymen. There are few such situations.

9 · A miscellany

This chapter serves two purposes. The first section draws attention to the fact that the use of juries has never been restricted merely to the trial of issues between the parties in civil and criminal cases. As we saw in Chapter 1, the Norman Kings used the 'group inquest' for administrative purposes before Henry II turned the jury to account in the royal courts. Juries which find facts rather than try issues have continued in use ever since. Today there are only two of these special kinds of jury which require discussion: the jury which is empanelled to try the preliminary question of whether a person accused of crime is fit to stand trial, and the jury summoned by the coroner to inquire into a sudden or unexplained death. The other examples are mainly picturesque ceremonies which have a jury character, such as the trial of the pyx, an annual occasion when six or more goldsmiths attend at the Royal Mint to see that coins are being properly compounded.[1]

The second part of the chapter refers to two kinds of juries, those which used to determine questions of compensation for compulsorily acquired land, and those which decided whether a person was a lunatic; both have now disappeared in favour of other special tribunals. The purpose of mentioning these juries is to draw attention to the absence of any similar institutions among modern administrative tribunals. These special tribunals are now so various as to rank in importance beside the ordinary courts, and it must be relevant to the future role of the jury that such tribunals are not constituted on the jury model.

THE JURY

FACT-FINDING JURIES

Criminal trials: ancillary questions

There have always been certain ancillary questions, relating to criminal trials, which require facts to be settled by a specially empanelled jury. For instance, a jury was called upon to determine whether a woman already under a sentence of death was pregnant. If she was, her sentence was commuted to one of life imprisonment. Until 1931, this jury was composed of matrons, the one occasion on which women performed jury service before 1919.[2] Now such a jury would be chosen in the ordinary way, but the virtual abolition of capital punishment for the present has rendered it obsolete.

Before a criminal trial begins, there may arise the question of whether an accused is fit to plead and stand his trial. He may be quite unable to communicate with the court, for instance because he is a deaf mute. Or he may be insane to such a degree that he cannot understand the charge or the difference between pleading guilty and not guilty, and is not able to challenge jurors, instruct counsel or follow the evidence. The defence, the prosecution, or even the judge may raise the question of whether the accused is suffering from one of these disabilities, in which case he is detained without trial. The judge is able, if he thinks it expedient, to postpone the trial of this question until after the prosecution's case on the charge in the indictment has been given. This power has been conferred because otherwise the defence will be precluded from raising questions about whether the accused committed the crime at all. When the fitness of the person to be tried is dealt with at the outset, and the jury finds that the accused is not 'under disability', then a new jury must be empanelled to try the case proper. Where the question is delayed, then the jury which has so far been hearing the case may also be used to decide the question of 'disability', if the court directs it to do so. Alternatively, a new jury may be used.[3]

If there is a real dispute about a defendant's sanity at this stage, then the same kinds of expert medical and psychiatric evidence will be given as would be given where the defendant raises a defence of insanity or diminished responsibility to the charge itself. The same problems arise concerning the ability of a jury to assess such evidence. It does, however, seem right that the same method of trial should be applied to the question of insanity at the time of the trial and at the time of the crime. If an accused is found to be insane on either occasion the consequences are that he will be detained in hospital for an unspecified period of time. The restriction of liberty is the same. If a jury tries the one question, it should also try the other.

Coroners' juries

In the Middle Ages the coroner was a local official of considerable importance. He was appointed by the Crown to carry out a wide variety of inquisitorial duties, many of them connected with protecting and enforcing royal property rights and payment of fiscal dues to the Crown. One function was the investigation of unnatural death, for the Crown derived various forms of revenue from the estates of dead men. This has now become the coroner's principal duty, though he may also find himself investigating treasure trove, or, in the City of London, the cause of a fire.[4] If, after a first look at the matter, he has reasonable cause to believe that a death was violent, unnatural or from an unknown cause, or if it took place in prison, he is bound to hold an inquest. Formerly a jury was always summoned. Like a grand jury, it was composed of between 12 and 23 members. In 1926 it was reduced in size to between 7 and 11 members, able to decide by majority if there were no more than two dissentients. At the same time coroners were given power to dispense with the jury altogether and hold the inquest alone, except where they suspected homicide, or the death occurred in prison or was caused by an accident (including a motor accident), poisoning, or certain diseases or conditions prejudicial to the health or safety of the public.[5] Coroners' juries have never been subject to precise qualification rules and it was formerly quite common for the coroner's officer to summon inmates of the workhouse as jurors or to use the same jurors time and time again. Such practices were disparaged and coroners were encouraged to see that a broader selection of jurors was made.[6] But there has never been any implementation of the recommendation of the Wright Committee that coroners' juries should be selected in the same manner as trial juries.[7]

A full inquest with a jury, to investigate a death where there is suspicion of foul play, can be an unsatisfactory proceeding because it may develop into something akin to a trial of some person implicated in causing the death. But this person is not himself accused before the coroner, and will have no right to cross-examine witnesses – though he may be permitted to do so – nor to address the jury. Moreover, the coroner will be more closely involved in the conduct of proceedings than is usual in an ordinary court. His role is inquisitorial. He may order that investigations be carried out. He will decide which witnesses to call and will conduct the examination of them himself. He is not bound to adhere to the rules of evidence, and this may result in the publication of prejudicial information which would not be admissible evidence at a trial. The jury may return a verdict of murder, manslaughter or infanticide against a named person, and thereupon the coroner must issue a warrant for that person's arrest and he will be committed for trial upon the coroner's inquisition. There is no need for a preliminary hearing (though sometimes one is held). This will happen only if criminal proceedings are not already in progress, for once they are instituted the coroner must normally adjourn his inquest until they are terminated. The most likely reason for not beginning criminal proceedings is that the police do not feel that they have enough evidence on which to base a charge. If a coroner's jury does implicate a named person, the result is unsatisfactory, because an insufficient case may proceed to trial and there result in a finding of not guilty, which directly contradicts the verdict at the inquest. For instance, in 1965 the Deputy Coroner for Wakefield held an inquest on the death of a fourteen-year-old schoolgirl. The jury returned a verdict of murder against a man who had given evidence at the inquest. He was arrested and sent for trial at assizes, where the prosecution offered no evidence against him and he was directed to be found not guilty.[8]

The objection to this is not that sending a man for trial on a coroner's warrant is a waste of time. This is not so, for in the period 1950–66 some 203 committals by coroners occurred, and in the end 15 persons were convicted of the crime for which they were committed, and another 73 of a lesser charge, 67 were acquitted because no evidence was offered by the prosecution; what happened to the other 48 was not revealed[9]. The objection is that if the accused man is ultimately acquitted there will be conflicting verdicts outstanding against him, and he may find himself treated in society as though he had been convicted by the processes of the criminal law. The result is profoundly unsatisfactory.

It has been argued that we no longer need coroners to investigate cases of sudden death at all. But death is too serious an occurrence for those concerned with it – especially institutions like hospitals, old people's homes and prisons, which are concerned with it regularly – to be left without any duty to account for its causes to some independent official. It is important that some competent person should examine the causes of deaths in order to be able to criticize lax practices in the course of medical or institutional treatment, and carelessness about the possibility of danger to life or health. The more difficult question in an age where the investigation of criminal conduct is in the hands of large-scale, professional police forces is whether a coroner should follow the old formula of a public investigation, which may resemble in many ways trial by jury in a criminal court but lacks the same protection against prejudice as is afforded to an accused man. There is much force in the suggestion that a coroner should now conduct his investigations in private, referring cases in which there is a suspicion of criminal conduct to the police. In Scotland, the Procurator-Fiscal – whose role as public prosecutor has already been noted (p. 67) – performs such an office, and it is not there considered necessary to have a formal proceeding in public.[10] If so complete a reform cannot be achieved in England, then at the very least the use of a jury in the proceedings before the coroner should be abandoned.

The Coroners' Society has expressed its view that in the majority of cases juries have no useful contribution to make, and merely act on the coroner's direction.[11] However, the Society would like the jury to be retained where there is a suspicion of murder, manslaughter or infanticide, or where death has occurred in prison or a police station. Certainly in the case of prison or police-station deaths there ought to be some special procedure to ensure that officials employed by the state do not collaborate to conceal details of a death in questionable circumstances. But to retain the present procedure in all cases of suspected homicide would be to perpetuate the chance of a person being found to have committed a criminal act in proceedings in which he is not accused. The Coroners' Society admits that it is not unknown for juries to return perverse verdicts of manslaughter in accident cases where there is no criminal negligence. The time has now come for removing this possibility by discontinuing the use of juries in such cases and it is to be hoped that the present Departmental Committee which is considering the functions of the coroner will make such a recommendation.

JURIES AND ADMINISTRATIVE TRIBUNALS

The use of special tribunals that are not part of the structure of the ordinary courts has grown continuously during the last hundred years. Increased participation and regulation by the state in many spheres of economic and social activity is one of the principal causes. Special tribunals hear claims in respect of national insurance and national health rights, land development, taxation and rating assessments, and many other matters involving the private citizen on the one hand and a government department or local authority on the other. Some issues between private citizens are settled by similar bodies: the rent tribunals and rent assessment committees are well-known examples.[12] A further group of special tribunals comprises the disciplinary boards of many professions – bodies such as the General Medical Council and the Architects' Registration Council. None of these tribunals, whatever its function, is now constituted on a model of trial by judge and jury. Occasional examples did, however, occur in former times. It is worth mentioning two, and noting the form of the tribunal which performs the same function today.

One is the jury which was summoned upon an inquisition to find whether a person was a lunatic. This was a special procedure of the Court of Chancery and one of considerable antiquity. It was a formal method employed only when the person in question was possessed of considerable property, in the eventual disposition of which others were interested.[13] For the less well endowed, a warrant issued by two justices generally sufficed for a person to be incarcerated in an asylum as a lunatic. The special procedure for Chancery lunatics continued in theory to be available until 1959, where the person objected to his certification. In the nineteenth century it enjoyed some popularity for a period after the administration of the ordinary system through the magistrates became more strictly controlled. But in this century it has been of little significance, and advances in medical knowledge of mental illness have made the cumbersome process of submitting the question to a jury of unskilled persons seem wholly inappropriate.

Under the Mental Health Act 1959, orders for compulsory admission to a mental hospital have to be made by two doctors having prescribed qualifications. Protection is now provided by special Mental Health Review Tribunals. A person who is in a mental hospital under the provision for compulsory admission may apply during his first six months in the hospital to one of the Tribunals for his release. There are also certain other circumstances in which he can apply to a Tribunal. The Tribunal reviews the question whether the patient is suffering from a condition or disease which justifies his continued detention.[14] The members of the Tribunals are selected by the Lord Chancellor in consultation with the Minister of Health, and are lawyers, medical practitioners and others having suitable experience such as social workers. They act in committee as a composite group.

The other jury of interest was summoned to determine the proper compensation to be paid to a person whose land was compulsorily acquired under an Act of Parliament. In practice it was not very popular, because an alternative way of settling the amount was also introduced into the first statute providing generally for juries: each side could appoint an arbitrator, who themselves could bring in an umpire if they could not agree. Both sides soon showed that they preferred the greater reliability, speed and flexibility of arbitrators.[15] Today, an independent body, the Lands Tribunal, performs this function (among others). It has a judge, or barrister of at least seven years' standing, as its chairman. Its other members are barristers, solicitors or experienced land valuers. Again the Lord Chancellor holds the power of appointment. The composition of the Tribunal will vary, depending on whether the issue is primarily legal, or one of valuation.[16]

When a statute creates a tribunal to deal with a new area of disputes, the practice of constituting the body as a committee of several members having equal voting rights and acting by majority decision is now so common that the form is rarely questioned. Argument will be about size, method of selection and qualification of the members. These will be settled with regard to the complexity and technicality of the subject matter. Often a lawyer is included as chairman in order to deal with questions of interpretation of the law and of proper procedure. The Mental Health Review Tribunals and the Lands Tribunal are good examples of tribunals which perform specialist functions and which are made up of appropriate legal and extra-legal experts. The recently created Rent Assessment Committees, which sit to review the rents fixed as fair by rent officers acting under the Rent Act 1965, are drawn from panels settled by the Lord Chancellor and the Minister of Housing and Local Government. No qualifications have been prescribed by law, it being left to civil servants in the two departments to find members of the panels who have sufficient general experience to be able to fulfil the task of reviewing rents.[17] Industrial Tribunals are another new form of tribunal. They deal with a number of matters, including disputes arising out of the new scheme for redundancy payments to dismissed employees. Their form is borrowed from the structure of other bodies, such as wages councils and joint industrial councils, that are concerned with different aspects of labour relations. They have a chairman who is legally qualified (seven years' standing as a barrister or solicitor), one representative from the employers' side of industry and one from the employees' side. No special experience in the management of personnel is required from the two members from industry.[18]

It is very much to be hoped that a series of studies of how different tribunals work will take place over the next few years, and that attention will be given to the question of what contribution to decisions comes from persons put on these bodies to provide a particular skill, or represent some point of view. For the present, it must simply be stressed once more that it has been widely accepted that the proper body to settle new forms of dispute is a committee acting by majority vote, and composed of persons with various forms of appropriate experience. No use is made of the judgment of members of the community selected at random, nor are lawyers and laymen formally separated and allotted their own spheres of decision.

10 · Revision or replacement?

At the end of the Middle Ages the breakdown of closely knit feudal society and the growth in size and importance of the towns meant that courts could no longer depend on the local knowledge of jurors for the settlement of disputes. Trial by jury was gradually developed by the judges to meet these changes. Jurors, instead of deciding the case on what they themselves knew, listened to evidence provided by the parties and so came to their verdict. In this new form the jury proved sufficiently successful to remain ubiquitous in the common-law courts for three centuries.

In the great transformation to an industrialized and more democratic society, the courts came under pressure to deal with many new kinds of dispute, and to modernize and simplify their procedure. Under these strains trial by jury did not adapt so successfully. The need for simpler and speedier processes to deal with a growing volume of work led to the setting-up of County Courts in which juries never attained much popularity, and to ever-increasing jurisdiction for the magistrates. Gradually, over the past century, the jury has lost its traditional place in common-law matters tried in the High Court, as well as the temporary popularity which for a time it held in contested divorce and probate cases. It has not developed new functions; as we have just seen, it has been accorded no place on administrative tribunals.

There are many reasons for the jury's decline: they include the need to keep expenses down, to keep court timetables flexible, to cut down the length of trials, to avoid inconveniences and delays which the summoning of juries occasions. Then there are the more fundamental objections to juries, such as the modern need for judges who are able to deal with long and complex cases and who have adequate experience of the subject-matter and procedure of litigation. It is unlikely that the jury will acquire new roles in the fields of civil or administrative law. The question now is merely how much longer it will be before some other tribunal replaces the jury in the remaining areas of the civil law in which it still has some place. These special cases we have already discussed. It is necessary, in this final chapter, to try to decide whether trial by jury of serious criminal offences should be considerably revised or totally replaced.

The slow and cumbersome process of trial by jury, and the complex administrative machinery for summoning jurors are disadvantages which apply just as much with criminal as with civil proceedings. They add up to so much inconvenience, expense and delay that a positive case has to be presented by those in favour of retaining the jury. If in the end one believes that there is some other system which is as good as or better than trial by jury, and if at the same time it is cheaper and simpler to run, then it ought to be introduced. The traditional view – one rarely challenged until recently – has been that the jury system has unique advantages which easily outweigh its inconveniences. We have already said a good deal about those advantages in an attempt to arrive at a true evaluation of their worth, and now they may be summarized under two heads: the need to secure disinterested adjudicators, and the need to have adjudicators whose views and experience will be those of the man-in-the-street. In regard to disinterestedness, we saw in Chapter 5 that in the changing social structure of early industrial England the jury probably did bring to the courts a measure of impartiality which could not be expected from the judges and magistrates of the time. But immense social changes since that time have brought new methods of ensuring that governments pursue political and industrial troublemakers by charging them with serious criminal offences only when they are sure of their ground. With adequately organized police forces to regulate demonstrations and public meetings, people who are alleged to have committed offences at such gatherings will most likely be charged with some relatively minor offence triable summarily before magistrates. In the early days of the industrial revolution, juries, being landowners or tradesmen, only showed very sporadic sympathy with political radicals and strikers. Today they may be more representative; but still they may not be able to eliminate prejudices aroused by present social conflicts – of colour, race or nationality. The jury certainly plays its part in setting the balance of respect and disinterestedness between the senior criminal courts and the police. We do not know enough of the attitudes of jurors towards the police to be able to judge whether the present balance is a fair one, or whether juries are often swayed by irrelevant and extreme anti-police prejudice. This is one of the secrets of the jury-room that particularly needs to be investigated.

Juries are given special power to bring their own sense of justice into play by departing from strict application of the law to the facts. If the Chicago evidence is any indication of how English juries behave, the power is freely used. We are entitled to know when and for what reasons it is so used, for what may appear at a casual glance to be lay common sense may well on closer scrutiny prove to be undeserved sympathy or bigoted obtuseness. We explored in Chapter 6 the assorted factors which combine to shape a person's judgment and noted that a jury may be free from the kind of prejudice which a judge may acquire from constant contact with the courts. And in Chapter 7 we considered a number of areas in the criminal law where inexperience may make it difficult for a jury to reach a just verdict in a doubtful case. Here again ignorance of what goes on in the jury-room makes it impossible to arrive at any certain conclusion about the seriousness of the problems and the degree of difference between the judgments of lawyers and laymen. Until something is done to fill these lacunae in our knowledge no final rational judgment can be made on this central issue.

Of course, to many people, the appeal of the jury system is primarily an emotional one, representing both a commitment to the ideal of individual liberty and a link in the traditional chain of impartial administration of justice in England. It would certainly be foolish to dismiss too hastily the obvious fact that a great many people simply *believe* in the jury system. A measure of trust in the fairness of its criminal courts is something which it is difficult for any state to establish or to maintain. The present public faith in the criminal courts has undoubtedly been encouraged by conscientious juries, and the system has the intrinsic advantage that in drawing upon a steady stream of ordinary citizens it is not only educating them in the work of the courts, but also, since they are generally satisfied with their own performance, sending them back to their ordinary lives with a sense of the fairness and propriety of the judicial process in this country.

However, it is an essential argument of this book that the general public's faith in the jury system should not be enough to ensure for it everlasting life. The fact that it has often been seen to function less well than it might is evidence enough that all is not well. We have had occasion to examine a number of recent instances in which the jury has not functioned successfully and have adduced reasons why another kind of tribunal might have done better. The extent of the breakdown now deserves proper investigation, and it has been one purpose of this book to suggest the various possible lines of inquiry that ought to be undertaken. Until this comes about, no one can have any proper basis for a true evaluation of the jury system.

It is useless to discard without replacing, and even before this research produces results we should be wise to consider possible reforms. These may be grouped under three heads: administrative changes, fundamental changes in the character of the jury system, and alternative tribunals.

ADMINISTRATIVE CHANGES

As well as its major recommendations on qualification for jury service the Morris Committee made many useful suggestions for smoother, more efficient and more equitable operation of the jury system: these included properly random selection of jurors by computer; revision of the procedure for summoning jurors in the light of the recommended extension of the qualification rules; provision of handbooks for jurors giving clear explanation of their principal duties as well as their hours, payment and facilities; increases in the maximum reimbursements for loss of earnings; a system to ensure that no juror should have to serve more than once in five years; various ways of avoiding wastage of jurors' time and a number of more minor reforms. These are all matters which could lessen inconvenience to jurors and improve their comfort as well as making them better informed about their duties. Every step taken along these lines will assist jurors to discharge their task to the best of their abilities.

The Morris Committee's Report was welcomed by the Government with the announcement that it intended to introduce a bill to implement the whole of its provisions. But the Home Office proceeded first to the enactment of the Criminal Justice Act 1967. While this Act dealt with some jury matters, including majority verdicts, it did not touch the administrative reforms proposed by the Morris Committee. Many of these are interrelated with changes in the qualification rules, and it is very much to be hoped that pressure of parliamentary business will not result in the shelving of the proposed Juries Bill. In the meantime, there are one or two points at which the Morris Committee's views deserve further thought. In particular, the time has come when all jurors ought to be informed that they may take notes and may ask questions through the judge. It is lack of knowledge of these rights that seems often to cause anxiety and lack of certainty among jurors. If we are prepared to give juries the considerable responsibility of deciding issues of fact, we ought to trust them over these lesser matters.

Not all of these administrative changes need wait for an Act of Parliament. In some cases a direction from the Home Secretary, and in others a Practice Direction from the Court of Appeal would be enough. Already the Home Secretary has made regulations increasing the payments to jurors, though not quite to the maxima suggested by the Morris Report.[1]

BASIC CHARACTERISTICS OF THE JURY SYSTEM

The Morris Committee was charged with the investigation of one fundamental principle of the jury system, the qualification for service. They recommended that the jury be made fully democratic, and sought to limit excusals and disqualifications as far as possible. They deliberated upon the assumption that jurors should be representative of the community at large and sought to achieve a true cross-section. Since we discussed these recommendations in Chapter 2 we have examined a variety of matters which suggest that a random cross-section of the community does not produce a tribunal which is always able to dispose adequately of the cases before it. Implementation of the Committee's recommendation will exacerbate the difficulty rather than diminish it, and this is the greatest risk involved in making the change. Our present state of ignorance makes it impossible to estimate the real extent of the danger. The Committee was not impressed even by proposals for special juries on difficult financial fraud cases, but they did not come to this decision on any stronger evidence than the impressions of lawyers connected with cases where there may well have been some deliberate inclusion of jurors with suitable professional qualifications. There is no worthwhile purpose to be served by retaining the property qualification as it operates at present. The Committee's recommendation is a sensible alternative. The inherent risks deserve investigation.

There are other ways in which basic characteristics of the jury system might be altered. The principle followed in England is that while in civil cases the jury decides both liability and damages, in criminal cases its functions are to return a verdict as to the defendant's guilt but not as to punishment. We have already considered the suggestion that in defamation cases it would be desirable to leave the assessment of damages to the judge, and rejected it partly because it might lead to unsatisfactory verdicts on liability in certain cases, and partly because it is undesirable to do anything to alter the jury's standing in such cases, while invasions of privacy do not give any right of action in English law.

As far as criminal procedure is concerned, we have examined whether the jury could be given power to assist in deciding the degree of punishment, in order to deal with the problem of cases (their number as yet unknown) where the jurors will not convict because for some reason they think that an inappropriate punishment will follow. Although it is a practice which has been introduced in some places, the serious objection to it is that sentencing is becoming a complex process and one in which knowledge of the general practice is essential in order that like cases shall be treated alike.

The jury gives no reasons for its decision. While it might be possible to require special verdicts from criminal juries to ensure that they do consider each legal aspect of the case, it would be impracticable to require a reasoned judgment from them. In any case, to take either step would seriously reduce the special value of the inscrutable verdict: that the jury may avoid the consequence of a strict application of the law, if it wishes to do so. This is surely a characteristic which is bound to last as long as the jury system itself – once the inscrutability principle has gone, the time has come to set up another kind of tribunal.

There remains the question of unanimous and majority verdicts. The principal reason for the introduction of the ten-to-two majority verdict was to prevent the 'nobbling' of jurors. The efficacy of the move was discussed in Chapter 5. At the same time it was obvious that a majority system would render nugatory the opinions of a juror who was in some other way 'unreasonable' and it was clear that a separate reason for wanting the change was to end the power of the crank to prevent a conviction. But while a jury system may throw up the occasional juror who will not agree with his fellows either to convict or acquit for some prejudiced or fantastic reason which ought not to be taken into account, it may also produce juries in which only one man can see that there is a legitimate ground of defence.

Needless to say there was no information from which a researcher could estimate how frequently either of these situations arose. There was not even much evidence of the proportion of cases in which juries disagree. The Morris Committee (which was not directly concerned with the desirability of majority verdicts) did show that the percentage of 'hung' juries in 1963 was 4 per cent at the Old Bailey and 3 per cent at London Sessions.[2] Subsequently it was reported that 1,185 persons were tried at the Old Bailey in 1965, and in 49 (4·1 per cent) of the cases the jury disagreed; 1,159 persons were tried at London Sessions, and in 41 (3·5 per cent) of the cases there was disagreement. Moreover, 89 of these cases were retried and resulted in 51 convictions, 25 acquittals and 13 second disagreements.[3] This suggests that 'hung' juries do not seriously prejudice the proper administration of justice, but it should be remembered that the length and seriousness of the cases in question should also be taken into account.

In the debates on the majority verdict proposal, a good deal of attention was given to the position in Scotland. A Scottish jury has fifteen members, and for centuries it has been permitted to return a verdict by a bare majority. Moreover in criminal cases, the jury has the further power to return an intermediate verdict of not proven, so that there are three possible divisions of opinion.[4] No hard facts about the working of the Scottish majority system were brought to light. The protagonists of majority verdicts thought that bare majorities were acceptable and produced satisfactory results. The antagonists pointed out that there were some celebrated Scottish convictions for murder by majority verdict, which were widely thought to have been incorrect.[5] In addition there were important differences in Scottish practice for instituting prosecutions and in stricter rules of evidence, which together with the different structure and functions of the jury itself meant that no reliance could be placed on what happened north of the border. In some American and Australian states a majority system has been operated in conditions which appear closer to those of the English criminal trial. Unfortunately they received little attention.[6]

The case against the hasty introduction of a majority system in England was a strong one: the number of cases in which it would prevent interference with jurors was probably very small, yet it may now produce a measure of uncertainty about jury verdicts which is thoroughly undesirable. Public trust in the fairness of the system may be lowered by convictions where the presence of a minority shows that one or two jurors had reasonable doubt; and a man who is acquitted only by a majority may bear some stigma as a result. But for those who have any doubt about the ability of all juries to deal with every kind of case which may come up, the real strength of the case against the majority system lies in the possibility of a jury in which only one or two members can see a real obstacle to conviction, but the majority is unable to appreciate the force of their objection.

It was particularly surprising that the majority verdict proposal was pushed through at a time when the government was already pledged to implement the carefully considered proposals of the Morris Committee. Such are the vagaries of law reform at present that the sensible course of implementing the Committee's report, and then studying the altered system to see whether majorities were desirable, was not pursued. The order in which reform has proceeded will at least take account of Lord Devlin's warning that it might be dangerous to introduce wider qualification rules for jurors without allowing for more disagreements by adopting a majority verdict system.[7]

Now that the change is on the statute book, we are at least entitled to some check on its consequences. In the first place, some adequate record should be kept of the proportion of convictions and acquittals reached by majority verdict, and of the extent to which juries still continue to disagree. American experience suggests that overall the number of disagreements will be reduced by about a half, but it may be that on some juries the very possibility of a majority verdict will make a group of three or four jurors less ready to compromise than they would have been under a system requiring unanimity. It would be desirable to try to discover whether vital defence points are being ignored by all but an insufficient minority. It was pointed out previously (see p. 179) that when there is a division of opinion, a method of compromise may arise from the fact that the defendant has been charged with a number of offences of varying seriousness all relating to the same event. If minorities can be ignored, it may be that there will be a tendency to arrive at a verdict of guilty on one of the more serious charges than would be the case if the verdict had to be unanimous.

ALTERNATIVE TRIBUNALS

In the end the true value of the jury must be measured against the tribunals which might be put in its place. A host of alternatives could be devised, taking into account combinations and permutations of the qualification for membership. It is likely, however, that any particular formula will fall within one or other of three main categories: trial by a single professional judge, trial by a number of professional judges, and trial by a mixed tribunal of professional and lay judges. Something must be said as to the desirability of each of them in turn, as a means of constituting a criminal court.

Trial by a single professional judge

This alternative springs naturally to mind, because it has already become the regular method of trying civil actions, both in the County Courts and the High Court. As a matter of history, this mode of trial derives from courts such as the Court of Chancery which lay outside the ordinary common-law courts. The common-law courts almost invariably used trial by jury, and when occasionally it fell to the judges to decide a question of fact, a bench of judges would sit together for the purpose. In the administration of the criminal law, there are only two occasions upon which a single judge sits alone to try a case: where a stipendiary magistrate has been appointed to a Magistrates' Court, and where a Borough Quarter Sessions Court, composed solely of the Recorder, sits to hear an appeal by way of complete rehearing from a conviction by a Magistrates' Court.

In other common-law jurisdictions, trial by single judge has been more extensively adopted for criminal cases. For instance, most American states and some Canadian provinces have solved the problem of reducing the number of serious offences requiring trial by jury by offering the accused the choice of trial by judge alone in the higher court; whereas in England the alternative has been trial in the lower courts before the magistrates. The extent to which this 'jury waiver' is permitted by the law varies from place to place. In many states and provinces it is available for all or most charges of serious crime. In the United States, the right is generally subject to consent by the prosecution and by the court, but normally this is given without question. In practice, the frequency with which 'jury waiver' actually occurs varies greatly. In some American states it occurs in as many as three-quarters of the prosecutions for serious crime, in others it rarely occurs at all. Much seems to depend on the preferences and established practices of local legal professions. The Chicago Project has demonstrated that the waiver is less likely to occur in those categories of crime in which juries tend most often to be more lenient than judges.[8] Professional advisers are well aware of the special factors influencing juries that were so carefully analyzed by the Project.

England has not developed a system of jury waiver because most of the higher criminal courts do not sit in permanent session. Judges at Assizes, and Recorders, Chairmen and justices at Quarter Sessions have other tasks to perform. In consequence, the steadily increasing number of prosecutions has produced pressure on these courts which has been relieved by transferring work to Magistrates' Courts. It has been more convenient, and cheaper, to increase the number and frequency of magistrates' sittings rather than those of the higher courts.

There are strong reasons, apart from expediency, why trial by single judge should not be introduced into the higher criminal courts, even though the system has achieved a large measure of acceptability in civil cases. It is one of the obvious and much vaunted advantages of trial by jury that it prevents the question of a defendant's guilt being decided by one man. The point is sometimes put rather differently by saying that the presence of the jury relieves the judge of the heavy responsibility of settling the defendant's fate single-handed. But the degree to which a judge should be expected to assume responsibility is a matter of subsidiary importance, and should not be allowed to obscure the fundamental issue. Not only is it wrong in principle that a defendant's guilt should be a matter for a single opinion reached without discussion, but it is also necessary for a system using pro-fessional judges to incorporate some protection against a judge whose abilities are seriously affected by age, ill-health or prejudice. It is paradoxical that while trial by jury ensures that the question of guilt will be decided by a large number of persons, the decision on punishment remains one for a single judge. But for the presence of the jury, it is unlikely that one judge alone would have retained this power for so long. Yet until 1907 the sentencing power of the judge was virtually absolute. In that year, the Court of Criminal Appeal was first set up, and as we have already noted it has in the course of time done a good deal in its supervisory capacity to secure that the sentences passed by the judges are more uniform, and better informed in the light of penological developments, than used to be the case.

Nonetheless, it is not easy to ensure that the considerable number of judges are kept abreast of current developments in sentencing policy. The best solution may well be to remove the question of sentencing altogether from the courts, at least under certain conditions, and place it in the hands of a specialist sentencing board. The members of this board could include lawyers, criminologists, social workers, and medical and psychiatric experts. To make such a change would be to recognize that there are a number of disciplines which have a vital contribution to make to the development of a humane and reformative system for dealing with criminals. But it is appropriate in this book to add one word of warning: there might be particular difficulties in establishing sentencing boards while leaving the issue of guilt still to be tried by jury. We have seen that juries tend in some cases to acquit because they do not agree with the severity of the sentence that might be passed. This attitude might be even more prevalent if the jury knew that by convicting they would be consigning the accused to be sentenced not by the judge who has tried the case with them, but by some unknown committee with no direct knowledge of the facts that emerged during the trial, but only a report of what happened.

There are two reasons why the objections to trial by a single judge do not apply with full force to the stipendiary magistrate: his sentencing power is limited, and there is a right of appeal by way of a full rehearing to Quarter Sessions. Yet there are also particular dangers: a stipendiary's work involves a constant series of prosecutions for minor offences. Moreover, the position is one from which there is little chance of promotion, so that not all such magistrates are of the highest calibre. Inevitably there are some who fall short of desirable standards of impartiality and good temper. A group of Bow Group lawyers summed up their experience in this way:

A visit to many of the courts presided over by stipendiary magistrates will reveal justice being administered with speed, efficiency, courtesy and good humour, all of the highest order: administered that is to say in a way with which the finest bench of lay magistrates would find it difficult to compete. However, a visit to some other courts of the same sort will reveal a very different state of affairs. Sufficient to say that in them, both laymen and women are bullied and chivied and treated in a way which some-times ignores even the most elementary rules of civilized be-haviour; the sentencing of offenders tends to be haphazard and sometimes almost savage. Fortunately such courts are rare, but no practitioner would deny their existence or think the picture painted a false one. One bad stipendiary magistrate sitting alone can do more harm than a dozen bad lay magistrates whose deficiencies will be tempered by right-thinking colleagues.[9]

The office of stipendiary magistrate was introduced late in the eighteenth century, and has been used in London and in other large cities where the need to keep Magistrates' Courts running day in, day out, has obviously made it convenient to appoint a permanent magistrate. But stipend-iary magistrates have never been markedly popular even during periods when the lay magistracy was a good deal more unpopular than it is at present. In part this has been a question of the additional costs involved. In part also, the initiative for establishing a new stipendiary post has had to come from the local authority – and local authority members are likely to favour the system of lay justices: the two offices belong to the same tradition of local administration by laymen. But the resistance to stipendiaries also represents an awareness of the dangers of allowing single judges to sit and administer justice unaided in the criminal courts. At least with this experience, it is highly unlikely that trial by a single judge would ever spread to the higher criminal courts as a replacement for jury trial.

Trial by a bench of professional judges

One obvious way of avoiding the objection to judges sitting alone is to increase their number: a bench of three is the smallest workable number, unless a court of two judges is obliged to act by unanimous decision. In England this has been the regular manner of constituting appeal courts, but the practice has not been extended to trial courts. Even staunch supporters of trial by jury have been prepared to admit that such a court would offer an adequate alternative. For instance Mr Justice Humphreys, in the course of a paper drawing attention to the jury's particular virtues, viewed a court composed of three judges with equal favour.[10] But he foresaw not the slightest chance of such a system being introduced because of the increase in judicial manpower that would be necessary. No doubt the first objections would be practical ones of this kind: the English legal system has traditionally operated with only a small number of judges, and since High Court judges in particular are highly paid there is always a reluctance to increase their number on grounds of expense. Yet, as already noted, the jury system is by no means cheap to run. Its true cost is much less easy to estimate than that of judicial salaries and pensions. It involves not only the direct payments to jurors themselves, but all the costs of administration, including such things as police protection for jurors when intimidation is feared. An accurate cost analysis of maintaining the jury system – and one is certainly required – would reveal that the expenditure involved is much greater than is often imagined. Moreover, in calculating the comparative costs of courts composed of judge and jury, and those consisting of three judges, allowance must be made for the fact that a court made up entirely of professional lawyers will work with greater speed. It may well be that there is no significant difference in the expenditure involved in maintaining the two systems.

Another practical objection would be the difficulty of finding suitably qualified lawyers to staff an expanded judicial service. It is a well-established tradition that all the higher judicial appointments are made from members of the Bar of sufficient seniority and standing, so that the possible field of selection is always quite small. Attempts to break away from this practice are generally rejected on the ground that barristers alone have adequate knowledge and experience of court procedure and the proper practice of advocates. Yet solicitors have gradually extended their rights to appear in the lower courts. They may appear in County and Magistrates' Courts and the recent extension of the jurisdiction of County Courts to the hearing of undefended divorce actions has provided solicitor advocates with new territory. It is too early yet to know to what extent the Bar will lose divorce work in consequence.

For some time, the two professions have been considering whether solicitors should be given a right of audience at Quarter Sessions.[11] At present, this is permitted at only a few Sessions, but the matter has been aired before the present

Royal Commission on Assizes and Quarter Sessions and doubtless its report will deal with solicitors' rights of audience. As well as rights as advocates, certain of the lesser judicial offices are now open to solicitors; for instance, those of stipendiary magistrate and chairman of Quarter Sessions. Other offices, such as clerk to the justices in a Magistrates' Court and that of coroner, which in many respects resemble that of a judge, are also open to them. As the number of judicial positions on tribunals that have to be filled by lawyers has increased, it has been usual to stipulate that the person appointed may be a member of either profession. Only a few specially important offices on tribunals have been reserved for members of the Bar. In the case of judges being appointed to share their responsibilities with two fellow judges, there would be nothing inappropriate in extending the field of selection to include solicitors as well as barristers.

In this century there has been a considerable increase in the number of professional lawyers serving as part-time judges in the higher criminal courts. Recorders, legally qualified chairmen of Quarter Sessions and their deputies are considerably more numerous than they were, and have in the main come from the Bar. It is generally recognized that an incidental effect of this system has been the establishment of means of judicial training and testing from which the best candidates may be selected for permanent High Court and County Court judgeships. Formerly judges were appointed on the sole assumption that good advocates make good judges – a risky premise, which in the past has been sorely shaken by events. If an increased number of trained lawyers were required to act as judges in a new form of criminal court, there would be much to be said in favour of extending the number of part-time judgeships. Provided that a lawyer does not sit on a court in the area in which he also practises, it should be quite possible to avoid conflicts of interest between the two functions. Complaints are not at present heard that legal practitioners who have part-time offices at court allow embarrassments to arise between their practice and their court duties. Not only does the existence of a series of part-time judicial offices provide a means of training and selecting men as full-time judges; it is also a means of avoiding the dangers of boredom and cynicism which are especially likely to prey upon a judge who spends a large part of his time deciding criminal cases.

One argument that is regularly deployed against every extension in the number of judges is that the respect and trust at present shown to the judiciary arises from its high quality, which can be maintained only so long as the body is a small one.[12] Of course, if there are to be extensions in the number of judges, care must be taken to ensure that a high standard is maintained. It is for just this reason that it would be valuable to extend the opportunities for members of both professions to serve in a part-time judicial capacity, so that their abilities as a judge may be assessed at the same time as they are themselves gaining experience. But references to the relation between the small number and the quality of the judges are generally made with the High Court bench alone in mind. Just as important, though less exclusive, are the ranks of County Court judges, stipendiary magistrates and part-time recorders and chairmen of Quarter Sessions. Indeed, it is in respect of criminal trials that the need to ensure that the judges are wholly trusted is greatest. Yet it is in this sphere that part-time judges are most numerous. It is a corollary of extension of the ranks of the judiciary that the idea of a 'career' as a judge should become more tenable. It would not be necessary to go so far as to copy the continental practice of a judicial service entirely separate from the other legal professions, in which a man works all his life. A man with several years of experience as a practitioner could be enabled to take up one of the lesser judicial positions and from there to progress towards the High Court and Appeal Court benches, if his record marked him out as being of sufficiently high calibre.

So far we have been concerned with the practical difficulties which would arise in respect of a criminal court composed of three judges. But even if they are satisfactorily answered, there remains the root question of principle: whether it is right to entrust questions of criminal liability solely to lawyers. There are countries such as Holland in which lawyers alone constitute the bench in criminal cases, but they are few in number. Many countries of Western Europe that tried a variation of trial by jury and found it unsatisfactory did not altogether repudiate the use of laymen in the criminal courts. Instead they introduced a system in which judges and laymen sit as a combined bench. They were prepared to concede to the judges the power to exert greater influence over the lay members by allowing them to take part in the joint deliberations. But they were not prepared to lose entirely such advantages as may flow from the presence of lay judges, free from responsibilities to the state, unfettered by any narrow, legalistic approach, unaffected by lengthy experience of the police and criminals, and drawn from wider social backgrounds than professional lawyers. These are values which have a widespread appeal in England, with its long tradition of lay judges, both jurors and justices of the peace. So long as the majority of criminal cases are in essence relatively simple, so long as techniques for assessing the weight to be attached to the evidence of witnesses represent nothing more scientific than the application of sound commonsense, it is not likely that a change to trial by lawyers alone would ever win much support. This leaves one possible alternative: a tribunal which follows the pattern of the continental courts just mentioned, in which judges and laymen sit together in a combined committee.

A composite tribunal of lawyers and laymen

We have already noted that composite bodies are the normal method of constituting administrative tribunals. In the civil courts there has been a reluctance to venture far in the same direction. Save for the traditional use of nautical assessors as advisers in Admiralty cases, the judges have shown no readiness to share their position with others, though it is an obvious expedient for developments in certain areas, such as family courts. There, as with many administrative tribunals, the purpose of the composite tribunals would be to place the power of decision in the hands of appropriate experts drawn from non-legal as well as legal professions.

In the criminal courts there are two forms of composite tribunal that are now well established, though their growth has been gradual and scarcely the product of deliberate policy. Where a stipendiary magistrate has been appointed, he may sit with one or two lay justices serving at the court on criminal cases. This happens sometimes outside London, though it is not the practice in the Metropolis. Yet it is interesting to observe that in London stipendiaries have been required to sit with two justices in matrimonial cases. Even more interesting is the constitution of County Quarter Sessions when it sits to hear appeals from Magistrates' Courts. If the accused pleaded not guilty in the lower court, and has appealed against his conviction, there is a complete rehearing of the case. But there is no jury; instead, the bench of justices is headed by a chairman or his deputy, who, as we have seen, is nowadays legally qualified. This court is just as much a trial court as the ordinary sessions sitting with a jury to try a case on indictment.

In both these courts the lay element is supplied by justices of the peace, and they are of course not complete novices, as are most jurymen. Newly appointed justices now receive some instruction over a period before taking up their duties,[13] and they are expected to serve with some regularity so that with time they build up considerable court experience. On the other hand, they are never given extended legal training of a formal kind, and if none of the bench is incidentally a lawyer, they will have to rely on their clerk for guidance on matters of law.

The forms of composite tribunal that have been evolved in Western European countries provide a varied selection of examples of combinations of lawyers and laymen, and laymen with different degrees of experience. France, for instance, tried a number of variations of the English jury system but found none that produced uniformly satisfactory results. In 1943, the whole structure of the criminal courts, which up to that time had used a jury, was changed: nine laymen (later reduced to seven), still called jurors, were required to sit together with three judges as one bench to decide questions of guilt and punishment jointly. A similar step was taken in Germany in 1924. A court of six lay members and three judges was established to try the most serious criminal offences, and for the medium-range offences a smaller version comprising one judge and two laymen was created.

The same kind of development has occurred in the Scandinavian countries. The closest parallel to the composite courts in England are those of Sweden. The traditional constitution of courts serving country districts is a professional judge and from seven to nine lay members known as *nämndemän*.[14] These are drawn from a body of local citizens chosen for their position of responsibility and their record of service in the community. The choice is made by a committee of the local government authority, so those selected may well have been politically active. A person appointed to the *nämnd* is expected to serve regularly, but not to attend every time that the court sits. Hence the selection committee has to cast its net reasonably wide. This bears a distinct resemblance to the appointment of justices of the peace in England, for although the Lord Lieutenant's committee, which puts up names to the Lord Chancellor, has an undisclosed membership and operates in secret, the justices who are appointed are often people with service to local political parties behind them. In the Swedish country courts the judge acts as chairman and his vote is given special weight. A case can only go against his opinion if at least seven of the lay members would decide it the other way.

In the town courts the traditional method of trial was by single judge, but recent changes have introduced the *nämnd*. Since 1948, serious criminal cases have been referred to a court constituted in the same manner as the country courts. Ten years later, a reduced version – judge and three *nämndemän* – was established for the middle range of crimes. An increasing number of *nämndemän* have had to be found, and many of them who are in a position to do so serve with some frequency. But unlike justices of the peace, *nämndemän* are paid for their service and this provides a useful means for retired people to supplement their pension.

In Denmark and Norway, no equivalent traditional institution survived in the same way; in both countries the jury has been introduced but given a restricted role.[15] Again criminal offences of medium seriousness have come to be tried by a court consisting of judge and lay members – in these instances two in number, following the German pattern. The basis of selecting lay members is the same – through a local authority committee. But it is not expected of a layman that he will serve with the same frequency as in Sweden, or as a justice of the peace in England. In Denmark, the average is once or twice a year. Appointment to the general panel is in the first instance for four years, but reappointment is common. The panel of laymen also constitutes the panel from which jurymen are selected for the trial of very serious criminal offences.

While lawyers in those countries are apt to express dissatisfaction with some verdicts reached by juries, it is widely thought that trial by judge and two or three laymen has been a successful method. In the course of visits to observe the operation of courts in Denmark, Norway and Sweden, I was able to discuss the combined courts with a number of judges and lay members, and I came away impressed with the merits of the system. There is no doubt – every judge to whom I spoke confirmed it – that the judge generally takes the leading part in reaching the final decision. He will normally start the discussion of the case, and put forward his own opinion on it, which in all likelihood will carry considerable weight with the lay members. But there will inevitably be cases in which he feels uncertain and will find the views of the others most useful. Even if he has made up his own mind before discussion begins, he has to justify his opinion to the laymen, for they in the end have the power to outvote him. This is surely the real value of the system: the judge's view, reached with all the resources of his experience, is nevertheless open to discussion and criticism by laymen. If the panel of lay members is so large that a judge is unlikely to sit regularly with the same persons, then there is the additional important advantage that he is having constantly to ensure that his judgment is acceptable to different members of the community. On questions of guilt, it is not uncommon for quite lengthy discussions to take place; on sentence, the judge's view is generally adopted without much demur. There is thus a direct interplay of lay and legal views on the issues, and the judge with all his lawyer's experience knows that any assumption that he makes may be challenged and will then have to be justified. The system seems to make for deliberation in an atmosphere of healthy rational criticism.

The Law Society has recently proposed that each Magistrates' Court should have a legally qualified chairman, and that there should then be a senior division at each court composed of the chairman and a small number of justices.[16]

This division would be empowered to hear certain cases which are at present beyond the magistrates' jurisdiction, such as charges of fraudulent conversion, burglary and housebreaking, perjury, bigamy and concealment of birth (the right to jury trial being preserved); it could also deal with the cases already classified as indictable offences triable summarily with the accused's consent, and any other case which gave rise to argument on points of law. The chief impetus behind the proposal was to put an end to the system whereby legal arguments in a Magistrates' Court must be addressed to a bench of laymen in the hope that the clerk will take the point and explain it to the bench afterwards. The Law Society's scheme would have the effect of creating an intermediate court to deal with most of the offences of the middle range.

It is by no means a new proposal that composite tribunals should play a more extensive role in the criminal courts. Learned writers such as Professor Glanville Williams and Professor Mannheim have argued that it should be a general substitute for trial by jury.[17] The Bar Council suggested to the Royal Commission on Justices of the Peace in 1947 that the number of stipendiary magistrates should be increased so that they might visit local benches in the country and help them with difficult cases.[18] This did not prevent their attacking the Law Society's recent proposal as 'totally unrealistic' because of the difficulties of finding the 250 or so men who would have to fill the appointments of chairman of the bench. It has already been suggested that neither this problem nor that of cost would be by any means insuperable, and might confer certain collateral advantages that would be well worth having.

Two general issues arise out of the Law Society's proposal. The first is whether it is really desirable to find the lay members of a new composite tribunal in the ranks of justices of the peace appointed under the present system. It has just been suggested that one advantage of a regularly changing membership of such a court is that the legal chairman is constantly sitting with different laymen and so cannot rely on being able to get his own way, as he might if he constantly sat with the same group of colleagues. The chance to build up a spirit of comradeship in which everything is left to the chairman is thus avoided. If the proposed Senior Division of a Magistrates' Court had lay members drawn from a larger panel than the ordinary justices, it would have the advantage of allowing many more people to accept nomination for appointment. Men and women whose employment would prevent them serving regularly as justices of the peace might well be able to hear a case once or twice a year. This in turn might ensure adequate representation of most classes and age-groups of society on the bench in at least one division of a magistrates' court. Recently there have been complaints that some benches are drawn exclusively from a rather narrow range of the middle and upper classes. Part of this problem is no doubt finding working-class recruits who can spare the time for regular work as a justice of the peace.

The other issue is the extent to which the establishment of such a court would and should lead to the further atrophy of trial by jury. If offences at present excluded were added to the list of indictable ones triable summarily, then there would be an increase in the proportion of offenders dealt with by the quicker and less expensive procedure in the lower court. If such offences included burglary and housebreaking, the saving of time would be significant. But the question would also arise as to whether some at least of the offences now triable summarily, or before a jury if the accused elects, should not be removed entirely into the forum provided by the new court. This is simply one aspect of the more general question of the jury's replacement by other tribunals, and it has been one purpose of this book to emphasize that this is a question which cannot be finally answered until more specific information is available about the extent to which juries function successfully. One fundamental part of further inquiries must relate to the reasons why juries acquit where judges would have convicted. It is usually his hope of such an outcome which induces a defendant who has the choice to risk the delays, and the danger of a heavier sentence, in order to be tried by jury. A system of law which offers a party a lottery for winning his case by choosing his court must in principle need special justification.

Some of the areas discussed in Chapter 7 might provide classes of case which ought to be moved exclusively to the new composite court in advance of others. The solution to cases of financial fraud, for instance, may well be that they should be tried by a judge and laymen, drawn from a roster of businessmen made up for the purpose. Cases involving complex medical issues might be dealt with by a court in which qualified doctors are included on the bench. Sexual offences might also be suitable for special treatment; a less formal and frightening forum could be provided for cases involving child victims, in order to spare them the possibly damaging ordeal of a full trial by jury. A composite tribunal offers opportunities for flexibility in the constitution of courts to take account of the varying nature of different cases in a way which would make it the modern equivalent of the special jury.

Recently the Lord Chancellor remarked, in commenting on the quality of benches at quarter sessions:

It has often seemed to me that the choice which we give to people, whether in criminal law or in civil cases – and in civil cases more particularly – when we say, 'Would you like the facts decided by one lawyer or twelve laymen?', is a very extraordinary choice. We do not realize it because we are so used to it, but usually any sensible man would say, 'I do not think I should like either. I think I should like it to be decided by one lawyer and two laymen sitting together, or one lawyer and four laymen.'[19]

Couple with this the view expressed by the Secretary-General of the Law Society at the last Commonwealth Legal Conference, that juries will have vanished from English courts by the end of the century, and the Lord Chief Justice's recently expressed opinion that juries are no longer suitable for the trial of criminal fraud cases. Among the leaders of the legal professions there are those who are contemplating reforms of the judicial system that would involve abrogation of jury trial at least to some extent. These opinions would perhaps be more frequently and forcefully expressed were it not for the regrettable fact that many people still adopt a 'sacred cow' attitude to the jury system. In any case as there is little precise knowledge of the differences in result produced by juries and by other tribunals, so there is at present every justification for not moving too hastily toward reforms.

But the fact remains that the courts have now to provide a service for a very different society from that of even a century ago. Their business involves people from a wider span of society than ever before; the growth of legal aid from the state and through bodies such as trade unions has made the civil courts more readily available to the poor, and the introduction of new forms of criminal liability – especially in relation to motor vehicles – has brought the rich as well as the poor before the criminal courts. At the same time, greater social equality and new means of ensuring that governments and civil servants are sensitive to public opinion have reduced the need for a guarantee against the partiality or bias of judges in the courts themselves. A much higher proportion of the lay public is educated and informed about the administration of justice in general, and therefore the general quality of jurors may well be on the up-grade. On the other hand the increased complexity of modern life has produced a wider variety of difficult cases and so the problems of providing a suitably constituted court to deal with questions involving specialist knowledge have increased considerably.

The effect of these social changes on the courts has been marked by developments in the jurisdiction and on the amount of business in the lesser courts, the Magistrates' and the County Courts, and by the confining of jury trial to special areas when it has retained some degree of appropriateness. The time has now come for careful exploration of the whole problem of constituting courts so as to give a reasonable share of power to ordinary laymen and to non-lawyers who are specialists in other fields. The long English tradition of using lay judges still has many benefits to confer on the administration of justice, but the actual manner in which they are turned to advantage is capable of many variations. A search for the best uses for laymen is likely to produce far-reaching changes on many aspects of the law and its administration that are bound to contribute to the common good.

Notes

1: INTRODUCTION

1. Recent accounts of the origins of jury trial which discuss the views of earlier historians are J. P. Dawson, *A History of Lay Judges* (1962), pp. 118–20, and Doris M. Stenton, *English Justice, 1066–1215* (1964), pp. 13–21.

2. The classic accounts of the development of trial by jury in England are Forsyth, *History of Trial by Jury* (1851), J. B. Thayer, *Preliminary Treatise on Evidence at the Common Law* (1898), chs. 2–5, and Pollock and Maitland, *History of English Law before the Time of Edward I* (2nd ed., 1898), I, pp. 138–50, II, pp. 618–50. See also W. S. Holdsworth, *History of English Law* (3rd ed., 1922), I, pp. 312–50, and Dawson, op. cit., pp. 122–9.

3. For the development of the office of justice of the peace, see Holdsworth, op. cit., I, pp. 286–98, Dawson, op. cit., pp. 136–45. There was a property qualification for justices, but it was abolished in 1906.

4. For a full description of judicial offices and the qualifications of judges, the standard work is R. M. Jackson, *The Machinery of Justice in England* (5th ed., 1967), chs. 2, 3 and 4 (section 5).

5. For the history of stipendiary magistrates see Stanley French, [1965] Criminal L.R. 213, 281; [1967] Criminal L.R. 224, 269, 321.

6. I. D. Willock, *The Origins and Development of the Jury in Scotland* (1961); T. B. Smith, *British Commonwealth: Scotland* (1962), pp. 92–3, 226.

7. J. H. Jearey, 'Trial by Jury and Trial with the Aid of Assessors in the Superior Courts of British African Territories', J. African L. [1960] 133; [1961], 36, 82; R. Knox Mawer, 'Juries and Assessors in Criminal Trials in some Commonwealth Countries' (1961) 10 International & Comparative L.Q. 892.

8. F. X. Busch, *Law and Tactics in Jury Trials* (1949).

9. Law Commission of India: 14th Report (1961); Jearey, op. cit., pp. 40–46.

10. H. R. Hahlo and E. Kahn, *British Commonwealth: South Africa* (1960), pp. 257–62.

11. H. Mannheim, 'Trial by Jury in Modern Continental Criminal Law' (1937) 53 L.Q.R. 99, 388; R. C. K. Ensor, *Courts and Judges*

in France, Germany and England (1933): A. von Mehren, *Law in Japan* (1963), pp. 312–21.

12. *The Listener*, 31 October 1966.
13. Jerome Frank, *Courts on Trial* (1949), chs. 8, 9; Glanville Williams, *The Proof of Guilt* (3rd ed., 1963), ch. 10.
14. For a list of publications of results of the Project to 1966 see H. Kalven and H. Zeisel, *The American Jury* (1966), pp. 541–5.
15. Criminal Law Act 1967, s. 13.
16. Morris Report (Cmnd 2627), para. 355.
17. *R.* v. *Armstrong* [1922] 2 K.B. 555, 568; see also similar criticisms by Bankes L. J. in *Ellis* v. *Deheer* [1922] 2 K.B. 113, 118. The Criminal Law Revision Committee has recently recommended that it should not be made a specific criminal offence for a juror to disclose what happened in the jury-room: Tenth Report (1968 Cmnd. 3750).
18. H. Kalven and H. Zeisel, *The American Jury* (1966).
19. ibid., ch. 5.
20. ibid, App. C.
21. Rita J. Simon, *The Jury and the Defense of Insanity* (1967).

2: JURORS

1. E. Halévy, *History of the English People in the Nineteenth Century*, I, 110–15.
2. Bentham, *The Elements of the Art of Packing as Applied to Special Juries* (1821), and the attacks of Wooler in *The Black Dwarf* were particularly influential.
3. Juries Act 1825, s. 1. Somewhat different rules apply in the City of London (s. 50).
4. Cd 6817, para. 236–7.
5. Cmnd 2627, paras. 41–3.
6. Criminal Justice Act 1967, ss. 13–17.
7. Cd 6817, para. 180.
8. Sex Disqualification (Removal) Act 1919, s. 1.
9. Morris Report (Cmnd 2627), para. 44. The estimates were made by the Social Survey Division of the Central Office of Information.
10. *Trial by Jury*, p. 20.
11. Gray, Corlett and Jones, 'The Proportion of Jurors as an Index of the Economic Status of a District' in F. Edwards (ed.), *Readings in Market Research* (1956).
12. Morris Report, paras. 39–44.
13. Morris Report, paras. 45–8; 53–64.
14. Strodtbeck and Mann, 'Sex Role Differentiation in Jury Deliberations' (1956), 19 Sociometry 715; Strodtbeck, James and Hawkins, 'Social Status in Jury Deliberations' (1957), 22 American Sociology R. 713; James, 'Status and Competence of Jurors' (1959), 64 American J. Sociology 563; Simon (James), *The Jury and the Defense of Insanity*, Part III. An all-female jury has recently been ordered for the first time in England: *R.* v. *Sutton* [1968] C.L.R. 402.

15. C. H. S. Fifoot, *Lord Mansfield* (1936), pp. 105–15.
16. Mersey Report (Cd 6817), para. 241.
17. See Juries Act 1949, s. 19; *Young* v. *Rank* [1950] 2 K.B. 510.
18. See 5 Stanford L.R. 247 (1953); 26 Cornell L.Q. 677 (1941); F. X. Busch, *Law and Tactics in Jury Trials* (1949), ch. 4.
19. *Glasser* v. *U.S.* 315 U.S. 60, 86 (1942).
20. 65 Yale L.J., 531 (1956).
21. The trial took place at the Old Bailey before Mr Justice Elwes: *The Times* 30 November and 1 December 1961.
22. Morris Report, paras. 53, 76–80.
23. Juries Act 1922, s. 2(1); this provision does not apply to nuns; nor to those disqualified by their previous convictions: Criminal Justice Act 1967, s. 14(7).
24. Criminal Justice Act 1967, s. 15.
25. Morris Report, paras. 101, 236–8.
26. Morris Report, paras. 68, 75.
27. *R.* v. *Thomas* [1933] 2 K.B. 489.
28. Morris Report, paras. 122–8.
29. *R.* v. *Kelly* [1950] 2 K.B. 164.
30. Morris Report, paras. 143, 242.
31. Criminal Justice Act 1967, ss. 14, 15.
32. Morris Report, para. 87.
33. Many persons connected with legal administration are at present exempt, though the list is not as wide as that given by the Morris Committee. Recently the term of these exemptions has been extended to include the period of ten years after the person leaves the occupation: Criminal Justice Act 1967, s. 16.
34. Morris Report, paras. 105, 115, 121, 149, 150.
35. Juries Act 1922, s. 3.
36. Juries Act 1922, s. 2(1).
37. Morris Report, paras. 215, 216, 245–7.
38. A list is given in the Morris Report, para. 201.
39. Morris Report, paras. 338, 339.
40. In the City of London, an official called the Secondary bears the duty of summoning jurors.
41. *R.* v. *Solomon* [1958] 1 Q.B. 203.
42. Morris Report, para. 346.
43. Mr Edward Iwi, *The Times*, 7 November 1963.
44. Morris Report, paras. 195–8, 234–5.
45. Common Law Procedure Act 1852, ss. 106, 107. Alternatively a party is entitled free of charge to inspect a copy kept for the purpose by the summoning officer, at any time during the seven days before the sitting of the court.
46. Para. 312.
47. *R.* v. *Dolley and Thelwall* (1821).
48. Criminal Justice Act 1948, s. 35(2).
49. Criminal Justice Act 1948, s. 35.
50. *R.* v. *Chandler* (*No. 2*) [1964] 2 Q.B. 322.
51. Morris Report, paras. 324–7.

52. Devlin, *Trial by Jury*, p. 30.
53. See the comments in *The Times*, 1 and 15 May, 1966.
54. Morris Report, para. 343.
55. It has recently been held that a challenge for cause ought to lie against jurors who have already tried and convicted another person concerned in an affair: *R. v. Gash* [1967] 1 All E.R. 811.
56. *R. v. Caldough* (1962) 36 W.W.R. 426.
57. F. X. Busch, *Law and Tactics of Jury Trials*, ch. 5.
58. *The Listener*, 11 August 1966.
59. Morris Report, paras. 331–3.
60. Juries Acts 1908–61, s. 107A.
61. [1965] Criminal L.R. 191.
62. Morris Report, para. 276; the Committee was quoting *The Economist*.
63. ibid., paras. 278–83.
64. Criminal Justice Act 1965, s. 1. Consent is still needed in a murder case.
65. See, e.g., *R. v. McNeil* [1967] Criminal L.R. 540; *R. v. Flower* [1957] Criminal L.R. 118; *Ellis* v. *Deheer* [1922] 2 K.B. 113.
66. *R. v. Box* [1964] 1 Q.B. 430; *R. v. Thompson* (1962) 46 Cr. App. R. 72; *Vaise* v. *Delaval* (1785) 1 T.R. 11.
67. This rule was most recently discussed and applied in *Boston* v. *Bagshaw* [1966] 1 W.L.R. 1136 and *R. v. Roads* [1967] 2 Q.B. 108; for its development see (1962) 233 Law Times 188; J. A. Andrews (1962) 25 Modern L.R. 345.
68. For examples where outside evidence was available see *R. v. Willmont* (1914) 10 Cr. App. R. 173; *R. v. Hood* [1968] 2 All E.R. 56. In the latter case the Court of Appeal did additionally look at a juror's affidavit.
69. *Ras Behari Lal* v. *King Emperor* (1933) 50 T.L.R. 1.
70. Juries Act 1949, ss. 1–17; Jurors' Allowances Regulations 1967. The latest increases followed a recommendation of the Morris Committee that the amounts should be raised; but the Committee wanted slightly higher maxima: Report paras. 289–98.
71. *Practice and Procedure of Magistrates' Courts* (1967), p. 2.

3: TRIAL METHOD AND PRACTICE

1. Summary trial of indictable offences was first introduced for juvenile offenders in 1847. The present list of offences which fall within the category was substantially settled in 1925 (see now Magistrates' Courts Act 1952, s. 19, App. I), but there have been important additions: see note 2. The development is traced by R. M. Jackson, 'The Incidence of Jury Trial during the Past Century' (1937) 1 Modern L.R. 132.
2. Report of the Streatfeild Committee on the Business of the Criminal Courts, Cmnd 1289 (1961), paras. 104, 107; Criminal Justice Administration Act 1962, s. 12, Sch. III; see further n. 4 below.
3. See Magistrates' Courts Act 1952, ss. 18, 25.
4. In 1879, when a number of offences (including larceny to the value

of 40 shillings) were added to the list, the work of the higher criminal courts decreased by 7 per cent but the work of the magistrates increased by 23 per cent (Jackson, op. cit., p. 136). When the breaking offences were added in 1962, the number of persons over 17 charged with these offences increased from 3,690 (in 1961) to 23,625 in 1963, 16,428 of them being dealt with in the Magistrates' Courts.

5. *The Times*, 1, 11 and 15 March 1966.
6. Criminal Justice Act 1967, ss. 76–9.
7. (1966) 116 New Law Journal 928–9.
8. J. J. Tobias, *Crime and Industrial Society in the Nineteenth Century* (1967), pp. 226–7.
9. Indictable Offences Act 1848, s. 17; Administration of Justice (Miscellaneous Provisions) Act 1933, s. 1.
10. Report of the Tucker Committee on Proceedings before Examining Justices (1958, Cmnd 479). See also E. Gardner and M. Carlisle, *A Case for Trial* (1966).
11. Tucker Report, paras. 45–50.
12. Criminal Justice Act 1967, ss. 1–4.
13. If the defendant is committed for trial without a full hearing and then pleads guilty, the case against him will be stated by the prosecution so that the judge can assess the punishment. Where there is no need to assess punishment because there is only one sentence that can be given (i.e. life imprisonment for murder), there would be no need to do this and so no occasion on which the facts were stated in open court. When this happened in a recent murder case (*R. v. Sokol*) there was an outcry in the press, and a new Practice Direction requiring the prosecution to state the facts to the court: [1968] 2 All E.R. 144.
14. See the proceedings reported in *The Observer*, 31 March 1968.
15. L. O. Pike, *A History of Crime in England* (1876), pp. 283–5.
16. Criminal Justice Act 1967, s. 11.
17. Criminal Procedure (Right of Reply) Act 1964, s. 1.
18. *R. v. Young* [1964] Criminal L.R. 347.
19. *R. v. Green* (1949) 34 Cr. App. R. 33.
20. Criminal Justice Act 1967 s. 13; *R. v. Elia*, [1968] 2 All E.R. 587.
21. See the discussions of the cases by J. A. Andrews, 'Legal Realism and the Jury' [1961] Criminal L.R. 758; D. W. Elliott, 'The Verdict of Them All', in *The Law in Action* (1965).
22. *R. v. Wallett* [1968] Criminal L.R. [1968] 2 All E.R. 296.
23. *Cooksey* v. *Haynes* (1858) 27 L.J. Ex. 371; it was unusual for a new trial to be ordered unless the sustenance was provided by one of the parties. Juries Act 1870, s. 23, abolished the old rule.
24. *R. v. McKenna* [1960] 1 Q.B. 411.
25. See generally *Archbold's Criminal Practice* (36th ed., 1967), para. 1395.
26. J. P. Dawson, *A History of Lay Judges* (1962), p. 129.
27. Criminal Evidence Act 1898, s. 1.
28. Professor Glanville Williams (*The Proof of Guilt*, pp. 45–63)

favours putting the accused in the witness-box and requiring him to listen to questions from the prosecution; he would then be faced with the choice of answering or damaging himself in the eyes of the jury by refusing to answer. In a recent broadcast, Lord Shawcross agreed with this approach, while Lord Dilhorne was in favour only of allowing judge and prosecution to comment on the accused's failure to present himself as a witness (*The Listener*, 11 August 1966). In *The Silence of the Accused*, Sir John Hobson and others considered that the present position should be only slightly altered: where an accused refuses to answer police questions, but goes into the witness-box and for the first time offers an explanation, the defence should be permitted to cross-examine him as to why he would not talk to the police. Lord Devlin, in summing up to the jury in the Bodkin Adams trial, strongly defended the accused's right under English law not to give evidence (S. Bedford, *The Best We Can Do*, 1961, p. 217). The case was one in which the judge was concerned to stress to the jury the weakness of the prosecution's case.

29. Dawson, op. cit., pp. 150–8.
30. The proportion of divorce cases tried with a jury between 1896 (39 per cent) and 1935 (6 per cent) is given by Jackson (1937) 1 Modern L.R. 134–5. The highest proportion was in 1918 (73 per cent).
31. Holdsworth, *History of English Law*, II, p. 633.
32. *re Enoch and Zaretsky* [1910] 1 K.B. 327.
33. See *re Brock* (1908) 24 T.L.R. 839; *re Fuld* [1965] P. 405.
34. J. B. Thayer, *A Preliminary Treatise on Evidence at the Common Law* (1898), p. 47; E. M. Morgan, *Some Problems of Proof* (1956), p. 106; G. D. Nokes, 'The English Jury and the Law of Evidence' (1956) 31 Tulane L.R. 153.
35. See O. E. Bodington, *An Outline of The French Law of Evidence* (1904); R. David and H. P. de Vries, *The French Legal System* (1958), ch. 10.
36. *R. v. Deputy Industrial Injuries Commissioner, ex p. Moore* [1965] 1 All E.R. 81, 94.
37. The leading English text on the subject is Rupert Cross, *Evidence* (3rd ed., 1967). For a valuable account of the present operation of the rules of evidence in criminal cases, and proposals for their reform, see Glanville Williams, *The Proof of Guilt* (3rd ed., 1963).
38. See Williams, op. cit., p. 91.
39. *Berkeley Peerage Case* (1811) 4 Camp. 401.
40. For these and other exceptions see Cross, op. cit., chs. 18–20.
41. *Uniform Rules of Evidence* (1953), r. 63; *Myers v. D.P.P.* [1965] A.C. 1001; Criminal Evidence Act 1965.
42. Law Reform Committee: 13th Report (Cmnd 2964); Civil Evidence Bill 1968, cls. 1–10, C. Tapper (1966) 29 Modern L.R. 653.
43. [1943] K.B. 587.
44. Law Reform Committee: 15th Report; Civil Evidence Bill 1968,

cls. 11–12. See J. A. Andrews, 'The Criminal in the Civil Courts' [1967] Criminal L.R. 441; M. Dean (1968) 31 Modern L.R. 58.

45. Civil Evidence Bill 1968, cls. 13.

46. *R.* v. *Smith* (1915) 11 Cr. App. R. 229; see generally Cross, op. cit., ch. 14, s. 1.

47. Criminal Evidence Act 1898, s. 1(f); Williams op. cit., pp. 216–26.

48. *The Times*, 3 October 1964.

49. *R.* v. *Davies* [1962] Criminal L.R. 569.

50. For these cases, see Cross, op. cit., pp. 87–9; Williams, op. cit., pp. 190–4.

51. Cross, op. cit., ch. 9 esp. pp. 169–73; Williams, op. cit., ch. 6.

52. *Ali* v. *Ali* [1966] 1 All E.R. 664.

53. *Barkway* v. *South Wales Transport Co. Ltd* [1948] 2 All E.R. 460, 471; Cross, op. cit., pp. 125–8.

54. *D.P.P.* v. *Smith* [1961] A.C. 290; Criminal Justice Act 1967, s. 8.

55. In 1964 the Court of Criminal Appeal was given a limited power to order a new trial when fresh evidence was introduced on appeal. But the Court requires the evidence to be relevant and credible, and there has to be a reasonable explanation of why it was not advanced at the trial, if it was then available: see Criminal Appeal Acts 1964, s. 1, and 1966, s. 5. A 'reasonable explanation' does not include the fact that the defendant or his advisers chose not to advance evidence as to one line of defence rather than another: *R.* v. *Williams*, noted in (1966) 29 Modern L.R. 82.

4: JUDGE AND JURY

1. *Shaw* v. *D.P.P.* [1962] A.C. 220.

2. *Qualcast (Wolverhampton) Ltd* v. *Haynes* [1959], A.C. 743.

3. *Holmes* v. *D.P.P.* [1946] A.C. 588.

4. Report (1953, Cmd 8932), paras. 141–53.

5. Homicide Act 1957, s. 3.

6. *Young* v. *Rank* [1950] 2 K.B. 510 contains a review of the earlier cases.

7. If the verdict is for the plaintiff against the weight of the evidence, the judge may enter judgment for the defendant, but in the contrary case he will normally order a new trial. The historical reason for this was that when the plaintiff failed to produce evidence to substantiate his case, he was simply non-suited and the judge was not obliged to take any verdict from the jury. But if the verdict were for the defendant against the weight of the evidence, the judge would have had to substitute a *verdict* for the plaintiff before entering judgment for the defendant, and only the jury could return a verdict. But see Devlin, *Trial by Jury*, p. 75, n. 12, for an account of some defamation cases in the 1930s in which the Court of Appeal showed a tendency to allow a verdict for the plaintiff to be entered because it felt that no twelve reasonable men (unlike the jury in the case under appeal) would reach any other conclusion.

8. *Ryder* v. *Wombwell* (1868) L.R. 4 Ex. 32.

9. See the instances reported in *The Times*, 13 October 1933, and

25 September 1945, and C. G. L. Du Cann, *Miscarriages of Justice* (1960), p. 81.

10. Criminal Justice Act 1967, s. 17.

11. *R.* v. *Dollery* (1911) 6 Cr. App. R. 255.

12. Criminal Appeal Act 1907, s. 4(1), now amended by the Criminal Appeal Act 1966, s. 4.

13. H. L. Debates, Vol. 274, cols. 837–8.

14. *R.* v. *West* (1910) 4 Cr. App. R. 179; *R.* v. *Frampton* (1917) 12 Cr. App. R. 202; *Woolmington* v. *D.P.P.* [1935] A.C. 462.

15. See generally Devlin, *Trial by Jury* (3rd imp., 1966), App. II. The cases which exemplify the new trend are *R.* v. *Larkin* [1943] 1 All E.R. 217; *R.* v. *Eastwood* [1961] Criminal L.R. 414; *R.* v. *Draper* [1962] Criminal L.R. 107; *R.* v. *Healey* [1965] 1 W.L.R. 1059, per Ashworth J. Lord Devlin makes the important additional point that if it is wrong for a jury to be directed to convict, the defendant should be entitled to have his conviction quashed on appeal; the Court of Appeal should not allow the conviction to stand by virtue of the proviso to s. 4(1) Criminal Appeal Act 1907. This proviso permits the Court to uphold a conviction despite a successful appeal, because it considers that no substantial mis-carriage of justice has occurred. The proviso should not permit the Court of Appeal to agree with the trial judge's view that there was no defence and so to circumvent the need to leave the question to the jury.

16. e.g. *R.* v. *Wheat and Stocks* [1921] 2 K.B. 119. See Devlin, *Trial by Jury*, p. 90, n. 35, for a note on how far appeal from a special verdict may permit the Court of Appeal – Criminal Division, to consider a verdict of acquittal on another count.

17. *R.* v. *Bourne* (1952) 36 Cr. App. R. 125.

18. But in *R.* v. *Jameson* (1896) 12 T.L.R. 551, a prosecution which arose out of the Jameson Raid on the Transvaal and which aroused great public sympathy for the defendants, the Lord Chief Justice required special questions to be answered in order to prevent an acquittal, and he all but told the jury that it must do what he asked. In the past, therefore, judges had been known to exert strong pressure to get a special verdict. The case was, however, decided before the establishment of the Court of Criminal Appeal.

19. The accused has a right to remain silent in the face of police or other questioning. If he says to the police: 'I am saying nothing', the trial judge may not pass any comment suggesting that an inno-cent man would have given his explanation: *R.* v. *Leckey* [1944] K.B. 80; *R.* v. *Davis* (1959) 43 Cr. App. R. 215.

20. Sir T. Humphreys, *Criminal Days* (1946), p. 75.

21. L. Kennedy, *The Trial of Stephen Ward* (1964), p. 220.

22. H. Montgomery Hyde, *Norman Birkett* (1964), p. 540.

23. Williams, op. cit., p. 326.

24. *New Statesman*, 1 May 1964.

25. Difficulties of communication may be even more rudimentary. A juror recently told a reporter that he was prevented from hearing what was going on in court by the sound of repairs to the court building. *Daily Mail*, 2 May 1966.
26. Busch, *Law and Tactics in Jury Trials*, ch. 23.
27. M. E. Otis, 21 Oregon L.R. 1.
28. L. Blatt, 23 J. American Judicature Society 56.
29. The complex history of the movement to reform the criminal law by reducing the number of capital offences is extensively traced by L. Radzinowicz, *A History of English Criminal Law* (1948), Vol. I. For the role of juries, see esp. pp. 94–7.
30. ibid., I, pp. 512, 592, 595–9.
31. S. Davies, *The Modern Approach to Criminal Law* (1948), p. 301.
32. H. L. Debates, Vol. 191, cols. 85–9.
33. Kalven and Zeisel, *The American Jury*, ch. 19.
34. *R.* v. *Ball and Loughlin* [1966] Criminal L.R. 451; *Yeandel* v. *Fisher* [1965] 3 All E.R. 158; *Sweet* v. *Parsley* [1968] 2 All E.R. 337 (the last two cases were tried summarily, but the defendant might have opted for jury trial); cf. *Warner* v. *Metropolitan Police Commissioner* [1968] 2 All E.R. 356.
35. *Gowar* v. *Hales* [1928] 1 K.B. 191, 196.
36. *Shaw* v. *D.P.P.* [1962] A.C. 220.
37. *Joshua* v. *R.* [1955] A.C. 121.
38. Lord Devlin, *The Enforcement of Morals* (reprinted with other essays under this title, 1965), pp. 15–17.
39. ibid., pp. 77–9.

5: THE BULWARK OF LIBERTY

1. *Commentaries*, Vol. III, p. 379, ff.; Vol. IV p. 342, ff.
2. Devlin, *Trial by Jury*, p. 164.
3. For a complete statement of the law of treason and sedition, see Smith and Hogan, *Criminal Law* (1965), ch. 19.
4. The medieval method of attacking a jury's verdict, in the period when juries were expected to act on their personal knowledge, was to seek a writ of attaint, under which a larger jury (usually of twenty-four) was called upon to give its verdict on the same case. If the second jury reached an opposite conclusion to that of the first, the second verdict would be substituted and the first jurors fined or imprisoned for being false to their oaths. As jurors ceased to be able to decide on their own knowledge and evidence was heard in court, the cumbersome attaint jury disappeared. It was apparently not used in criminal cases anyway. The judges assumed power to punish jurors for a false verdict just as they had always had power to punish them for other misconduct such as receiving bribes. See Thayer, *Preliminary Treatise on Evidence*, pp. 137–60.
5. (1535) 1 Howell's State Trials 395.
6. *Throckmorton's Case* (1554) 1 St. Tr. 869 (see D. M. Loades, *Two Tudor Conspiracies*, p. 97; the jury that tried Throckmorton was severely punished, and shortly afterwards his brother was success-

fully prosecuted). *Lilburne's Case* (1649) 4 St. Tr. 1270 (Lilburne was subsequently banished by the Rump Parliament but returned, whereupon he was again unsuccessfully prosecuted: C. Hill, *A Century of Revolution* (1961), p. 135).

7. (1670) 6 St. Tr. 999; Vaughan 135.
8. (1688) 12 St. Tr. 183; see also Shaftesbury's acquittal of treason in 1681, 8 St. Tr. 759.
9. (1793) 24 S.T. 199, 25 St. Tr. 1. For a lively account of Erskine's achievements see L. P. Stryker, *For the Defence* (1949).
10. *R.* v. *Francklin* (1731) St. Tr. 626.
11. *R.* v. *Woodfall* (1770) 20 St. Tr. 895.
12. *R.* v. *Shipley* (1783) 21 St. Tr. 847.
13. See generally the cases reported in Howell's State Trials, Vols. 22–7.
14. See the cases reported in 23 St. Tr. 118–1013.
15. J. Bentham, *Elements of the Art of Packing as Applied to Special Juries* (1821), and the account of jury-packing given by Horne Tooke in respect of his trial for sedition in 1777: 20 St. Tr. 685–92.
16. See generally Wickwar, *The Struggle for the Freedom of the Press* (1928).
17. J. L. and B. Hammond, *The Skilled Labourer 1760–1832* (1919), ch. 12; F. O. Darvall, *Popular Disturbances and Public Order in Regency England* (1934), pp. 85–6, 104.
18. F. C. Mather, *Public Order in the Age of the Chartists* (1959), p. 227; G. D. H. Cole and R. Postgate, *The Common People 1746–1946* (1946), pp. 279–91, 323–9; L. Radzinowicz, 'New Departures in Maintaining Public Order in the Face of Chartist Disturbances' [1960] Cambridge L.J. 51.
19. The recent history of public order and the police is traced in D. Williams, *Keeping the Peace* (1967).
20. D. Williams, op. cit., pp. 74–5, 182–6; *The Times*, 7 March 1917.
21. *R.* v. *Leese and Whitehead*, *The Times*, 19 and 22 September 1936; *R.* v. *Casement* [1917] 1 K.B. 98; *Joyce* v. *D.P.P.* [1946] A.C. 347; *Chandler* v. *D.P.P.* [1964] A.C. 763.
22. See generally R. Y. Hedges and A. Winterbotham, *The Legal History of Trade Unionism* (1930), pp. 42–51.
23. Cole and Postgate, op. cit., pp. 239–40.
24. H. C. Debates, Vol. 162, cols. 1632, 1635; Mersey Report (Cd 6817), para. 180; *G. Scammell & Nephew Ltd* v. *Hurley* [1929] 1 K.B. 419.
25. W. Cobbett, *Works*, VI, pp. 355–8.
26. Race Relations Act 1965, s. 6.
27. ibid, ss. 1–4.
28. G. Myrdal, *An American Dilemma* (1962 ed.), p. 553; recently juries in the Southern States have consistently refused to convict persons accused of the manslaughter or murder of civil rights workers: *The Times*, 1 October 1965.
29. B. Whitaker, *The Police* (1964), p. 15. The Royal Commission glossed over these figures in its Final Report and managed to

convince itself that the survey constituted 'an overwhelming vote of confidence in the police': 1962, Cmnd 1728, paras. 338–50.

30. Kalven and Zeisel, *The American Jury*, ch. 23.

31. Willett, *Criminal on the Road*, p. 120; *The Times*, 7 and 12 December 1965.

32. See Bow Group, *Scales of Justice*, pp. 9–10; Jackson, *The Machinery of Justice in England*, p. 174.

33. Juries Detention Act 1897; S. R. & O. 1940, No. 1869. For the history of the right to separate see *Fanshaw* v. *Knowles* [1916] 2 K.B. 538, and *R.* v. *Taylor* [1950] N.I.L.R. 57.

34. *R.* v. *Williams and others* (unreported).

35. After six months' experience of majority verdicts (during which 1·8 per cent of offenders were convicted by majority) the Home Office is satisfied that jurors are no longer being interfered with: *The Times*, August 1968.

6: CRIME: THE JUDGES OF FACT

1. (1966) New L.J. 928–9. The published analysis is taken from police records and is given for each of the Assizes and Quarter Sessions held in England and Wales for 1965. Of 28,674 accused persons, 7,029 were committed only after conviction in a Magistrates' Court to be sentenced in the higher court. Another 13,880 pleaded guilty; 7,765 were tried by jury and of these 3,029 were acquitted and 4,736 convicted. The proportion of those acquitted was lowest for the breaking offences, burglary, housebreaking and the like – 30 per cent; and highest for the various forms of larceny – 47 per cent.

2. *The Times*, 25 June 1966.

3. H. C. Debates Vol. 734, written Q. 33; on the same day the Home Secretary put the proportion of acquittals in England at 37 per cent (written Q.9).

4. D. Broeder, 'Functions of the Jury: Fact or Fiction' (1954) 21 U. Chicago L.R. 386.

5. Blom-Cooper, *The A6 Murder*, p. 14. The practice of allowing the jury a transcript of a difficult portion of the evidence was deprecated by the Court of Criminal Appeal in *R.* v. *Terry* [1961] 2 Q.B. 314.

6. Lord Denning, *The Road to Justice* (1955), pp. 29–30. The principle that judges ought to give reasons for their decisions is often ignored in Magistrates' Courts, where the issue is often which witnesses the court believes on a simple factual dispute, and the reasons are clear from the finding. If there is an argument about the law, the magistrates may be required to state a case to the Divisional Court in order that the point may be decided by that court; this will involve the magistrates setting out their findings of fact so far as they are relevant.

7. Tribunals and Inquiries Act 1958, s. 12, following the recommendation of the Franks Committee on Administrative Tribunals and Enquiries (1957, Cmnd 218), paras. 98, 99, 107.

8. R. DuCann, *The Art of the Advocate* (1964), pp. 38–9; Lord Birkett, *Six Great Advocates*, p. 13; W. Roughead, *Notable British Trials*: *Oscar Slater* (1929), p. 100.

9. *The Times*, 1 January 1965.

10. Hoffman and Brodley, 'Jurors on Trial' (1952) 17 Missouri L.R. 235.

11. Kalven and Zeisel, *The American Jury*, ch. 28.

12. ibid., pp. 154–8.

13. Rita M. James, 'Status and Competence of Jurors' [1959] American J. Sociology 563.

14. *R. v. Blick* [1966] Criminal L.R. 508.

15. Ely Devons, 'Serving as a Juryman in Britain' (1965) 28 Modern L.R. 561, 569–70.

16. Cecil Whiteley, *Brief Life* (1942), p. 101, describes a notable instance of this effect: a single jury was put on to try a succession of drunken driving charges at London Sessions; the jurors became much readier to convict as their service wore on. See also, G. Williams, *The Proof of Guilt*, p. 275.

17. (1965) 28 Modern L.R. p. 567.

18. Kalven and Zeisel, op. cit., chs. 11–14.

19. See Common Law Procedure Act 1854, s. 27; Criminal Procedure Act 1865, s. 8; *R. v. Pilcher* (1910), described in C. A. Mitchell, *A Scientist in the Criminal Courts* (1945), p. 23; (1942) 20 Canadian Bar R. 794, 798.

20. Dale Broeder, 'Occupational Expertise and Bias as Affecting Juror Behavior' (1965) 40 New York U.L.R. 1079.

21. Kalven and Zeisel, op. cit., chs. 15–18, 22, 27.

22. *R. v. Black* [1963] 1 W.L.R. 1311; L. Blom-Cooper (1964) 27 Modern L.R. 233.

23. (1965) 28 Modern L.R. 567.

24. Kalven and Zeisel, op. cit., chs. 20, 21.

25. Much of the relevant work, mostly American, is reviewed by H. Toch, *Legal and Criminal Psychology* (1961), pp. 100–102. On the accuracy of the memory of jurors, see the discussion by J. F. Dashiell, in C. Murison (ed.), *Handbook of Social Psychology* (1935), pp. 1097–1158. For a British appraisal of psychological contributions to the evaluation of evidence, see L. R. C. Howard, 'Some Psychological Aspects of Oral Evidence' (1963) 3 British J. Criminology 342.

26. As well as the references in notes 25 and 27, see F. K. Berrien in Dudycha (ed.), *Psychology for Law Enforcement Officers* (1955), ch. 8.

27. Williams, *The Proof of Guilt*, pp. 86–93, 158–62; Bartlett, *Remembering* (1932).

28. H. L. Debates, Vol. 282, col. 1567.

29. See the instances discussed by Williams, op. cit., pp. 173–8.

30. E. R. Watson, *The Trial of Adolf Beck* (1924).

31. *The Case of Timothy John Evans* (1966, Cmnd 3101).

7: CRIME: SOME SPECIAL PROBLEMS

1. The cases on joint trials of different defendants have recently been reviewed by J. A. Andrews, 'Joint Trials' (1967) 30 Modern L. R. 645. See also G. Williams, *The Proof of Guilt*, p. 141-3, 155-7 and ch. 9. Professor Williams has also pointed out (ibid., p. 141) that the prosecution can gain tactical advantages from a joint trial, e.g. an accomplice who is jointly indicted can be questioned by cross-examination (if he goes into the witness-box); if he is not prosecuted but permitted to turn 'Queen's Evidence' he can only be examined in chief.

2. *R.* v. *Dawson and Wenlock* [1960] 1 All E.R. 558, 563.

3. The Home Office Research Unit's study of a sample of offenders tried in higher courts in 1956 showed that the proportion of those charged with felonious wounding who were acquitted (23 per cent) ran noticeably higher than average; it was thought that this was because the offenders were often convicted of the lesser offence of malicious wounding: see *Time Spent Awaiting Trial* (1960), App. C.

4. *R.* v. *Griffiths and Others* (1965) 49 Cr. App. R. 279.

5. Morris Report (Cmnd 2627), paras. 312-13, 343.

6. Report of the Commissioners for Uniformity of Legislation, 1965, p. 39.

7. Administration of Justice (Miscellaneous Provisions) Act 1933, s. 6.

8. One of the last instances was the trial of the financier, Whitaker Wright, in 1901; for an account see Lord Birkett, *Six Great Advocates*, p. 57.

9. R. C. Baker (1950) 35 Iowa L.R. 409; Note (1956) 65 Yale L.J. 531.

10. *The Times*, 16 September 1966. Two of the defendants appealed to the House of Lords, where they were successful in establishing that admissions had been extracted from them involuntarily and had therefore wrongly been admitted in evidence: *Commissioners of Customs and Excise* v. *Harz* [1967] 1 A.C. 760. Fifty-three days is by no means the longest fraud trial. In 1966, a case at the Old Bailey lasted for eighty-one days: *The Times*, 17 May 1966.

11. *R.* v. *M'Naghten* (1843) 4 St. Tr. (N.S.) 847, 926.

12. *R.* v. *Rivett* (1950) 34 Cr. App. R. 87.

13. See the cases mentioned in the note accompanying *R.* v. *Latham* [1965] Criminal L.R. 434.

14. Royal Commission on Capital Punishment, Evidence (Cmd 8933, 1953): Lord Goddard (Qs. 2127 – 8, 2203); see also Sir John Anderson (Qs. 4497–8); Viscount Simon (Q. 7738); and see the Report (Cmd 8932), pp. 81–8.

15. See E. Hall-Williams, 'Trusting the Jury' [1954] Criminal L.R. 434.

16. Homicide Act 1957, s. 2.

17. Rita J. Simon, *The Jury and the Defense of Insanity* (1967).

18. ibid., pp. 47–50, 57–8.

19. ibid., p. 67–74, chs. 4 and 8.
20. ibid., ch. 6.
21. ibid., ch. 8.
22. ibid., App. A.
23. ibid., chs. 4, 5.
24. The dilemma of pleading an alibi and insanity arose in the A6 murder case. The accused, James Hanratty, did not raise the question of his mental condition: Blom-Cooper, *The A6 Murder*, p. 73.
25. See *R. v. Williams*, mentioned above, ch. 5, note 34.
26. See Home Office, *Criminal Statistics*, 1960–66.
27. D. W. Elliott and H. Street, *Road Accidents* (1968), pp. 90–1.
28. H. Kalven and H. Zeisel, *The American Jury*, pp. 293–7.
29. T. Willett, *Criminal on the Road* (1964), p. 201. His general conclusion is that it is doubtful that the serious motoring offender is predominantly of 'white-collar' status; but this conclusion depends on his including in his statistical analysis charges of driving while disqualified or uninsured: see Steer and Carr-Hill [1967] Criminal L.R. 214 and cf. the American study of H. L. Ross [1960] Social Problems 231.
30. [1957] Twentieth Century, August, pp. 146–7. See also Willett, op. cit., p. 103.
31. Elliott and Street, op. cit., ch. 6.
32. Road Traffic Act 1967, s. 1.
33. See above, note 28.
34. Kalven and Zeisel, op cit., App. C.
35. Sex Disqualification (Removal) Act 1919, s. 1.
36. Children and Young Persons Act 1933, s. 38; Cross, *Evidence*, p. 165.
37. *R. v. Campbell* [1956] 2 Q.B. 432; *R. v. Chandor* [1959] 1 Q.B. 545.
38. There are indications that juries are specially reluctant to convict of certain sexual offences, e.g., indecently assaulting a female under 16 and having unlawful intercourse with a female between the ages of 13 and 16: see the Home Office Research Unit Report, *Time Spent Awaiting Trial* (1960), App. C. See also C. Whiteley, *Brief Life* (1942), p. 96.
39. Report of the Departmental Committee on Sexual Offences against Young Persons (1925) Cmd 2561, paras. 42–52. Report of a Joint Committee of the British Medical Association and Magistrates Association (1949), pp. 13–15; G. Williams, *The Proof of Guilt*, pp. 334–8; C. Breaks (1962) 126 Justice of the Peace J. 801.
40. N. St John Stevas, *Obscenity and the Law* (1956); H. Street, *Freedom, the Individual and Law* (1963), pp. 126–45.
41. *R. v. Hicklin* (1868) L.R. 3 Q.B. 360, 371; Obscene Publications Act 1959, s. 1.
42. *D.P.P. v. A. and B.C. Chewing Gum Ltd* [1967] 2 All. E.R. 504.
43. See Stevas, op. cit., pp. 111–21. The summing-up of Stable J. in

the case of *The Philander* (*R.* v. *Martin Secker & Warburg* [1954] 1
W.L.R. 1138) was treated as an important statement of a liberal
approach to questions of obscenity.

44. C. H. Rolph, *The Trial of Lady Chatterley* (1961).
45. *The Times*, 21 January, 11, 13, 14 February; 9, 12, 17, 21 March.
46. *The Times*, 12 December 1966; Criminal Justice Act 1967, s. 25.
47. *The Times*, 24 November and 2 December 1967. The conviction
    was quashed on appeal because of inadequacies in the summing-
    up: *The Times*, 1 August 1968.
48. Report on Censorship in the Theatre (H.C. 503, 1967), paras.
    40–55.
49. Theatres Act 1968, S.I.
50. See, generally, H. Street, op. cit., pp. 155–76, Z. Cowen, *Sir John
    Latham and Other Papers* (1965), ch. 2; and the Reports of 'Justice',
    Contempt of Court (1959) and *The Law and the Press* (1965).
51. For early contempt cases tried by jury see Sir J. Fox, *The History
    of Court* (1927), App. p. 234. A general review of present
    problems is found in the Report of 'Justice', *Contempt of Court*
    (1959).
52. *R.* v. *Colsey, ex p. D.P.P.*, *The Times*, 9 May 1931; A. L. Goodhart
    (1931) 47 L.Q.R. 315. The prevailing attitude at present seems
    more moderate: see *R.* v. *Metropolitan Police Commissioner ex p.
    Blackburn*, (No. 2) [1968] 2 All E.R. 319.
53. *Almon's Case* (1765), Wilmot's Notes (1892) p. 255, cited in *R.* v.
    Davies [1906] 1 K.B. 41.
54. *R.* v. *Duffy* [1960] 2 Q.B. 188, where the prejudicial report could
    only have influenced the Court of Criminal Appeal.
55. *Rideau* v. *Louisiana*, 373 U.S. 723 (1963); and see, generally,
    Cowen, op. cit., pp. 76–82.
56. *R.* v. *Odhams Press Ltd* [1957] 1 Q.B. 73; *R.* v. *Griffiths* [1957]
    2 Q.B. 192.
57. Administration of Justice Act 1960, s. 11.

8: CIVIL ACTIONS

1. A useful account of the law of defamation and its role im limiting
   freedom of speech will be found in Harry Street, *Freedom, The
   Individual and the Law* (1963), pp. 147–54.
2. *Capital and Counties Bank* v. *Henty* (1882), 7 App. Cas. 741.
3. [1936] 2 All E.R. 1237.
4. See the Report of a Joint Working Committee of 'Justice' and the
   International Press Association, *The Law and the Press* (1965),
   para. 111. The report is cogently criticized by Lord Lloyd as 'one-
   sided': [1967] Current Legal Problems, p. 43.
5. See H. Street, *Law of Torts* (4th ed., 1968), p. 318.
6. *Broadway Approvals Ltd* v. *Odhams Press Ltd* [1965] 2 All E. R. 523.
7. *Barnes and Gould* v. *Hill*, *The Times*, 24 June 1966.
8. [1966] 1 W.L.R. 1125, 1135.
9. Diplock L.J. in *Boston* v. *Bagshaw* [1966] 1 W.L.R. 1126, 1135.
10. *Gardner* v. *Moore*, *The Times*, 14 July 1966.

11. Report cited in note 5 above, para. 115.
12. An instance occurred in *Mosley* v. *The Star* (1932), according to Robert Jackson, *The Chief* (1959 – a biography of Hewart L.C.J.), p. 248.
13. *Yousoupoff* v. *Metro-Goldwyn Mayer Pictures Ltd* (1934) 50 T.L.R. 581. At the turn of the century shows that defamation actions were on a modest scale. In 1901 (a typical year) there were 34 libel actions in the High Court, bringing an average of £271 damages to plaintiffs; there were 21 slander actions with average awards of £34.
14. *Lewis* v. *Daily Telegraph* [1964] A.C. 234.
15. [1964] A.C. 1129, pp. 1220–31, *per* Lord Devlin. The High Court of Australia refused to accept the decision of the House of Lords as laying down a principle restricting the right to award punitive damages in defamation actions in Australia, and the Privy Council agreed that this was the law in that country: *Australian Consolidated Press* v. *Uren* [1967] 3 All E.R. 523.
16. *McCarey* v. *Associated Newspapers Ltd* [1965] 2 Q.B. 86.
17. *Manson* v. *Associated Newspapers Ltd* [1965] 2 All E.R. 954.
18. *McCarey* v. *Associated Newspapers Ltd*, above, note 16, pp. 104, 108.
19. ibid., p. 111, *per* Willmer L.J.
20. Cf. D. C. M. Yardley, *The Future of the Law* (1964), pp. 214–15.
21. Wayland Young, *The Profumo Affair* (1963).
22. op. cit., para. 119.
23. See Street, op. cit., pp. 243–7: G. Dworkin, 'The Right to Be Left Alone', *The Listener*, (1962) 503. Private member's bills to introduce a right of privacy were unsuccessfully introduced by Lord Mancroft in 1962 and Mr A. W. Lyon in 1967. For the decisions of the Press Council see its Annual Reports, and Phillip Levey, *The Press Council* (1967).
24. Street, op. cit., ch. 1.
25. The rule goes back to the sixteenth century, and was authoritatively affirmed by the Court of Exchequer Chamber in 1786: *Johnstone* v. *Sutton*, 1 T.R. 492.
26. *Glinski* v. *McIver* [1962] A.C. 726; *Dallison* v. *Caffery* [1965] 1 Q.B. 348.
27. *Dallison* v. *Caffery* [1965] 1 Q.B., p. 368.
28. *Allum and Hislop* v. *Weller and Jackson, The Times*, 25 February 1966.
29. [1937] 2 K.B. 130.
30. Lord Devlin, *Trial by Jury*, p. 133, note 11.
31. For a discussion of the need to introduce contributory negligence principles in order to encourage plaintiffs to waive their right to trial by jury in the United States, see H. Zeisel, H. Kalven and B. Buchholz, *Delay in the Court* (1959), pp. 90–1.
32. For a full discussion of the 'heads' of personal injury damages, see H. Street, *The Law of Damages* (1962), chs. 3–6. Equally difficult problems arise when the injured person has been killed and his

dependants are claiming. In particular, the judges have disliked having to guess at a widow's chance of remarrying, but the Court of Appeal has said that the prognostication has to be made under the present law: *Goodburn* v. *Thomas Cotton Ltd* [1968] 2 W.L.R. 229.

33. Only occasionally trial judges relax their usual refusal to listen to the citation of other cases. The matter is entirely for their discretion: *Bird* v. *Cocking* [1951] 2 T.L.R. 1260; *Waldon* v. *War Office* [1956] 1 W.L.R. 51; cf. *Bastow* v. *Bagley* [1961] 3 All E.R. 1101.

34. *Watson* v. *Powles* [1968] 1 Q.B. 596.

35. *Singh* v. *Toong Fong Omnibus Co.* [1964] 3 All E.R. 925, *per* Lord Morris; *Ward* v. *James* [1966] 1 Q.B. 273; *Gray* v. *Alanco Development Co.* (1967) 61 D.L.R. (2d) 652.

36. Comment (1957) 32 New York U.L.R. 186. For the rule in England see *Watt* v. *Watt* [1905] A.C. 115.

37. *Morey* v. *Woodfield* [1964] 1 W.L.R. 16n; *Warren* v. *King* [1964] 1 W.L.R. 1. H. Kalven, 'The Jury and the Damage Award' (1958) 19 Ohio S.L.J. 158, states that the Chicago Project's research into personal injury awards shows that a well-publicized high award produces a noticeable impact on later juries.

38. *Fletcher* v. *Autocar and Transports Ltd* [1968] 1 All E.R. 726.

39. *Grey* v. *Alanco* (1965) 50 D.L.R. (2d) 17.

40. Melvin Belli, *Ready for the Plaintiff* (1956), describes his tactics as a plaintiff's attorney in seeking high awards of damages from U.S. juries. Kalven and Zeisel, *The American Jury*, p. 64.

41. [1966] 1 Q.B. 273. The previous cases were *Hennell* v. *Ranaboldo* [1963] 1 W.L.R. 1391; *Sims* v. *Howard* [1964] 2 Q.B. 409 – the first case to indicate that very serious injuries might not constitute a reason for awarding a jury; and *Watts* v *Manning* [1964] 2 All E.R. 267. In Scotland, a majority of the Strachan Committee recommended the retention of trial by jury in a few types of civil action, including personal injury cases (Report, 1959, Cmnd 851).

42. *Davies* v. *Smith*, Kemp and Kemp, *Quantum of Damages* (2nd ed., 1961), p. 353.

43. *Waldon* v. *War Office* [1956] 1 W.L.R. 51, 54, *per* Singleton L. J.

44. H. Street, *Law of Damages* (1962), ch. 5; cf. Kemp and Kemp, *Quantum of Damages* (3rd ed. 1967), I, ch. 4.

45. D. C. McGregor, 'Use of Retail Price Indices' in Law Society of Upper Canada, *Lectures on the Assessment of Damages for Personal Injuries*.

46. D. P. Derham, 'Some Notes on the Role of Juries in Running-Down Cases' (1962) 36 Australian L.J. 59.

47. An interesting judgment in this respect is that of Harman L.J. in *Morey* v. *Woodfield*, note 37 above.

48. For analyses of the defects of the present system of compensation together with suggestions for radical reform see T. G. Ison, *The Forensic Lottery* (1967), and, in relation to road accidents, D. W. Elliott and H. Street, *Road Accidents* (1968), Part II. A Committee chaired by Winn L.J. has now recommended changes in

pleading and procedure designed to speed up existing methods of conducting personal inquiry litigation. They recommend interim payments pending trial in certain cases as well as a limited number of 'split trials' dealing separately with liability and damages. No changes are suggested with regard to the present system of fixing the mode of trial of cases heard by a jury. (1968) Cmnd 3691. The New Zealand Royal Commission on Workmen's Compensation has recently recommended that negligence actions be abandoned in favour of a national system of insurance compensation for road, industrial and domestic accidents: see (1968) 31 Modern L.R. 544.

49. Report (Cd 6817), para. 176. Similar views were expressed by the House of Lords in the *Sunshine Roof* case (*Mechanical and General Inventions Co.* v. *Austin* [1935] A.C. 346). The action was a complex one involving questions of licence under a patent covering a sunshine roof for a car, and breach of confidence. Viscount Sankey L.C. remarked: 'I cannot help thinking that in the present case, after a prolonged trial and thousands of questions in examination and cross-examination, it was impossible for the jury to have kept all the facts in their minds.'

50. R.S.C., o. 75 r. 22 (2), [1965] 1 W.L.R. 853; C.C.R. o. 31; the Registrar keeps a special list of persons willing to act as assessors.

51. *S.S. Australia* v. *S.S. Nautilus* [1927] A.C. 145, and the other cases there noted: *The Marinegra* [1960] 2 Lloyd's Rep. 1.

52. The High Court has a special power to appoint an independent scientific adviser to assist the court, or to conduct an inquiry and report thereon, in an action for infringement of a patent (R.S.C., o. 103 r. 27); the power is not at present used. The High Court has a general power (R.S.C., o. 33 r. 6) to appoint assessors to sit with the judge at the trial or otherwise to advise him in reaching his decision: occasionally a judge may bring in such an independent adviser (see, e.g., *Southport Corporation* v. *Esso Petroleum* [1953] 2 All E.R. 1204). A judge may also refer a matter to one of the court's official referees and he may sit with assessors; or the reference may be made to a special referee; alternatively, in non-jury cases, the court may appoint a court expert to conduct an investigation of a specialist matter and report back to the court (R.S.C., o. 40). The expert may then be cross-examined by the parties. The County Courts also have powers to order trial with assessors but not the use of a court expert (C.C.R., o. 31). Under the Workmen's Compensation Scheme (superseded in 1946) County Courts referred medical questions to expert assessors. This procedure caused a good deal of dissatisfaction, which partly accounts for the present distrust of the assessor system.

The Evershed Committee on Supreme Court Practice and Procedure (Final Report, 1952, Cmd 8617) noted that official referees quite often used court experts, particularly in relation to disputes over building contracts, and the Committee favoured more general use of the power to appoint them (paras. 292–5). But they

did not favour the appointment of expert assessors, particularly
mentioning the recurrent problem of medical opinions as being
unsuitable for this treatment. More recently a Joint Committee of
the Bar Council, the Law Society and the B.M.A. has taken the
same view of medical assessors: '. . . the number of assessors would
have to be very large in order to cover all aspects of medicine
and in many of these aspects there is more than one opinion to be
followed. It would not therefore be right that any one medical
man should be in the influential position of a single assessor'
(Report, 1965, para. 36). But this leaves any conflict of opinion
to be resolved by lay outsiders: judge, or occasionally jury. How
can their choice be a more reliable judgment? This general distrust
of medical experts appointed by the courts has to be contrasted
with the well-established scheme by which medical inspectors are
appointed by the court in petitions to annul marriages. The system
is generally thought to work well: see Sir R. Ormrod [1968]
Criminal L.R. 240. Special steps have been taken to ensure that
the inspectors on the approved panel are adequately qualified.
In paternity cases it is becoming common to appoint a single
expert serologist; and in custody cases the High Court may in
some circumstances have the child examined by a psychiatrist
through the agency of the Official Solicitor: *Re S. (Infants)* [1967]
1 All E.R. 202.

For an interesting experiment using medical court experts in
New York, see Association of the New York City Bar, *Impartial
Medical Testimony* (1956).

53. Phillimore J. recently regretted that there was no jury to decide a
difficult issue of fraud in a civil case: *Ovenell* v. *Norwich Union Fire
Insurance, The Times,* 15 February 1967.

54. See above, ch. 3, note 30.

9: A MISCELLANY

1. Halsbury, *Laws of England* (3rd ed.), Vol. 8, p. 308.
2. Sentence of Death (Expectant Mothers) Act 1931, s. 2.
3. Criminal Procedure (Insanity) Act 1964.
4. Treasure trove juries have power to return a verdict very similar
to that in a trial, for they may deprive the finders of treasure or
their reward by finding that they attempted to conceal it; see for
instance the recent case at Mansfield: *The Times,* 17 December
1966. Fire juries in the City of London are rare; the first for twenty
years recently sat and found a fire to have been caused by arson.
5. Coroners (Amendment) Act 1926, s. 13.
6. *R.* v. *Watson, ex. p. Divine* [1930] 2 K.B. 29.
7. Report of Departmental Committee on Coroners (1936, Cmd 5070)
para. 216.
8. *R.* v. *Spencer, Sunday Times,* 20 February 1966.
9. H. C. Debates, Vol. 743, written Q. 243.
10. Save for inquiries into the cause of fatal industrial accidents:
D. M. Walker, *The Scottish Legal System* (1959), p. 162.

11. Morris Report (Cmnd 2627), App. II; and see G. Thurston, 'Coroners – a Few Points', *Law Guardian*, June 1967, p. 12.

12. A list of 150 bodies which act as special tribunals or conduct governmental inquiries is given in Lord Evershed (ed.), *Court Forms*, Vol. 40, pp. 28–51. The list is incomplete, but is the best available compilation.

13. Kathleen Jones, *Lunacy, Law and Conscience, 1744–1845* (1955), p. 189, App. II.

14. Mental Health Act 1959, s. 3, Sch. I.

15. Land Clauses (Consolidation) Act 1845, s. 23.

16. Lands Tribunal Act 1949, s. 1.

17. Rent Act 1965, s. 25, Sch. 2. It is also interesting to note that where the County Courts have been given new statutory jurisdiction over rent restriction and housing matters, juries are not permitted: County Courts Act 1959, s. 94.

18. The Industrial Tribunals were established under the Industrial Training Act 1964, s. 12, and now have jurisdiction in relation to industrial training levies, redundancy payments, contract of employment terms, selective employment tax and dock-work at certain ports.

10: REVISION OR REPLACEMENT?

1. Jurors' Allowances Regulations 1967.

2. Morris Report (Cmnd 2627), para. 356.

3. Basil Wigoder, *The Times*, 19 October 1966.

4. See T. B. Smith, 'A Scottish Survey' [1954] Criminal L.R. 500.

5. Oscar Slater's trial is described by W. Roughead in the *Notable British Trial Series* (1929).

6. In 1936, Mr Justice Evatt tried to assess the effect of introducing limited majority verdicts in criminal cases in the states of South Australia, Tasmania and Queensland. He was able to suggest from the available statistics that majority verdicts might have the unexpected effect of increasing the number of cases in which there was a 'hung' jury. Possibly the knowledge that there could be some disagreement made jurors less ready to swallow their differences of opinion 'The Jury System in Australia', (1936) 10 Australian L.J. 49. American experience suggests that there will be about half as many cases needing to be retried. For some of the hung juries studied in *The American Jury* a note was kept of the final division of opinion and it was found that 24 per cent were divided 11:1 and another 10 per cent 10:2 for guilty. A study of 150 other juries that 'hung' showed that in none of them was the jury divided 11:1 at the outset. The tendency was for there to be substantial initial disagreement. But the sample is too small for any very definite conclusions to be drawn: see ch. 36.

7. Lord Devlin, *Trial by Jury*, p. 22.

8. Kalven and Zeisel, *The American Jury*, pp. 22–30.

9. Bow Group, *The Scales of Justice* (1960), p. 9–10.

10. Sir T. Humphreys, 'Do We Need a Jury?' [1956] Criminal L.R. 457.

11. See, for instance, the Memorandum of the Law Society to the Beeching Commission on Assizes and Quarter Sessions.

12. Humphreys [1956] Criminal L.R. 458–9.

13. Justices of the peace appointed after 1 January 1966 are given a compulsory course of preliminary training: see the White Paper, *The Training of Justices of the Peace* (Cmnd 2856, 1965).

14. Ruth Ginsburg, 'The Jury and the Nämnd' (1963) 48 Cornell L.Q. 253.

15. For the operation of the Norwegian system see *The Administration of Justice in Norway* (1957), pp. 31–41.

16. Law Society, *Practice and Procedure in Magistrates' Courts* (1967), pp. 4–11.

17. G. Williams, *The Proof of Guilt*, pp. 299–300; H. Mannheim, *Criminal Justice and Social Reconstruction* (1946), p. 246–9.

18. Report of the Royal Commission on Justices of the Peace (Cmd 7463, 1948), para. 215.

19. H.L. Debates, Vol. 274, col. 852.

Index

DATE DUE

APR 2 0 1973			
MAY 3 1973			
			PRINTED IN U.S.A.